THINGS
REMEMBERED

Also by Georgia Bockoven
and available in Beeler Large Print

THE BEACH HOUSE

THINGS REMEMBERED

GEORGIA BOCKOVEN

BEELER LARGE PRINT
Hampton Falls, New Hampshire, 1999

Library of Congress Cataloging-in-Publication Data
Bockoven, Georgia.
    Things remembered / Georgia Bockoven.
        p.   cm.
    ISBN 1-57490-195-8 (hardcover : alk. paper)
    1. Large type books. I. Title.
[PS3552.0282T48   1999]
813'.54—dc21   99-18705
                                                                        CIP

This is a work of fiction. The characters, incidents, and
dialogues are products of the author's imagination and are not to
be construed as real. Any resemblance to actual events or
persons, living or dead, is entirely coincidental.

Published in Large Print by arrangement with
HarperCollins *Publishers*

BEELER LARGE PRINT
is published by
Thomas T. Beeler, *Publisher*
Post Office Box 659
Hampton Falls, New Hampshire 03844

Typeset in 16 point Times New Roman type.
Printed on acid-free paper and bound by
BookCrafters in Chelsea, Michigan

This book is a love letter to my mother,
Mary Ann Stephens,
and to Susan Grad's mother,
Jean Hulm.

ACKNOWLEDGMENTS

I couldn't have written this novel without the help of many people. A big thank—you to Dr. Marcia Smith, a veterinarian who gives extraordinary medical care to her patients and compassionate, insightful care to their owners; Dr. Elizabeth McClure, for ideas, laughter, enthusiasm, and knowledge, both personal and professional; and Dr. Dave Brauner, who steered me in the right direction and gave generously of his time.
A long overdue thank—you goes to Dr. John Morelli, who has listened with good humor, commented sagely, and given astute advice through several past books as well as this one.
Many thanks also go to Connie Cullivan for her enthusiastic history lesson on a community she loves with passion and dedication, Rocklin, California

PROLOGUE

THE OLD WOMAN RAN HER HAND OVER THE CHENILLE bedspread, smoothing the traces of her late afternoon nap. Giving the spread a final pat, she allowed herself to enjoy the accompanying sense of accomplishment. She may not have control over the large things in her life anymore, but she could still handle the day—to—day. If only the imprint the spread had left on her cheek and hand could be erased as easily.

She glanced out the bedroom window at the brilliant red leaves struggling to stay attached to the liquidambar and was momentarily startled to see how long the shadows were on the lawn. In the next instant she remembered it was daylight savings time, not her failing body, that had upset her internal clock, and the insidious, unwelcome feeling of panic subsided.

Her hand left the bedpost, reached for the dresser, and then the door frame as she made her way out of the bedroom and into the hall. For months now the furniture and walls had provided the support her doctor insisted should come from a cane. But she wasn't ready to let herself be stamped an invalid. As soon as she did, her life would be perceived as over. The world wouldn't see her meandering toward the end, it would have her standing with one foot in the grave.

Well, she'd be damned if she'd let that happen.

Orange and gold shards of light cut through the kitchen window and into the hallway. The sunset would be spectacular that night. The rice farmers were burning again, the smoke from the remnants of their crop as much a part of fall in the Sacramento Valley as the

1

barren fields. Their burning days were numbered; the environmentalists had just about won the battle.

But fall days without smoke in the air were beyond the old woman's remaining time. She didnt mind. She'd been allowed more years than she'd expected when she was twenty and had believed old age to be fifty. Of course she'd changed her opinion as she neared the half—century mark and discovered age was a state of mind. The accumulation of years, the gathering of wrinkles only mattered if you let them. Now, at eighty—five, she told herself that old age began tomorrow.

The kitchen still held a lingering smell of lunch, a spicy meat loaf meant to entice long—dead taste buds. Somewhere, sometime—without her even noticing—she'd lost her desire for food. She didn't know whether to lay the blame on the medicine she took or the realization that after a lifetime of counting calories she could eat anything she wanted with out consequence.

Not even crème brûlée tempted her anymore. It seemed crème brûlée had to be a forbidden food to be fully appreciated. The richness had to be a sin, the transgression filled with guilt. Now it was a free food, like celery on a diet.

She made a cup of apple cinnamon tea, one of her remaining pleasures. She would cradle the cup between her hands and breathe in the memory—evoking aroma as she gently rocked and waited. For six months she'd waited, awakening each morning with renewed hope that this would be the day, refusing to feel discouraged when it wasn't.

She had not been so patient as a young woman. Now she knew things in her heart as well as her mind, and it gave her a confidence she'd lacked then.

She would come. Not out of love, but out of duty. The love she'd buried too deep too long ago. Together they would find it again. This was the reason the old woman hung on to life, this one job left undone, the lone failure she could not forgive herself.

Her teacup in her hand, the woman sat in her rocker facing west. And waited.

CHAPTER 1

"I DON'T UNDERSTAND WHY YOU ASKED JIM—OF ALL people—to run the coffee shop for you while you're gone," Heather called from the kitchen. "It was a mistake. You know it. I know it. From the way he sounded, I think even Jim knows it."

Finally, after an entire afternoon discussing pregnancy, labor, baby formula, first steps, first words, throwing up, and potty training, Karla Esterbrook's sister had said something that caught her attention. She stopped distributing silverware around the dining room table and went into the kitchen.

"You talked to Jim?" she asked. "When?"

"He called about fifteen minutes before you got here." Heather motioned Karla out of the way and opened the oven door.

"That was five hours ago. And you're just now telling me?"

"He said it wasn't important, that he'd catch up with you later."

"Was it about the shop?"

Heather ignored the question, instead breathing in the smells of the lasagna, her lips forming a small, satisfied smile. "I know I shouldn't admit this, but I just love my

3

own cooking, even when it is Grandma's recipe."

Heather had the lead. Karla either followed or made a fuss about the phone call, which would be tantamount to an announcement that her interest went beyond business. "Mom's was better."

"You can't possibly remember how Mom's lasagna tasted. You just think you do. In your mind everything she ever made was better than anything you've tasted since. Martha Stewart couldn't compete with your memories."

They were on the brink of an old, never—to—be—won argument. Heather had been eight when their parents died, too young to have carried any but the most profound memories of their mother and father into adulthood. Karla had been twelve and believed without reservation that she remembered everything—from the softness of her mother's hair to the smell of her father's aftershave.

"From the wonderful smell, I'd say you've added your own touches to Anna's recipe," Karla said in conciliation. She wanted this to be a good visit for them, not like the last time when they'd just learned Anna was dying and had gone from one argument straight to the next as they tried to sort through feelings and decide what needed to be done. She adored her sister and wished they lived next door to each other. As it was, they spent half of every visit working through emotions and misunderstandings before they got to the fun of just being together. "I can hardly wait to eat. I'm starved."

"Good. I made twice what I usually do, and Bill hates leftovers."

"Back to Jim's call." Karla had played the game long enough. "Did something happen at the shop?"

"Would you cut it out? You've only been gone for

4

three days. What major catastrophe could happen in that time that Jim couldn't handle?"

Karla looked at her watch. If there really was something wrong, she could be back in Solvang in a little over four hours. "I'm going to call."

"Dinner's ready."

The dinner thing took Heather's evasiveness a step too far. Something was going on. It seemed Heather hadn't been playing coy before, she'd been trying to avoid the subject altogether. "Bill and the kids aren't even back from the store yet. Were you planning to eat without them?"

"They'll be here any minute."

"And I won't be long." She was testing to see how far Heather would go.

Heather put her hands against the maroon tile counter and leaned into them, her belly protruding as if she were nine months pregnant instead of six. The easy—care pixie hairstyle she'd chosen for this pregnancy made her look as if she were just entering her twenties instead of on the verge of leaving them.

"I shouldn't have said anything. At least not until after dinner. Now everything will be ruined—and I've been working for days to make tonight special."

Guilt. Heather was really good at it. "Nothing will be ruined unless you insist on dragging this out through dinner. If you want me to wait to call Jim, tell me what he said."

"It isn't about the coffee shop—at least not the important part." She ran a possessive, protective hand over her softly rounded belly. "There's something you need to know before you talk to Jim. . . . Damn, I really don't want to be the one to tell you this."

Despite Heather's dramatics, Karla managed to focus

5

on the "at least not the important part." For the past two years she'd put her heart and soul into The Coffee Shop on the Corner, using work in place of therapy to get past a sense of personal failure. The business she and Jim had once owned together had become everything to her, her only constant relationship, her substitute child.

"Enough," Karla said. "If you wanted my attention, you've got it."

"I'm sorry. It's just that this is so hard. You tried to hide it, but I know what you were hoping for when you asked Jim to take over for you while you're gone."

"For cryin' out loud, Heather, would you please stop beating around the bush and tell me what's going on? Whatever it is, it can't be as bad as I'm imagining."

Still Heather hesitated, her lips moving as if practicing what she would say, but no words coming out. Finally, in a monotone rush, she blurted, "Jim isn't running the shop by himself."

The statement was so far from what she'd anticipated, at first Karla didn't know how to respond. "You mean he's hired more help?" But that didn't make sense—she'd only been gone three days, and it was the off season in Solvang. October was the month she set aside to catch up on the paperwork she'd let slide during the tourist rush of summer. There was hardly enough work for the two women she had working part—time.

"He brought a woman with him."

Karla was sure she'd heard Heather wrong. "What do you mean *with* him?"

I don't know for sure, but my guess would be that he had her hiding out at one of the motels while you were still there, then moved her in as soon as you left."

"Moved her in?" she repeated inanely. "Are you

6

saying Jim has someone—a woman—living with him? At my house?"

Heather nodded. "The story he's telling is that she decided she couldn't be without him for a whole month so she quit her job in Los Angeles and showed up on his, uh, *your* doorstep this morning. He didn't want you to hear about it from someone else, so he called to tell you himself. Only you weren't here, so he told me. Of course, if he'd really wanted to tell you himself he would have waited until tonight to call."

She was such a fool. Hanging on for two and a half years believing Jim would wake up one morning and realize he couldn't live without her. Asking him to take care of the shop had been a stupid, desperate ploy to bring him back into her life. Her only sanctuary from the embarrassment was that she hadn't told anyone, not even Heather, how she felt.

"I don't see what difference it makes whether he has someone with him or not." Karla almost choked on the words. "I hired him to take care of the shop. That's all I have any right to expect."

"He's got her in your *house,* Karla. They're sleeping in your *bed.*"

"Thanks for pointing that out. I doubt I could have figured it out for myself."

"She didn't just show up, they had this planned all along."

"You've said that twice now. What's your point?" All her life she'd used anger to hide pain. It seemed so obvious to Karla, but no one had ever made the connection. Everyone, her sisters included, simply believed her short—tempered and humorless. "If you're right, and I'm not saying you aren't, what do you suggest I do about it?"

7

"Throw him out. Make him find someplace else to stay."

"And what if he says it would be a pain in the ass for him to have to find another place and that if I insist he move out, he'll pack up and go back to Los Angeles? What would I do then, Heather?"

"There has to be someone else you could get to run the shop. It's only a month."

It was useless to try to explain. In her entire twenty—nine years, Heather had never had to face a crisis alone. There had always been someone ready to help with any difficulty encountered. From the moment she'd let out her first scream in the delivery room she'd attracted problem—solvers the way a full moon attracted crazies. Heather couldn't conceive of how hard it would be to find someone reliable to run the shop for "only a month."

"I don't have the time to find someone else. It's not as if Anna is going to wait around while I get my life in order. If I'm going to do this, I have to do it now." Finally, a point Heather couldn't argue.

"Then why don't you just close the place down? You could put a sign on the window saying you're taking a well—deserved vacation and will be back before Thanksgiving—plenty of time to fill your regular customers' gourmet coffee needs. Four weeks isn't that long. I'll bet most of the people around there wouldn't even know you were gone. As long as you're back before the holidays, I'll also bet you wouldn't even notice the loss in business."

"And I'll bet you're wrong on both counts. Then what? Are you going to come down and haul my regular customers out of the other coffee shops they've switched to and back into mine? People are

8

creatures of habit, Heather. Four weeks is a long time to most of us."

"You don't have to get nasty. I'm just trying to help."

Heather's world revolved around Bill and their two children. She'd gone straight from college to marriage, her work experience outside the home limited to the part—time jobs she'd taken for spending money. Karla softened her tone and tried to explain. "I've worked hard to build a base of repeat business. I can't take a chance that I might lose it and have to start all over again."

"No one switches loyalties that fast. Once they see you're open again, they'll come back."

Heather didn't have a clue what Karla was up against in her business, and there was no way to make her understand. She gave up and moved on. "You may be right, but it doesn't matter. As long as Jim doesn't try to charge me for her time, I don't give a damn who he brings in to work with him."

"Yeah, right. And you don't give a damn that he's screwing her brains out in your bed either. That's assuming she has any brains, which I doubt, or she wouldn't have gotten hooked up with Jim in the first place."

"The way I did?"

"You know that's not what I meant."

"It's past history. He can do whatever he wants in my bed. I've—"

"That's not the way you felt three years ago."

"Please—don't hold back," Karla snapped. "Let me know what you really think." If Heather hadn't shown up for an unexpected visit the day Karla and Jim split for good and he moved out, Karla would never have told her about his affairs. She would have said

9

something about irreconcilable differences and left it at that. But she'd been vulnerable that day and had needed someone to talk to. She'd told Heather everything, knowing it was a mistake the minute the words were out of her mouth.

Karla hadn't wanted or needed her friends and family to take sides after the divorce. She'd never believed any marriage survived or failed on the actions of one partner alone, and she refused to accept what appeared to be the obvious and easy answer when it came to Jim's infidelities. Jim was bright, and caring, and had been unfailingly loving and considerate with her. He'd worked as hard at making the coffee shop a success as she had. Only, as she'd discovered three years into the marriage, when he'd taken off in the afternoons to attend community affairs, there had been no community, only an affair.

What she'd never shared with Heather were her personal doubts. Maybe if she'd tried harder to please Jim, had been more adventuresome in the bedroom during the marriage, he wouldn't have looked else where to fulfill his needs. But when she came home and discovered him in their bed with another woman, there was no turning back.

"As I was about to say," Karla went on. "I've been thinking about trading my king—size bed in for a double anyway. It would give me more room, and the sheets are cheaper. Jim bringing his girlfriend just gave me the push I needed."

"When you end up with lemons, make lemonade, huh?" Heather said.

"If you want to look at it that way."

"Do me one favor."

"What now?"

"Deduct the cost of the new bed from his final paycheck." Her eyes sparkled with mischief at the suggestion.

Karla would have laughed but was afraid if she let one emotion go another would follow. Reason should have dulled the disappointment or at least numbed the pain, but she'd allowed the hope that she and Jim could work things out between them to ride too high too long for it to be brought down so easily. "I think I could manage that. Thanks for the idea."

Heather took the salad out of the refrigerator.

"I'm sorry, Karla. I know you don't want to hear any more, but I can't believe you're going to let him get away with this without fighting back."

"Why should I care who's he living with? I'm over him. I have been for a long time now." Finally she sounded convincing, even to herself. Maybe Heather would let it go if she added just a little more. "I admit it would have been nice if he'd been more up—front about the whole thing, but then that's not Jim's style. It never has been."

They seemed to be the words Heather needed to hear. "You know, Jim doing this could be a blessing in disguise. Maybe all you needed was for him to do one more really shitty thing to prove he was never going to change. Now you can really get on with your life instead of simply going through the motions and telling everyone you are."

"Tell you what—I'll get on with my life if you get on another subject." Karla took the salad bowl and headed for the dining room.

"I didn't say that to hurt your feelings. You know as well as I do—"

The front door opened. "We're home," Bill called

11

out.

"We got ice cream," Jamie shouted as he tore through the living room. "And cookies."

"I hope you got the salad dressing, too," Heather said, reaching for the brown bag Jamie held aloft.

Bill came in with the three—year—old, Jason, tucked under his arm. "It smells great in here." He gave Heather a quick kiss, smiled at Karla, and lowered Jason to the ground. He instantly attached himself to Heather's legs. "Daddy let us ride the horsey. Two times. I got to go all by myself because Jamie was being mean."

Thankful for the distraction and for having the focus shifted to something other than herself, Karla busied herself filling glasses with water and milk and putting hot pads on the table for the lasagna.

CHAPTER 2

DINNER WAS LIVELY AND FULL OF CHILDHOOD chatter as both Jamie and Jason fought for their parents' and Karla's attention. When a lull finally appeared, Bill took advantage of it to ask Karla, "How did the car buying go?"

At the last minute, Karla had made an inconvenient detour to L.A. in response to Grace's impassioned plea for help. It seemed that it had suddenly become critically necessary for their little sister to have a new car. There was no way she could wait until Karla came home and no way she could ever make the purchase without her oldest sister's expertise.

"Fine," Karla said. She was still feeling put—upon by Grace but past the point of needing to vent.

12

Bill grabbed a piece of lasagna noodle as it left Jason's fork and headed for the floor. He put it on the corner of his plate without missing a beat in the conversation. "What kind did she get?"

"A Saturn." The sporty one Karla would have liked to have for herself but couldn't fit into her budget.

Pausing midbite, Heather said, "Wait a minute. I thought she said she needed you with her to negotiate the deal. Aren't those the cars they sell at a set price?"

Karla nodded, knowing what was coming, wishing she could head it off, feeling as foolish as she always did when Grace managed to manipulate her into doing something she knew better than to do.

"Don't tell me she talked you into buying it for her." Anger created twin red circles on Heather's cheeks like some 1920s makeup artist gone crazy with rouge.

"There's no way I would let her do that."

"Then what?"

Reluctantly, Karla admitted, "I cosigned the loan."

Bill put his napkin on the table and sat back in his chair but didn't say anything. He didn't have to, his actions said enough.

Heather took a drink of water and sat for several seconds with her jaw clamped tight. It appeared that she, too, was going to let the news go without comment. Then it was as if the frustration had nowhere to go but out. "God damn it, Karla—" She glanced at Bill and then the kids. "'I'm sorry," she said to Jamie, "I shouldn't say words like that. No one should. Not ever."

She wasn't so distracted by the swearing she didn't finish. She glared at Karla. "Grace is never going to grow up if you don't stop dancing to her tune. You either back off and let her learn to depend on herself or she's going to turn into an emotional cripple."

13

"All I did was cosign. She made her own down payment." Minus the thousand dollars her trade—in didn't cover, which Karla had insisted was a loan, not the early Christmas/birthday present Grace had suggested.

"Which means if she stops making payments you either make them for her or lose your own credit rating," Heather said.

"That's not going to happen."

"Did she say why she needed a new car when all the rest of us get by with used?"

Karla knew the answer wouldn't satisfy Heather, but gave it anyway. "She needed something she could count on to get her to auditions."

"And you bought into that?"

"Her auditions are all over town. Some days she has half a dozen and might as well not go as be late."

"All those auditions and no jobs. Wouldn't you think she'd at least have had a commercial by now?"

"She doesn't go out on commercials."

"Oh? And why is that? Too good for them?"

"She's afraid they'll typecast her."

"Oh, you mean the way they have Rosie O'Donnell and Candice Bergen. And what about all the famous people who got their start in commercials?"

Bill reached over to wipe sauce from Jason's chin. I think we're going to let the two of you work this out by yourselves." He reached for Jason and said to Jamie, "Come on—let's see what we can find to watch on television."

"I'm sorry, Bill," Karla said. "You don't have to go. We'll behave."

"That's all right. I shouldn't have brought up the car, but I think the two of you have a few other things that

14

need to be worked out, too." He smiled, leaned over and pressed a kiss to her forehead. "If you're still talking to each other when you finish, I'll take you over to Monterey to check on the sea lions."

When he was gone, Karla got up and started clearing the dishes.

"Leave them," Heather said. "I'll get it later."

She sat back down, in Bill's chair this time which was closer to Heather's. "You know Grace thinks you don't like her."

"She could be right."

"You don't mean that."

Heather propped her hands over her belly. "What I really don't like is the person Grace is becoming. She's turning into a user. And you're not only facilitating the transformation, Karla, you're encouraging it. You've got to let go. How is Grace ever going to learn that if she falls she can get up under her own power if you're always waiting around to pick her up? You're denying her any sense of accomplishment from doing something herself."

"Wow, that's quite a speech. How long have you been working on it?"

"Don't you dare use that superior—sounding, condescending voice on me. It's not a speech, it's a fact."

Karla backed off fighting the need to defend herself. "All right. So what do you think I should have done about the car?" When Heather started to answer, Karla held up her hand to stop her. "Wait a minute. Before you say anything, you should know Grace checked into having the old one fixed and it was going to cost more than it was worth. Also, if she can't get to auditions she can't get a job. Without a job she can't pay her rent—let

15

alone car payments."

"What would you have done if you were faced with the same circumstances?"

The question took Karla by surprise. "That's beside the point."

"Why?"

"Grace isn't me."

"And why is that?"

Karla hated losing ground in any argument, let alone one to Heather. "Do you really want to get into a discussion about birth order?"

"That's a cop—out and you know it. Grace being the youngest has nothing to do with this. She can't take care of herself because you won't let her."

Karla got up again. "I'm sorry I ever told you about the car."

"You had to. At least you had to tell us about it or come up with some other reason for cutting short your visit." Heather stood now, too. "That's another thing that pisses me off. Grace gets to see you whenever she wants. She snaps her 'poor little me' finger and you're there before her crocodile tears are dry. I get you once a year, twice if I'm really lucky. It's been ten months since you were here last and yet she sees nothing wrong in summoning you to L.A. even when she knows it means you have to cut days off your visit with me."

This was not the time to point out that the road between their houses ran both ways. "Would it help if I promise to try to make it back for Christmas?" They hadn't spent a Christmas together in six years.

"And how are you going to manage that?"

"I don't know, I'll figure something out." With Halloween and Thanksgiving to get through yet, Christmas seemed a lifetime away.

16

"I'd love it. But you know what I'd like even more? If you could be here when the baby's born."

"Me, too, but I don't think you'd love how long you had to stay in labor for me to get here in time."

"You could—" She shook her head. "Never mind. Get through your month with Anna first, and then we'll talk about it."

"Speaking of Anna—I know you have your mind made up about having her come to live with you, but I wish you'd reconsider." Karla had hoped that by going to Anna's herself she would take the burden of responsibility off of Heather. But Heather was convinced that in the end Anna's care should fall to the person who loved her most, and neither Karla nor Grace could lay claim to that position.

"I know you do, but my mind's made up. I can't turn my back on her now. Not after everything she did for us."

"You'll be taking her away from her home. All of her friends are—"

"I know. But it's family that matters. You taught me that, Karla."

"No fair."

Heather laughed. "Come on. I've decided you can help me with the dishes after all. Then we'll let Bill drag us over to see his sea lions and come home and have Jamie's ice cream and cookies." She handed Karla a plate. "I've got to find a way to get through to Bill that not everyone is as enchanted with sea lions as he is."

"Don't. I love that he wants to share them with me."

Heather laughed. "And I love that you make him think he's doing you a favor."

Karla finished stacking the plates and carried them into the kitchen. She thought about being with Heather a

17

lot when they were apart, but it wasn't until they were together that she realized just how much she missed her sister. More than that, how much she missed being part of a family that did things together. A family that had time for each other. She wanted to go back to the family they had once been, the family of her childhood, the one only she remembered.

CHAPTER 3

THE SUN SETTLED BEHIND THE GENTLY ROLLING mountains of the coast range, leaving the western sky in the Sacramento Valley awash in purple and orange and salmon.

As she traveled I—5 up from Stockton to Sacramento, her appreciation for the display was limited to quick glances out the side window of her car. She'd thought she was leaving Salinas in time to miss the rush hour traffic in Sacramento. Instead she was caught in the middle of it.

Alone, confined, and without distraction for her thoughts, Karla used the time to search for a way to cope with the crushing disappointment that Jim had found someone else. When she'd shown him around the shop, pointing out the changes she'd made, his excitement at being back was palpable. For the first time he admitted that he'd floundered since leaving, that nothing he had done since came close to the pleasure he'd received from running their business. She'd chosen to believe that she was part of what he'd missed.

Now, with someone in his life again, she could no longer nurture the fantasy of a reconciliation, letting herself believe his late—night calls and spur—of—

the—moment visits were a sign that he couldn't get her out of his system instead of simply being part of the slow process of breaking a habit.

Still, there was a part of her that wondered how he would have reacted had he known she was willing to try again. Would it matter if he knew that for over two years she hadn't dated anyone more than twice, that she'd stopped letting her friends set her up with their friends, that she went to bed every night and got up every morning with the hope that he would finally realize he couldn't live without her? Would knowing provide the jolt that made him change?

She'd never find out. It was better that she moved on—as he had. She'd already wasted two and a half years.

But her heart wasn't ready. She wasn't sure it ever would be.

A sea of red taillights flashed, bringing the traffic to a stop one car at a time. Karla braced the steering wheel with her knee and stretched, rolling her shoulders and moving her head from side to side. There had to be a corner of hell reserved for the people who made sleeper sofas—a corner where they spent eternity going to bed every night on their own product. Next time she stayed at Heather's, she was going to sleep on the floor no matter how much her sister protested.

As the cars ahead inched forward, she looked down from her elevated position on the freeway to what had been a bustling railroad yard decades ago. Now it was an environmentally chancy, incredibly valuable piece of downtown real estate waiting to be developed.

The city had changed dramatically in the six years she'd been away, almost as if there'd been another gold rush, only this time the flush of immigrants had built up instead of spreading out. The new skyline erased the old image of California's capital as a sleepy, overgrown cow town. While a long way from being mistaken for San Francisco or Los Angeles, Sacramento had definitely and defiantly awakened from its nap.

Karla wasn't sure she liked the city's new look. She did know, however, that she didn't think much of the traffic the change had brought with it. She didn't like waiting for anything, but when the payoff was simply getting from one side of the city to the other, it tried her patience.

Once through the city, it took another half hour to drive the twenty miles to Rocklin. The sky was a star—speckled black when she finally pulled into her grandmother's driveway.

A single light burned inside the living room of the Queen Anne—design house. Once a mansion in a town of Finnish immigrant laborers, a hundred years later it was as out of step with the modern world as the woman who lived inside.

The same lace curtains that had covered the windows nineteen years ago when Karla first came to live with her grandmother still covered them now. Karla looked for signs of movement behind the lace but saw nothing; it was as quiet inside as out.

Even knowing her grandmother was in the house and likely wondering about the headlights that had flashed across the windows, Karla couldn't summon the emotional energy she needed to get out of the car. It was as if the past nineteen years had disappeared and she was fourteen again, foisted off on a woman she hardly knew, aware that after two years of being shifted from relative to relative on her father's side of the family this was the last stop for her and Heather and Grace together. They either made it work here or they would be split up forever, sent to live with aunts and uncles and cousins states apart from each other.

Her gaze shifted to the second—story corner room with the turret window alcove where she'd studied more than played during the four years she'd been here, determined to make the grades that would get her a scholarship to a school far away from Rocklin and her grandmother and all they represented.

Finally, reluctantly, she got out of the car. She had almost reached the front door when she saw her grandmother sitting in the straight—backed rocker that was as much a fixture on the porch as the fake ferns in their redwood pots.

"What are you doing out here in the dark?" The question came out more accusation than query.

"Waiting for you," Anna said simply, as if it had been hours instead of years since Karla's last visit.

"How did you know I was coming? Did Heather call?" She'd specifically asked her sister not to say anything, deciding it would be easier for her and Anna both if she waited until she was there to explain why she'd come.

"No . . . Heather didn't call," Anna said. "How long are you staying?"

"A month." She still didn't understand what had prompted her to come for an entire month. No matter how complicated Anna's estate, what they had to do wouldn't take near that long. "If that's all right with you, of course."

"This is your home, too. I've always told you and your sisters that you can come as often as you want and stay as long as you like."

Karla crossed her arms, leaned against the post and

openly studied her grandmother. She'd thought some of the fire would have left her eyes, dampened by fear of what was ahead. But she should have known death wouldn't scare Anna the way it did normal people. "When did you stop coloring your hair?"

Anna brought up her hand to touch the cap of soft white curls that surrounded her face. "A couple of years ago. I was getting so thin on top I figured gray would blend in better with the bald spots."

That was Anna, brutally honest, even about herself "Well, you look good," Karla said. "Better than I'd expected."

"I hope that's not disappointment I hear in your voice."

"What a terrible thing to say." A defensive anger as old and familiar as the pain of being misunderstood wiped away any hope that somehow this visit would be different. Some chores fell to Heather and Grace, this one fell to Karla. Someone had to see Anna through her death, to assist with her estate, to give her some small peace of mind that she would have the final say over the disposition of the money she had so carefully hoarded all her life. But from the moment Karla had decided to come, she'd feared it was a mistake. She just hadn't imagined she'd be proven right so soon.

Anna came forward in her chair, paused, and sat back again. "Yes, it was," she said after several seconds. "I've been waiting for you for so long I started getting scared that you weren't going to come. It's not much of an excuse for such an inexcusable statement, but I'm afraid it's all I have."

"I spent a lot of time looking for reasons to stay away," Karla admitted.

Anna turned tired eyes to her granddaughter. "I know.

But I'm so glad you came. We have a lot of things we need to get settled between us before I go."

Karla drew her crossed arms closer to her body to ward off a sudden chill. She hadn't come there to visit the past. Anna needed to know that before it created problems between them. "We tried going down that road the last time I was here, Anna, and look where it got us. We've barely spoken to each other for six years. I don't want to do that again. I can't. I especially don't want to spend the rest of my life feeling guilty because we fought through the end of yours."

"Why did you come, then?"

"To help you settle your estate." Lacking another, she'd finally accepted this as the reason for her being there. None of the rest—the compulsion, the nagging need, the voice insisting she go—made sense. "It's about time you got a return on all the money you spent sending me to college. I was a pretty good accountant before Jim and I opened the coffee shop.

"If you don't want my help, tell me," Karla said. "I didn't come here to force myself on you. I can get back in the car and leave right now, if you don't want me here."

Anna put her hand out to Karla. "Right now the one thing I need from you is help up."

Karla hesitated. "Answer me first."

"What is it you want me to say?"

Again Karla hesitated. Emotions she didn't understand stuck in her throat like a pill swallowed without water. "Whether I go or stay is up to you. Either way, I want you to promise me we won't spend the whole time I'm here fighting."

Anna's outstretched hand began to tremble. "How can I promise that, Karla? All we've ever done is

23

fight—from the day you first stepped off that plane from Tennessee."

With resignation, she went to Anna and helped her out of her chair. "Your hand is like ice." The skin was as soft as a newborn's. "You have no business being outside without a coat."

Anna paid no attention to the chiding. "The sunset was beautiful."

"I know. I saw it." Karla put her arm around Anna's waist and was horrified at how little of her there was under the baggy dress. "When was the last time you ate anything?"

"I had a peanut butter and jelly sandwich for lunch, and Susan—" Before she could finish, a car pulled into the driveway. "There she is now." Anna straightened her shoulders and smoothed the front of her dress. "Susan brings me dinner two or three times a week. I think Heather put her up to it the last time she was here." She paused to catch her breath. "She's such a dear. I don't know what I would do without her."

"Susan?"

"Susan Stephens. You remember her. She went to school with Heather. Her name was Grad back then. Susan Grad. They were on the swim team together."

Karla had been in her freshman year at UCLA when Heather started high school. She'd missed out on most of her sister's friends and activities. "The one who got the scholarship to Stanford?"

"Yes, but she never went. Her brother was the one who got into trouble with the Perkins girl. Her parents said it was rape, because she was only fifteen and he was twenty—two when she got pregnant. Susan stayed home to be with her mother during the trial."

"I see you've got company," Susan called as she

24

came up the gravel walkway carrying a paper grocery bag.

"It's Karla," Anna said.

"So it is." There was no missing the it's—about—time—you—got—here look Susan gave Karla.

Karla nodded. "Susan . . . it's been a while."

"Too long." She climbed the steps and gave Anna a kiss on the cheek, then looked affectionately into the old woman's eyes. "How are you feeling today?"

"Wonderful—even better now that Karla's here."

"Still, it's a little chilly for you to be out here without a sweater, don't you think?" Susan put her arm through Anna's and guided her inside the house. "I stopped by the pharmacy today. They said your doctor needs to authorize the refill on the Lasix, so it won't be ready until tomorrow, but I got everything else."

"You're an angel." Anna led the way into the small kitchen, lightly touching the walls for balance.

"I appreciate all you've done for Anna," Karla said, feeling chastised. She was embarrassed that she hadn't figured out what needed to be done for Anna herself and made arrangements for someone to do it.

"Well, now that you're here, I'm sure you'll want to take over." She put the grocery bag on the Formica—and—chrome kitchen table.

Anna took the teakettle off the stove and filled it with water. "I hope that doesn't mean you'll stop coming by to see me."

"Not a chance." A genuine warmth filled her voice when Susan directed her words to Anna.

"What do we owe you for the medicine?" Karla asked, remembering she'd left her purse in the car.

"Anna and I have that all worked out." As comfortable as if it were her own kitchen, Susan began putting away groceries. "Allen and Bobby are at the coach's soccer meeting tonight," she said to Anna. "I was hoping I could talk you into going out to dinner with me. A little wine, a little pasta. . ."

Anna looked at Karla. "What do you think? Are you up to going out tonight after your long drive?"

How was it her grandmother inspired friendship and loyalty, even admiration, in everyone except her eldest granddaughter? "You two go ahead. I'll stay here and unpack."

As soon as Anna moved the teakettle to the stove and had her back to them, Susan shot Karla an angry look. "You have to eat. It might as well be with us."

She'd been there less than fifteen minutes, and already she'd infuriated one person and hurt another. If Jim and his roommate hadn't already set up house—keeping, she would have gotten in her car and headed south. She wasn't wanted here, she wasn't needed, and she didn't want to stay. "You're right, I do have to eat. And it's been a while since I had pasta."

"It doesn't have to be pasta," Anna said. "I'm sure Susan wouldn't mind going somewhere else. You'd be surprised how many new restaurants have opened since you were here last."

"How long has it been since you were here?" Susan asked.

"A while."

"Heather comes up pretty often, and I've seen Grace a couple of times during holidays," Susan said. "But it seems like . . . oh, I don't know, five, six years since you've taken that long drive up from Los Angeles."

"Solvang," Karla corrected her. "I would have thought—"

"Susan, why don't you tell Karla about that sweet

little boy of yours?" Anna said. "And then she can tell you about the wonderful coffee shop she owns in Solvang."

Two sentences and Karla felt like a misbehaving little girl again. She was only one sentence short of being told to stand in the corner. "Why don't we save it for dinner?"

They went to Macaroni's, an Italian restaurant in Roseville across the street from a new Kaiser Hospital and around the corner from an auto mall that advertised itself as the largest in the world. All had been empty fields the last time Karla had visited Anna.

After dinner, Susan took a circuitous route back to Anna's house. By way of an apology for her part in their earlier run—in, she assumed the role of tour guide, taking Karla to places that should have been familiar but were barely recognizable, showing her how in less than a decade, a population explosion and industry had turned what was long considered an isolated town in the foothills into a bedroom community for Sacramento.

When she was in high school, the big news had been the building of the new Safeway market. Now there were almost as many grocery stores as service stations. There were a Wal—Mart and Kmart, a Power Center with a Crown Bookstore, a Costco and a Toys "R" Us.

The day Karla and her sisters first came to Rocklin, there wasn't a traffic light in the entire town. Now there were several major intersections landscaped and paved in fancy brick, the light standards painted a peculiar color that Susan said her friend Connie, who was on the city council, had told her was called wine—not purple.

The once—sprawling Stanford Ranch now contained more houses than it ever had cattle, and Susan said she never heard coyotes howl anymore. The roadways tallied the cost of the missing open fields in the dispossessed skunks and possums and rabbits that littered the asphalt.

Karla was stunned into silence at the sense of loss she felt for a place she'd only that night come to realize she had once considered home.

CHAPTER 4

ANNA CRACKED AN EGG ON THE SIDE OF A LARGE ceramic bowl, her attention focused on a pair of Brewer's blackbirds and their enthusiastic morning dip in the birdbath. She'd been thinking a lot lately about weaning the finches and blackbirds and doves from their dependence on the feeders that she had hanging from trees and posts in the yard. If she did it slowly, letting the feeders stay empty a day or two at a time, the birds would begin to look elsewhere for food. Perhaps then it wouldn't be so hard on them when she was gone.

So much to do. So many things to think about. Still, she procrastinated. It was almost as if she believed she couldn't or wouldn't die until the last chore was finished. Part of the blame she laid on the good days, the mornings like this one, when her heart seemed to beat as strong and confident as it had when she was a young girl. But not only had those days come less often lately, by the time she was parked on the porch at night watching the sun leave the sky she was invariably back to believing in her own mortality again.

She shouldn't overdo on the good days, at least that's what her doctor had told her. After months of patiently listening to his well—intentioned advice, she'd asked him if not overdoing would make any difference at the end. He'd admitted it wouldn't, and they'd never talked about it again.

She was dying. She'd known it for a long time now. Slowly, a beat at a time, her heart was on its final countdown. Everything that could be done to make the going easier was being done. She had a cupboard filled with pill bottles, a book on living with congestive heart failure, and another on the light that would greet her at her death. Best of all, she had the sure, comforting knowledge she'd not wasted her eighty—five years. She considered herself one of life's fortunate ones. While she didn't like what was happening to her, it was a hell of a lot better than the way so many of her friends had gone. Especially her dear sweet Frank . . . He had suffered the pain of the damned before Saint Peter got around to opening the gates of heaven to let him through.

She'd been warned that the very end could be bad, that every breath would be a struggle as her lungs filled with fluid, but there was nothing the books or her doctor had described that she was worried she couldn't handle. However the end turned out, she wouldn't trade a quick easy exit for the time she'd been given to set things right with Karla.

Anna had never known anyone as lonely or as alone as her oldest granddaughter. She had an emptiness inside that nothing, no one, could fill, not even the sisters she cared for above all else. She'd come that way to Anna, a defiant fourteen—year—old determined to take on the world in defense of her sisters who, at six and ten, wanted nothing more than a safe haven, a lap to sit on, and arms always ready to wrap them in a hug.

Anna opened the drawer beside the sink and took out

a wire whisk to beat the eggs. She then added a splash of milk, the grated rind and half the juice from an orange, and a dash of cinnamon, blended them into the beaten eggs and put the bowl in the refrigerator. After months of her usual fare of tea and an English muffin for breakfast, French toast seemed downright decadent.

Upstairs, Karla fought an intrusion into her blanketed layers of sleep. Incorporating the shrill sounds of the finches outside into her dream, she drifted into the memory of her first morning at her grandmother Anna's house.

Alone and isolated in the upstairs bedroom while her sisters and grandmother slept on the ground floor, Karla woke to a raucous screeching outside. She crawled out of bed and went to the window, searching the trees and wires for one of the hawks her mother had told her lived in the area. She'd said they would lie in wait for the little birds to show up at the feeders and then swoop down for the kill, taking the unlucky finch back to the tree, where a macabre shower of feathers would rain onto the ground.

Karla opened the window, discovered the noise came from territorial battles over the feeders, and went back to bed. She closed her eyes and listened hard for sounds that would tell her that her sisters were finally up. She needed to know that they were all right, but the need was not great enough yet to let her chance getting caught creeping around the house by her grandmother. This place was the last for her and Heather and Grace. They had nowhere else to go, at least not together.

And it was her fault.

She was the reason they'd been sent here. She knew this because she'd hidden in the hallway and listened at her grandmother and grandfather Becker's house as they talked about what they were going to do with Karla and her sisters. Her aunt was willing to take Heather, and her uncle said Grace could live with them, but no one wanted Karla. Not even her grandmother and grandfather. She was a troublemaker, always interfering when her sisters got in trouble or needed discipline. She argued, she fought, she went her own way. She might make her bed and clean her room and do her homework without being told, but she never smiled. She was a difficult child.

Karla had pressed her back tighter into the corner of the hallway and told herself she didn't care that no one liked her. She could take care of herself, even preferred it that way. She looked a lot older than she was, everyone said so. She could get a job, and as soon as she'd saved enough money, Heather and Grace would come to live with her.

But then her grandfather said, "Maybe we should just let Anna have them."

Her grandmother waited a long time before she answered. "We'll have to tell her about the money."

"Do you think it will matter?"

"It would to me," her grandmother said.

Three days later Karla and her sisters were on their way to California to live with a woman they couldn't have picked out of a room full of old people. Obviously, Grandma Becker had been right. The money did matter to their grandma Anna.

The first morning that she was alone in her mother's old room, Karla had pulled the covers to her chin, curled into a ball, closed her eyes, and mentally reached for her mother. Somewhere in this old house there had to be something of her left—in the rooms, the walls, the closets. These were the stairs she had climbed for eighteen years, the yard she had played in as a little girl, the shower she had used as she prepared for her wedding.

Karla knew she wouldn't hear her mother's voice or anything crazy like that. All she needed was a small sign, a touch of wind on her cheek in the airless bedroom, one of the pictures stuck in the mirror frame to fall onto the dresser, her grandmother to appear at the doorway and tell her that she'd changed her mind and that Karla could sleep downstairs with her sisters after all.

Now, nineteen years later, the memory of that morning was almost as painful to revisit as it had been to live.

Rolling over in the softly protesting bed, Karla abandoned the lonely little girl who had never found her mother again and opened her eyes. A male house finch, its head and chest a blaze of bright red, sat on the windowsill and stared at her. Karla remained perfectly still, resisting even the urge to smile at this lone, tiny member of the welcoming committee.

She imagined the bird to be a part of the fifth or sixth generation of the finches that had visited her window when this had been her room. She'd had four years to make their long—lost relatives her friends—her grandmother never had let her move downstairs to be with her sisters.

Simultaneously, the finch flew away and Karla heard Anna moving around in the kitchen. She swung her legs over the edge of the double bed, stretched, and reached for her robe. An unexpected feeling of rightness and familiarity came over her, as if she actually belonged in this room. She passed it off as the rush that came with bobbing in the eye of an emotional hurricane. Still, she sat a minute on the edge of the bed and looked around the room, giving in to the sentimental trappings as she had the night before when Susan had shown her around town.

The same wallpaper her mother had looked at when she was a young girl covered the walls—a narrow green and white and peach stripe. When Karla went to college, Heather had moved in and added a flower border around the top, something Karla had never even considered a possibility. The only other changes were the green braided throw rug beside the bed and the peach and green bedspread. The furniture and curtains, even the mirror over the dresser with the pictures of her mother and her friends stuck between the glass and frame, were the same.

A second sound came from the kitchen, prompting Karla to get moving. If she didn't make it downstairs before Anna started the coffee, she'd lose the chance to substitute her own.

She opened her bedroom door to the strong odor of burnt coffee beans. Too late. Living at the top of the stairs, she'd never had to ask what they were having for dinner. Nor had she ever had to sneak around to listen in on Anna's private conversations with her friends. The narrow stairwell acted like a megaphone for the rest of the house. She only had to be very still and she could hear most of what Anna and her friends said when they were in the living room playing cards. What she didn't hear was easy enough to fill in.

This was how she'd slowly added more pieces to the puzzle about the money. Anna would sometimes talk to her friends about how Karla's aunts and uncles and even her grandmother and grandfather Becker had taken

Karla and her sisters in to live with them because of the money. But then not even the money was enough. Three girls were too much work.

Gleaning the bits of painful information by eavesdropping became a secret addiction. Every other Wednesday when the card club was there, Karla was in her room, sitting on the floor, her back to the wall beside the open door, her eyes closed in concentration. The four women had been friends for over twenty—five years and were as close, and at times as contentious, as Karla and her own sisters. They told each other everything, a lot of it embarrassing to a somewhat naive and innocent fifteen—year—old.

One particular summer afternoon was forever imprinted on Karla's memory, however. It was one of those moments that remain as clear as yesterday, as piercing as sunlight after rain. Every word of Rachel Winslow's gravely voiced sentences reached Karla as she sat with a book in her lap and listened. "You were right to step in when you did before all that money was gone, even if it did mean you had to take all three of them. Marie was your daughter. You deserved that money."

Anna's reply was lost in the sound of Karla's heartbeat as it thundered deafeningly in her ears. That afternoon was the last time Karla sat at the top of the stairs to listen to Anna and her friends. She'd heard enough to last a lifetime. Not until Karla was older had she understood that "the money" she'd heard talked about at both her grandparents' homes had to do with life insurance and lawsuits. Her parents' car was hit by a man driving a Mercedes. He was drunk and undeniably at fault. She had no idea how much the settlement had been, only that it must have been a lot and that neither she nor her sisters had ever received a dime directly.

Anna greeted Karla with a forced cheerfulness as she appeared at the doorway. "Good morning. How did you sleep in your old bed?"

"Fine—until the birds started in. I forgot how noisy they could be."

"I guess I'm just so used to them I don't hear them anymore. Come sit down." She motioned for Karla to come all the way into the kitchen. "Have a cup of coffee and talk to me while I finish making breakfast for us."

"Don't bother fixing anything for me. I haven't eaten breakfast for years." She stuffed her hands into the pockets of her terry cloth robe. "And I brought my own coffee." Realizing how needlessly cruel she sounded, she added, "It's a special blend I make up at the shop to get me going in the morning." And then, as an afterthought, "Would you like to try some?"

Anna smiled. "This special blend of yours wouldn't be called Self—Preservation, would it?"

Karla wasn't sure how to respond. Considering the circumstances of the visit, she hadn't expected Anna to put on a show of cheerfulness. But if Anna was going to make an effort, she could, too. "I'm sorry. I've become a bit of a snob when it comes to coffee. I tell myself it comes with the territory, but I was that way before I owned the shop."

"Are you sure you won't have some breakfast with me? I've already made it up, or at least the batter. It won't take but a minute to heat up the griddle."

"I told you, I never eat—" God, she was so inflexible. What possible difference would it make if she let Anna have her way about something as inconsequential as breakfast? "Sure. Why not?"

Anna opened the oven to take out the ancient cast—

iron griddle she stored there, hesitating a fraction of a second too long for the chore to look as effortless as she tried to make it seem. "You still like French toast, don't you?"

"I don't know. It's been years since I've had any." Karla took the bread and batter out of the refrigerator and put it on the counter. "It's Heather's favorite."

"I thought it was yours," Anna said softly.

"Mine is pecan waffles."

Anna thought for a minute. "I don't remember ever making pecan waffles."

"You never did. Mom used to make them for me."

"You should have told me."

"It wasn't important." Karla lit the burner, then adjusted the flame. "I figured when I got my own place I'd learn how to make them for myself."

"And did you?"

"Never did. Sometimes when I'm eating breakfast out and see them on the menu I'll give it a try, but I'm always disappointed." Why this morning—after all this time—was she was telling Anna about her mother's pecan waffles?

"With me it's peanut butter fudge."

"I don't remember Mom ever making peanut butter fudge."

"My mother made it. Your great—grandmother. It was her own recipe. I spent years trying to duplicate it, but finally gave up." She glanced up at Karla and smiled. "I'm looking forward to my mother meeting me at the pearly gates with a great big hug and a pan of fudge."

"When did she die?"

"A week to the day before your mother was born. It broke my heart that she never got to know her granddaughter. They would have been such great friends—as I'm sure they are now. Frank and I had picked out the name Marie Lynne for your mother, but when Frank filled out the birth certificate, he changed it to Marie Karla after my mother."

Karla felt a jolt of surprise followed by a peculiar, compelling connection to the woman who'd also carried her mother's name. "No one ever told me."

"Your mother knew she was named after her grandmother, but I never told her how it came to be. I didn't want her to know how sad I was when she was born."

Karla smelled something hot and remembered she'd turned the fire on under the pan. She reached over to turn off the burner.

Anna waved her off. "You go on up and get your coffee. I'll take care of this."

"It can wait until tomorrow. I suppose one cup of the stuff you've been drinking all these years won't leave too many permanent scars on my palate."

Anna yielded the stove and instead set the table. "Have I ever told you I take credit for your going into the coffee business?"

"Oh?" Karla stopped dipping bread to glance at Anna. "And why is that?"

"I was the one who taught you to appreciate a really good cup of coffee."

Karla was no more prepared for humor from Anna than she had been for the family history, and it took a minute for her to understand she was being teased. She didn't know how to respond, and emotion came before words. She was angry. "It's too late for us to become friends, Anna. You might as well save your time and energy for something that matters."

"It's my time and my energy," she snapped back. "I'll spend it and use it as I see fit."

"You never have listened to me about anything. I don't know why it should be any different now." She shoved the spatula under a piece of toast and flipped it over. If she had anywhere else to go, she would leave that day. It didn't matter to Anna whether or not her estate was in order; why should Karla care?

"How long did you say you were going to be here?"

"A month. Heather said you were only up to working a couple of hours a day, so I figured it would take at least that long to get everything done." Her answer rang true, but lacked logic. Most of what had to be done, Karla could do alone.

"Oh, at least."

She'd agreed too easily. Karla grew suspicious. "There are some things I want to get settled between us first. I was going to wait until later to bring them up, but since we're headed in that direction now, we might as well get them out of the way."

Karla stopped to finish the French toast and put it on plates before she went on. Facing Anna, looking her directly in the eye, she said, "Just so you know—I haven't come here to make sure I get 'my share.' I don't want to be included in your will. As a matter of fact, there isn't one thing you have that I want."

"Then you can give it away for all I care," Anna said. She took the syrup and butter out of the refrigerator and dropped them on the table. "There is no way I'm going to take you out of my will. I'm not saying there's anything I'm leaving that's worth having, but what's here is one—third yours. Now, if the real reason you came was to badger me until you got your way, you might as well pack up right now and head back to that fancy little town of yours."

By the time she'd finished, Anna was holding onto the side of the table and fighting for every breath. For the first time Karla saw real evidence of Anna's crippled heart, and it scared the hell out of her.

"Sit down," Karla said, her fear making it sound like a command rather than a request. "I'll get what we need."

Anna lowered herself into the chair. "I'm sorry. I shouldn't have yelled at you."

"You're supposed to stay calm? Is that what the doctor told you?"

It was a moment before Anna answered. "My God, Karla, is that what you really think?" Several seconds passed before she quietly added, "Have we always been like this with each other?"

"I don't understand what you mean."

"That's exactly what I mean. It's as if we're having two completely different conversations. The doctor had nothing to do with why I shouldn't have yelled at you. I can't even come up with a reason you would think that except you believe I'm so caught up in myself I can't see you standing in front of me." Anna paused to catch her breath. "We have this one month left to us. Why would I want you to go the rest of your life remembering me yelling at you?"

Karla could feel herself being pulled into the drama of Anna's dying, something she'd thought about long and hard before leaving home and had sworn she would not let happen. To do so was the worst kind of hypocrisy. For all of her faults, for all of the things she would change about herself if she could, there was one she wouldn't. She was not, and never had been, a hypocrite. "How we are now is the way we have always been, Anna. Sad, maybe, but honest."

Anna reached across the table to touch Karla's hand. "I can't leave it like this between us. Your mother will never forgive me."

It was everything Karla could do to leave her hand under Anna's. "My mother has nothing to do with how we feel about each other. And she doesn't care. If there is a heaven, and you do get there, the two of you will be so busy talking about Heather and Grace, you'll forget all about me."

"Oh, my dear, sweet Karla, don't you know you'll be the first person we talk about?"

Now she did take her hand back. "Don't play those games with me. All I'm saying is that people talk about the people who are important to them. If you think it bothers me that I'm not your favorite, you couldn't be more wrong. You're not my favorite person either, Anna. Being related doesn't mean you have to like someone. All we owe each other is loyalty. That's why I'm here."

Anna couldn't tell whether her heart was failing or breaking. She only knew that the pain in her chest was worse than it had ever been. How could she not have known how Karla felt? When the three of them had come to her, Heather and Grace had been so easy to love, so needy after two years of being emotionally ignored. Karla had only been angry.

"I owe you so much more than loyalty," Anna said. "If I could I would give you your childhood to live all over again."

"Why? Are you saying there's something wrong with the way I turned out?"

Anna put her hand to her heart and pressed, an automatic, futile gesture she'd adopted months ago to

40

try to help her struggling heart. Responding to the alarmed look in Karla's eyes, she dropped her hand and said, "It's nothing, just a catch in the muscle or some such thing, happens all the time."

"Isn't there something they can give you?" Her anger had turned to concern.

"I'm sure there is. It's just that I'm taking so many pills now I lose track of what they're all for. I'd just as soon not add another one if I can get along without it."

"You shouldn't be living here alone."

"I'm not. You're here with me."

"Only for a month."

"Susan—"

"I know. Susan has been terrific, but you're going to need someone full—time eventually. Or you're going to have to take Heather up on her offer to have you move in with her."

"I have other friends, too. Since I sold my car, there's always someone calling to see if I need anything or want to go somewhere."

"I thought most of your friends were gone. At least that's what Heather told me."

Anna had expected the subject to come up, just not so soon. She struggled for an answer, knowing how easily the wrong words could thrust them into the middle of yet another argument.

"I know it's something I'll have to consider one of these days, but I'm not ready yet. This isn't just a house to me, Karla, it's my home." It was suddenly deeply important that Karla understand what Anna was trying to tell her. "Your grandfather planted every tree in the yard and painted and papered every room in the house. When I leave here it will be like leaving him. I'm well aware that when I'm gone, this place will be torn down

41

and something big and beautiful and impressive built in its place—just like all the other houses on this street. No one wants a house like this anymore. I don't blame them. I just don't want to be around when it happens."

"Then we'll look for someone to hire to stay with you when it's time."

The statement brought a dichotomy of feelings. Anna had expected to have to put up a fight to be allowed to die at home. She was relieved at how easily Karla had conceded the point, yet a little sad, too. She didn't want the last face she saw to belong to a stranger. "I'm not sure who you would call for something like that, but there must be an agency. There is for everything else."

"You're going to have to let Heather know you won't be staying with her. She's expecting you."

"I know, and I love her for caring so much." Heather was Anna's bright spot, her success story, the child she'd managed to bring through the crisis of childhood with the fewest scars. She knew Karla would take her words as criticism, but Anna would not hold back from one granddaughter to save the feelings of another.

Not now. She'd tried for twenty years to put her words and thoughts for her granddaughters on a mental justice scale, trying to give to each equally. It hadn't worked.

Anna reached for the syrup and poured a thin layer over her French toast. "Can you imagine Heather trying to take care of me and Jamie and Jason and the new baby all at the same time?"

"I'll talk to Grace," Karla said. "Maybe she can arrange her schedule to come up to stay awhile."

That was as likely to happen as a permanent truce at the bird feeder. Anna had no illusions about Grace. She'd been taken care of so long and by so many people she'd never learned to take care of herself, let alone anyone else. "I haven't heard from her in a month or so." It had been more like three. "How is she doing?"

"She told me she talked to you just last week."

Even knowing it was a mistake, as usual, Anna covered for Grace. "Oh, did she? I must have forgotten."

They finished their breakfast in silence.

When it was obvious Anna would eat no more, Karla got up to clear the dishes. At the sink, her back to Anna, she asked in the breezy, impersonal tone they usually used with each other, "Do you have anything on your schedule for today?"

"A doctor's appointment. Susan said she would take me."

"What time?"

"Eleven—thirty."

"Give her a call and tell her that I'll take you. I assume you're still going to that guy in Granite Bay?"

"I haven't seen him in months. He referred me to a cardiologist in Sacramento."

"He couldn't come up with one a little closer?"

"If it's going to be a problem for you to take me, Susan—"

Karla turned around to face Anna. "Look, I think if we both give a little and don't jump on everything the other one says, we might make it through the month without constantly being at each other's throats. Agreed?"

"Agreed."

"Now, how long does it take you to get ready?"

"A half hour." No, that was how long it used to take. "Better make that an hour."

"It doesn't take me near that long, so why don't you get started while I finish the kitchen?"

Anna nodded. She placed her hands on the table, leaned forward and slowly stood. "After what's happened this morning, I know it might be hard for you to believe this, but I'm glad you're here."

"You knew I'd show up sooner or later. I'm the controlling one, the one with the compulsive need to put things in order. That's what you meant last night when you said you'd been waiting for me."

"There are things left unsettled between us, Karla. You may not know that here . . ." She touched her forehead with her finger. "But you do here. . . ." She put her hand over her heart. "You don't want me to leave before we take care of them any more than I do."

"I'm sorry, Anna, but you're wrong. I came here because I knew it would be easier to do what has to be done now than to have to do it later."

"I never gave you your answer last night," Anna said.

"About what?"

"Whether I wanted you to go or stay."

"I didn't expect an answer. I don't need one."

"Some things need to be said out loud anyway. I want you to stay, Karla—through the fights, through it all. I've never asked anything from you before. I'm asking now."

"I'll be here as long as I can, but I can't stay away from the shop forever."

"That's okay. I don't have forever."

CHAPTER 5

KARLA WIPED OFF THE TABLE AS SHE LISTENED TO THE sounds of Anna getting ready for the shower. As soon as she heard the water running, she would return the call Jim had made to Heather. She'd worked out a reason for not calling sooner and rehearsed it in her mind often enough that she was sure she could pull it off without letting him know how upset she was about the girlfriend. If she waited any longer, he would know. She had to call this morning.

She just didn't want to chance Anna's overhearing the conversation and then having to pretend to her, too, that the girlfriend didn't matter. The wound was too new to convince Anna it didn't hurt, and she never shared that kind of thing with her grandmother, especially where Jim was concerned.

Anna had said from the beginning that Jim was the wrong man for Karla. Karla had been furious the first time she expressed her opinion and unforgiving when it turned out that Anna was right.

The almost century—old pipes clanged as Anna turned on the shower. Karla wiped her hands on the kitchen towel and reached for the phone on the wall above the table. She had her hand on the receiver when the bell sounded.

"Anna Olsen's residence," Karla said.

"Karla—thank goodness you're there. I was afraid you might still be en route from Heather's."

At the sound of Grace's overly cheerful voice—the one she used when she wanted something—the French toast Karla had eaten turned to a lump in her stomach. "I got in last night. Why are you looking for me?"

"We forgot about the insurance for the new car."

"No, we didn't. You said you were going to call your agent first thing Monday morning."

"That's not what I mean. You forgot to figure how much it was going to cost when you arranged the financing."

Karla was suddenly, overwhelmingly weary. She leaned into the wall and cradled the receiver between her shoulder and ear. "You don't include insurance in an auto loan, Grace. That's something you take care of separately. The same way you did with your old car."

"I didn't have insurance on the old car."

"You must have. You can't renew your license in California without proof of insurance." The silence that followed lasted so long Karla began to wonder if they'd been disconnected. "I saw a current tag on your old car, Grace. If you didn't pay to have it renewed, how did it get there?"

"You don't want to know."

"I hope you didn't tell the insurance agent about this."

"I'm not stupid, Karla," she said testily. "And I don't need a lecture."

"So why did you call?"

"I need eight hundred and twelve dollars to pay the first six months' insurance or that idiot salesman won't let me pick up my car."

After all she'd already been through to help Grace get reliable transportation, it seemed stupid to stop at eight hundred and twelve dollars. Still, it grated that Grace had automatically assumed she was good for it. "Did you ask about making monthly payments?"

"What good would that do? You saw my bills. You know I barely get by on what I make now."

Much to Grace's annoyance, Karla had insisted on looking at her expenses to see whether she could handle monthly car payments. Between the cost of acting, singing, and dancing lessons along with being seen at restaurants the in—crowd frequented and the upkeep on the wardrobe she insisted she needed to impress the "right people," Grace barely made her portion of the rent each month. If her two roommates hadn't had the power to evict her, Karla doubted Grace would have taken that commitment seriously. Karla had refused to cosign the loan until Grace agreed to follow the budget she set up for her. A budget that accommodated the car payment, but not the insurance.

"So you're asking me for a loan?" Karla said.

"You know I'm good for it."

Karla opened Anna's junk drawer and poked around for a pen and paper. "Give me the name and address of the insurance agent. I'll get a check out to him today."

"Couldn't you just call and give him your credit card number? The car is going to be ready this afternoon."

It might be the reasonable thing to do, but Karla wasn't in the mood to be reasonable. "It's a check or nothing."

"I have an audition tomorrow. How am I supposed to get there?"

"Take the bus."

"The audition is in Burbank."

"Then take a cab."

"Do you have any idea how much that would cost?"

Karla exploded. "If it's important, you'll find a way."

"It is important," Grace said, a catch in her voice. "I'm trying for a part in the new James Bond movie, and my agent says I'm perfect for the role."

"What time is the audition?"

"Eight—thirty—in the morning. There's no way I can get there in time if I take the bus. And you know as well as I do that if I spend the money on a cab, I'll just have to be short somewhere else."

Karla knew she was being manipulated yet couldn't come up with a reasonable way to extricate herself What if this really was the audition that would give Grace the break she'd been looking for? Was she going to deny her the opportunity just to prove a point? "You're going to pay me back," Karla said. "The day you get a job I expect a check for thirty—one dollars and twenty—five cents from you every week. I don't care what you have to give up to get it to me, I just want you to know that if I don't get the check from you, you'll never get another thing from me as long as I live." It wasn't the first time she'd used threats with Grace, but this time she meant every word. Even knowing it was overkill, she couldn't resist adding, "I'm serious about this, Grace."

"Thirty—one dollars and twenty—five cents. Every week. I got it."

"Please don't let me down this time."

"I won't. I promise." Now that she'd gotten what she wanted, her voice changed to its normal, hurried cadence. "Why don't you just give me your credit card number and I'll call him for you."

"My purse is upstairs," Karla lied. "Besides, I should take care of it myself in case he has any questions."

Grace laughed. "You don't trust me. But that's all right. As long as you call him as soon as we hang up, I'm satisfied."

"I will."

Grace gave Karla the phone number. "Let me know if there's a problem."

"Why don't I just have the agent call you as soon as I'm finished? That way you'll know it's taken care of."

"You're the best, Karla." Almost as an afterthought, she breezily added, "I love you, Big Sister."

"I love you, too," Karla said, but Grace had already hung up.

As she passed the bathroom on her way upstairs, Karla heard Anna get out of the shower. Only then did

48

she realize Grace hadn't asked about Anna or bothered to pass on a greeting. The omission bothered Karla more than the loan. Grace had been six years old when they came to live with Anna. She had no real memory of their mother caring for her, only Anna. Anna was Grace's mother in every way except biological. How could she forget to ask about her now?

Karla tried to remember what she'd been like at twenty—five. Had she been so caught up in her own life that she was blind to what others were going through? The comparison was useless. Even at twenty—five, Karla had been an old woman. She hadn't seen it then, but it was painfully clear now.

The bathroom door opened as Karla passed again on her way back to the kitchen to call the insurance agent.

"Did I hear the phone ring?" Anna asked.

"I thought hearing was one of the things that went when you got old."

Anna grinned. "I'll let you know when I get there."

"Grace called."

"Oh, I'm sorry I missed her."

Karla flinched at Anna's automatic assumption that Grace had called to talk to her. "She sent her love and said she'll get back to you in a week or so."

Anna tucked her bathrobe closer. "Is she all right?"

It seemed a strange question even for Anna. "She sounded okay to me. Why do you ask?"

"Oh, nothing," she said unconvincingly. "It's just that Grace has been so busy the past couple of years she doesn't call very often. When she does, it usually means there's a crisis brewing."

"What you really mean is that she only calls when she wants something."

"We can talk about this later. I'd like to leave a little

early to stop by the grocery store and pick up my Lasix before we head downtown."

Karla didn't want to talk about Grace any more than Anna did and followed her lead. "I think we can manage that."

Anna's cardiologist's office was on the top floor of a building that overlooked the historical landmark of Sutter's Fort. Like most locals without school—age children, Karla had driven by the park for years without ever stopping. Now, she stared down at the crudely constructed shelter from the richly appointed waiting room of the man entrusted with keeping Anna alive as long as possible. She would have given the Gucci watch she'd received from Jim for her thirtieth birthday to be one of the women herding a group of five—year—olds out of a big yellow bus rather than the woman waiting to hear in clinical detail how much more her grandmother's heart had failed since she last saw her doctor.

When the nurse called Anna, Karla walked her to the door, then picked up a magazine and headed back to the chair by the window.

"I'd like you to come with me," Anna said.

"I think it would be better if I waited here."

"Oh, it's all right," the nurse said. "Dr. Michaels doesn't mind if someone accompanies the patient."

Karla didn't care about the doctor; she was thinking about herself She no more wanted to stand around in a cramped examining room than she wanted to walk back into her house knowing Jim had been there with another woman.

"I know you have questions," Anna said. "Now is the time to ask them."

Reluctantly, Karla dropped the magazine on the table and followed Anna and the nurse. Curious, she tried to see the weights when Anna stepped off the scale, but the nurse swept them back to zero before she had a chance. It was the same with Anna's blood pressure: the cuff was on and off and the numbers written in the file and the file closed before Karla could make them out.

A short time later, Anna looked up expectantly when she heard her chart being removed from the wooden pocket outside the examining—room door.

Several seconds passed. When the seconds became a minute, she glanced at Karla and then the door. "He probably hasn't had a chance to go over the tests he ordered last month."

"What kind of tests?"

"Blood tests."

"For what?"

"I don't know. He didn't say."

The answer angered Karla. She believed medical care was a team effort, with the patient being the most important member of the team. "It's your responsibility to ask."

"Why? What good would it do?"

Before Karla could answer, a man with a shiny bald pate opened the door. Dressed in a generic white lab coat, tailored dark brown slacks, striped shirt, and paisley silk tie, he looked like an expensive German chocolate cake with canned frosting. He was halfway into the small room before he noticed Karla pressed into the corner and held out his hand. "My nurse didn't tell me Anna had someone in here with her. I'm Mrs. Olsen's doctor—Harold Michaels."

Karla liked the firmness of his grip. "Karla Esterbrook—Anna's granddaughter."

"The actress?"

"The businesswoman."

"Ah, the one with the coffee shop in Solvang." Having categorized her, he focused on Anna. "Any new problems since you were here last?"

Anna shook her head.

"What about the breathing? Is it getting any worse?"

"It's fine."

"No, it isn't," Karla interrupted. Typically, Anna made light of something that was important to Karla. "You can't make it from the kitchen to your bedroom without hanging onto the wall and stopping to catch your breath."

"Dr. Michaels already knows that," Anna said patiently. "This has been going on for months now."

"Does it seem to be getting any worse?" he asked Anna.

"No worse, no better. I added another pillow to my bed."

"Did it help?"

"I don't seem to wake up as often, so I guess you could say it helped."

Karla half listened to the rest of the conversation as she tried to absorb how easily both doctor and patient seemed to deal with Anna's terminal condition. When it was clear the exam was over, Karla motioned to stop the doctor before he had a chance to leave. "It's plain I don't know as much about what's happening to Anna as I thought I did. Since I'm going to be staying with her for the next month, I'd like to know what to watch for. Would it be possible to make an appointment to come in and talk to you about this?"

He glanced at his watch. "I have a few minutes before I'm due at the hospital. If you think that would be enough, we could talk now."

"Now is fine."

"I'll meet you in my office as soon as I make a phone call. It's the one at the end of the hall. The nurse will show you."

Karla looked at Anna. "Do you want to come?"

"Lord, no. I've heard all I want or need to hear. I'll meet you in the waiting room."

Karla had barely settled into the leather chair opposite Dr. Michaels's desk when he came in and handed her several glossy pamphlets. "These are pretty general, but they answer some of the more obvious questions about congestive heart failure."

"Has she talked to you about dying?"

"Yes." Instead of sitting down behind the desk, he leaned his elbow on the file cabinet, propping his head against his hand. "As a matter of fact, we've talked about it a number of times."

For months Karla had thought about this conversation, knowing it was one she would have to have with Anna's doctors eventually, believing it would be easy because it was what Anna wanted. Still, there was a lump in her throat the size of a fist and a sadness that made the words almost impossible to speak.

"Anna has always insisted that the quality of life comes before the quantity. If it happens that a choice has to be made and Anna can't make it for herself, it will fall to me. I need to know what I'll be facing."

"Have you talked to her about this?"

"Not yet, but it's one of the reasons I'm here."

Again, he glanced at his watch, hesitated, then said, "I'm going to give you the basics this morning. I can guarantee you'll have questions when you've had time to think about what I've said. When that happens, call me and we'll talk again."

For the next ten minutes Karla listened while she heard in unemotional, clinical terms how the disease that had begun years earlier without warning or symptoms would eventually take Anna's life. How in its struggle to provide needed oxygen to the body, the heart had grown larger and less efficient until finally the disease manifested itself in the outward symptoms of shortness of breath, fatigue, and swollen limbs.

"How will she die?" Karla asked, purposely keeping her questions as unemotional as his answers.

"There's no way I can predict that," he said. "There are a dozen clinical things that can happen, but it all boils down to the fact that her heart will give out one way or another and stop beating."

"What about between now and then?"

"In the beginning, when she reaches a crisis point, there are a lot of things we can and will do."

It was one thing to know something—she'd come there knowing Anna was going to die—but it was another to feel it.

"What do you mean by crisis point?"

"She'll begin to swell, not just her legs, but her entire body. She won't be able to catch her breath and may even pass out."

"What do I do if I see that happening?"

"Get her to the hospital. As soon as possible."

What if it happened in the middle of the night? Or in the daytime when Anna was home and she was at the store? When her month was over and she was in Solvang again? Karla had stepped into a trap of her own making. No one had made her come. She could have stayed home and minded her own business, oblivious to the details of Anna's impending death, forgiven for her lack of attention by her ignorance. Now that she knew what was ahead, she'd closed that escape route and could only go forward. But what did that really mean?

She'd been there less than a day. How much deeper would she be involved in Anna's life in a month?

"What happens at the hospital?" she asked.

"Several things, depending on the severity of the episode."

"I guess what I really want to know is how much longer she has."

"That's impossible to say. I've have patients who are worse than Anna who have lived for years with the disease. I've had others who were not nearly as compromised and died a lot earlier than I had anticipated."

A woman dressed in the female version of Michaels's uniform appeared at the open door. "Ready?" she said, and then noticed Karla. "I'm sorry, I didn't see that you had someone with you."

"Hold up," Michaels said. "I'll be through here in a second." To Karla, he said, "Next time let the receptionist know that you'll be coming in with your grandmother and we can schedule a longer appointment for you." He began to move toward the door. "In the meantime, if you have any questions just give me a call."

Karla started to rise, but he was gone before she could get out of the chair. She felt a stirring of anger at his abrupt departure and contemplated letting the anger build. She needed a distraction, an outlet for what she was feeling, and anger had served her well all her life. But she instinctively knew it wouldn't work this time. No matter how explosive the temper tantrum, no matter how detailed her argument in favor of her cause, no matter how righteous her indignation, she couldn't erase the knowledge of what was ahead for Anna.

She found Anna in the waiting room calmly talking to the woman sitting next to her, as if she weren't the patient with the death sentence and all was right in her world. They rode the elevator in silence. Karla waited for Anna to ask what the doctor had said, dreading what she would tell her, wishing she'd insisted on not going in the examining room. Most of all, wishing she'd never come. What difference did it make whether Anna's estate was in order when she died? No one else seemed to care; why should she?

Karla opened the door that led to the parking garage and stood aside to let Anna through. "Wait here. I'll get the car."

"It's not that far." Anna tucked her hand into Karla's elbow and started up the ramp. "Besides, there's something I want to tell you, and if I wait until later, I'm afraid it will sound contrived. I really hate coming here. It reminds me that I'm dying and that there's not a damn thing I can do about it." She paused to catch her breath. "Having you with me made it easier somehow. I just wanted you to know that."

Of the dozen answers that came to mind, Karla was surprised at the one she chose. "Thank you for telling me. It was something I needed to hear."

CHAPTER 6

"WHY DON'T WE STOP SOMEWHERE FOR LUNCH?" Karla said as they drove away from the doctor's office. She was on the ramp for the elevated freeway before Anna answered her.

"If you don't mind, I think I'd just as soon go home and lie down for a while. If I have a nap, I'll be ready if we decide to do something tonight."

"Are you sure you're feeling all right? You don't look tired, you look exhausted." Even Karla flinched at the question—the third of its kind in less than ten minutes.

"There's something we have to get out of the way between us, Karla, and it seems now is the right time." Anna stuck her thumb under the shoulder strap on the seat belt and held it away from her body. "I really don't mind you talking to Dr. Michaels about me"—she turned to look at Karla for emphasis—"as long as you don't take what he tells you too seriously and start hovering. I have enough reminders of my own about whats happening without you adding to them."

"You would think I'd know better. I used to hate it when you would pick up on one of my moods and want to know what was bothering me. I swore I would never do that to anyone." She glanced at Anna with a self—effacing grin. "And here I am, doing it to you."

"Just what did you and Dr. Michaels talk about that's made you like this?"

"You—and what's ahead." She'd decided on honesty between them no matter how stark or brutal. Given a choice, it was the way she would want to be treated. Still, the words were hard to say aloud.

Anna returned her smile, only hers was accepting. "I'm sure he told you that I'm dying, but I'm just as sure he didn't tell you that it was going to be today. As a matter of fact, the last time I brought up the subject, he told me there wasn't any reason I couldn't last a couple more years. Good years, too. That's the only kind I want," she said insistently. "I suppose that's one of the things you've come here to talk about. At least I hope it is."

Karla needed time to think, to sort through all that she'd learned that morning, to regain some equilibrium. They traveled the next five miles with only the sounds of traffic to relieve the silence. Then, realizing that her retreat was a form of abandonment, she forced herself to ask, "Does it bother you to talk about what's happening?"

"You don't have to use euphemisms or dance around the subject. just say, does it bother me to know I'm dying. After all, it's why you're here. We both know that."

"I wish that weren't true," Karla said softly, as surprised at the revelation as she knew Anna was. "I'm sorry I can't tell you a convincing enough lie to make you believe I came here for another reason."

Anna turned to look out the window. "Maybe, by the time you leave you'll feel differently."

They'd had twenty years. There was no reason to think four weeks would change anything. Still, she conceded, "Maybe I will."

"We've talked about me enough. Tell me about you. At least tell me about the coffee shop. How were you able to leave it for a whole month?"

Karla wasn't ready for reciprocal intimacies. Her involvement in Anna's life was one thing; Anna's involvement in hers was another. Still, it was easier to answer than come up with a reason for not answering. "I had Jim come up from Los Angeles to run it for me."

"How is Jim?" Anna asked carefully.

"Fine."

"Is he still working for that movie company?"

The only way Anna could know about Winn Brothers Productions was through Grace or Heather. Karla

58

didn't like knowing her sisters were talking about her personal life to Anna. "They went out of business a couple of months ago."

"Oh, that's too bad. I know Grace was hoping he could help her get a job."

Grace had never said anything to her about talking to Jim. "Grace doesn't need Jim to help her. She's got one of the best agents in Los Angeles. All she needs is a break."

"I hope she can hold on long enough to see it happen. Living down there is so expensive."

"She's doing okay." Karla thought Grace had stopped dumping her problems on Anna, but wasn't surprised that she hadn't. Grace was a person who never let a thought go unspoken.

"It was lucky that Jim was free to take over the shop for you."

"Yes, it was."

"You don't want to talk about Jim to me, do you?"

"Not really."

"That's okay. It's none of my business anyway. It was just my clumsy way to let you know I was interested."

Karla hesitated over saying anything more. She couldn't remember one time she and Anna had talked about Jim that they hadn't ended up in a fight. "When I decided to come, it was either close up the shop or ask Jim to run it for me. I wasn't about to turn the place over to a stranger, and my part—time people already give me as many hours as they can. It happened that Jim was between jobs and willing to take it on for the month. He may have a lot of faults, but he's honest." She thought about what she'd said. To some, her grandmother especially, honesty included fidelity. "At

59

least he's honest when it comes to something like this."

"Seems to me he was the perfect choice, then."

Karla was aware how much the approval had cost Anna. "I'm pleased you agree."

"Do you think there's any chance the two of you will get back together?"

"No." As far as Karla was concerned, Anna had lost the right to ask about her and Jim when she'd refused to attend their wedding.

"Are you sure? There's no one else in your life right now—at least not according to Heather. Couples getting back together after a divorce isn't unheard of."

"You made it very clear that you never liked Jim. Why would you want me to get back together with him?"

"I was wrong. I never should have tried to stop you from marrying him. All I accomplished was to drive a wedge between us, and I've been sorry ever since."

"So now you think you can change that by giving your approval for us to get back together? It's not going to happen. Jim and I have gone our separate ways, and you and I are exactly where we have always been." She sounded cruel and didn't want to. "We may not have the best relationship, but it's foolish to waste time worrying about it now or trying to change things. At least we know where we stand with each other, Anna. That's something, don't you think?"

"I didn't mean to push you. It's just that sometimes I don't know when to stop."

"Me either. Maybe it's something genetic." It was the first time in Karla's memory she'd acknowledged they could have something in common.

"If so, it skipped your mother. We never argued—not about anything. That doesn't mean she listened to everything I said, mind you." Anna's smile at the memory was one of sweetness and longing. "She would just stand there with one of those innocent looks on her face, nodding her head as if she agreed with everything her father or I said, and then she'd go on and do whatever she'd had in mind to do in the first place."

"Daddy used to say she had a smile that could charm a general out of his stars."

"How lovely."

"He was always saying things like that about her. I used to love hearing him, especially when he said it in front of my friends." Grateful that they'd stumbled onto something neutral that they could talk about, Karla added, "They thought he was the most romantic man alive, straight out of the movies. I told him how they felt one day, even admitted I was proud that my friends thought he and Mom were special, and that I hoped when I grew up someone would love me the way he loved Mom." She'd never told anyone about that conversation, saving it the way she had the four—leaf clover she'd found at the cemetery on her mother's grave, giving the memory and clover special power without knowing what the power was. How ironic that when she'd finally told someone, it was Anna.

"And how did he answer you?"

What he'd said was so touching, so special, as she'd grown older she'd developed doubts about the accuracy of her memory. "He said I was destined to have one of the great loves of all time . . . poets would be unable to find the words to describe this love . . . that it would come to me so gently I wouldn't recognize it at first." She glanced at Anna and met her gaze. "Being the father of three daughters, it was almost a given that he'd develop a gift for telling fairy tales."

61

"There are so many things about your father I don't know. I was content that he made Marie happy and never thought to ask anything else. I missed so much of all of your lives."

"Why did you let it happen?" For once, she wasn't being judgmental, just curious as to how a mother could remove herself so completely from her own daughter's life. As far as Karla knew, her mother and grandmother loved each other, they just weren't particularly close.

"I didn't want your father to think I was interfering in their marriage. I had such a terrible time with Frank's mother that I swore I would never do anything like that to my own daughter and her husband. But I let it go too far. I thought I was giving her freedom, and now I'm afraid she actually saw it as disinterest. She must have thought I simply didn't care."

Again she reached up to loosen the shoulder harness. "Then you met Jim and I was so sure he was the wrong man for you that I rode that pendulum all the way to the other side. Frank's mother wouldn't have dreamed of doing what I did to you. I had no business telling you not to marry Jim, and I've regreted that I didn't go to the wedding every day since."

"And you still feel that way? Even knowing you were right about Jim?" Karla was testing. Anna wasn't the kind of woman who backed off easily or without laying groundwork for the retreat. Somewhere in the fractured apology was an "I told you so."

"Yes," Anna said without elaboration and then laughed. "Did I pass?"

Karla laughed, too. How could they know each other so well and be such strangers? "Mom said you never came to see us because you lived so far away. I told her I thought it was because you didn't like us. It must have

62

hurt her feelings. She didn't talk to me about you for a long time afterward."

Anna didn't say anything.

"It's so strange. . ." Karla went on. "I can reconstruct the entire conversation in my mind, everything except her answer." Again she looked over to Anna. "I know now why you never came to see us, but why didn't we visit you?"

"You did. A couple of times before Heather was born and then once after. You probably don't remember because you were so little. Then Frank died, and your father was transferred so often you barely had time to unpack before you were packing up to move again. Marie and I were always making grand plans to get together, but then something would come up and we would have to postpone the trip to another time." She opened her purse, took out a pill from a small container and stuck it under her tongue. "I thought we had so much time. I should have known better, especially after Frank died so young."

"She missed you," Karla said defensively. "I can't believe you didn't know how much. If I could see that, why couldn't you?" The moment her mother died, Karla had become her champion, a role she'd carried so long it had become as much a part of her as the scar on her chin. It was impossible not to defend her now, even if Anna was dying.

"At night I'd sit on the porch and make up stories in my mind about what she'd done that day. I always put myself in the picture, of course. We'd have long conversations while we prepared dinner together. Afterwards, when we were cleaning the kitchen, we'd get to laughing and carrying on the way we used to when she was at home. Your mother liked to laugh more than anyone I've ever known. She'd get tickled about some silly little thing and the more she thought about it, the more tickled she would get. She'd wind up sitting on the floor holding her sides, me right along with her. Half the time I wouldn't even know what we were laughing about."

This was a side to her mother Karla had never seen. She felt cheated. "I guess when you grow up things aren't as funny anymore."

"When I got the phone call in the hospital that she and your father had been killed in the accident, the first image of her that came to me was one of her laughing. It's stayed with me all this time."

"I see her in the car." Somehow, Karla had forgotten the reason Anna hadn't come to the funeral. She'd been in the hospital with a gallbladder attack, so ill the doctors had refused to release her.

"But you weren't there. At least that's what I was told. How is it that you know what she looked like?"

"I listened to everyone talk about the accident, every tiny detail over and over again, how many bones were broken, how long my father lived, how Mom's head went through the windshield, how much blood was in the car . . . everything."

"They had no business saying things like that in front of you. They should have been more careful. Someone should have protected you. I should have been there to protect you." She didn't say anything for several seconds, and then softly added, "I was told they both died immediately."

It would only take a sentence to destroy Anna's comforting image of a laughing daughter. Not only hadn't Marie died immediately, she'd lasted long enough to see her beloved husband die before her own

64

heart had run out of blood to pump. "She only lived a minute or two," Karla lied. "As I recall, it even says so on the death certificate," she added, compounding the lie.

"It would break my heart to think they suffered," Anna said.

"They didn't, so your heart is safe. At least from breaking." She cringed at what had been a stupid attempt at humor. "I'm sorry. That was a thoughtless thing to say."

"It's all right," Anna said. "We're new at this watching—what—we—say thing. It's a given that there'll be a little backsliding every now and then."

Karla changed lanes as they neared the Rocklin turnoff. "How long do your afternoon naps usually last? I looked through the cupboards this morning and there are some things we need from the store."

"Do as much shopping as you like. You don't have to worry about me."

"I was going to make an appointment at the bank for this afternoon to get into your safe—deposit box, but I think you've been through enough today. It can wait until tomorrow."

"I've been giving your being here some thought."

Karla exited and turned left, taking them under the freeway. "Oh?"

"I've decided you're right. There are some things that I need to put in order."

Karla had butted heads with Anna too many times to be drawn in by her seemingly easy capitulation. "What made you change your mind?"

"You have something I want. It seems only fair that I give you what you want in exchange."

"Okay, I'll bite. What do I have that you want?"

65

"All those years I missed with your mother."

Karla gave her a puzzled took.

"I want you to tell me about them. I want to hear everything you can remember, every detail, every moment."

If Karla had been instructed to draw up a list of a hundred possibilities, Anna's request would have been at the very bottom. "That doesn't make sense. What difference could it make now?"

"Why does it have to make sense?"

"As you said before, you'll be seeing her yourself soon. Why not ask her then?"

"I want the stories to come from you."

Karla felt as if she'd been backed into a corner. "If this is your idea of a way to foster some last—minute reconciliation between us, to . . . to . . . create some common ground to build a relationship on, it's too late, Anna. We can't erase nineteen years in four weeks. It's foolish to even try."

"Why?"

"Because you'll just be disappointed."

"At least I'll know we tried."

"The doctor said you're supposed to avoid things that upset you."

"If that's true, then the answer is obvious. Let me have what I want."

"I'm not going to let you blackmail me into this," Karla said. "You may be—"

"Why is it so hard for you to talk about your mother? I've tried since the day you first came here to get you to open up, but you were just as stubborn back then as you are now. Why?" The more agitated she got, the shorter and faster her breaths.

Upset at Anna's physical distress, at the obvious

signs of her grandmother's failing heart, at her own inability to control the situation, Karla burst out, "Because it hurts too much to talk about her."

Anna's eyes widened in surprise. "Even after all this time?"

"Even after all this time," she repeated woodenly. Her memories hadn't faded. They were as clear now as they had ever been, as poignant. She could still hear her father's laugh and see him coming up to put his arms around her mother as she worked at some chore. The way her parents had looked at each other, the smiles they gave no one else, the kisses they shared that had nothing to do with arriving or leaving were the guideposts Karla used to define love. After she started dating, it hadn't taken long to realize she'd set her standard impossibly high. If she wanted a man in her life, she would have to find a way to settle. And she had.

She waited for a car to pass and then turned into Anna's driveway. "If you were thinking about telling me how much better I'd feel if I got it all out, don't bother. I've already heard it from the best psychiatrist my HMO would provide."

"I didn't know you'd had therapy."

She stopped in front of the house so that Anna wouldn't have to walk from the detached garage. "If you want to call five sessions with a man who couldn't take his eyes off my chest long enough to look at my face 'therapy,' then I guess you could say I've had therapy."

"As much as I'd like you to believe this is for you, it's not," Anna said. "It's for me."

Karla sensed it was an argument she was going to lose. Anna had time and stubbornness on her side.

Without her grandmother's cooperation, Karla wouldn't get to finish half of what she'd planned to get done before she had to leave. "All right," Karla said, yielding. "You can ask your questions, but I reserve the right not to answer if I don't want to."

"Agreed."

Karla got out and went around the car to open Anna's door. She was about to add to the list of conditions that the questioning wouldn't start until they'd finished whatever Karla had planned for the day, when she saw how slowly Anna moved and decided it could wait. As she helped her out of the car and into the house, Karla was once again struck by how small Anna actually was. In her mind her grandmother was a giant figure, dominating the landscape of their time together. Karla wasn't sure where this diminutive, fading woman belonged in her life.

"Thank you for today," Anna said as Karla helped her into bed and turned to leave. "I know how you hate anything to do with doctors and hospitals."

There were some things she couldn't deny. She'd rather clean a friend's house than spend five minutes visiting her in the hospital. "You're welcome," she said.

Karla was inside her car, her seat belt in place, when she realized she hadn't given Anna her cell phone number in case she needed to reach her. She returned to the house, wrote her number on a slip of paper, and went to Anna's room. She was already asleep, propped up on a small mound of pillows, softly snoring, a pill bottle clutched in her left hand.

Karla had already propped the paper against the telephone and started to leave when she noticed a hand—knit afghan at the foot of the bed. The house was warm now, but in an hour or two the redwood tree beside the garage would put the bedroom in shade. Karla carefully opened the blanket and laid it over Anna, trying not to disturb her.

As she was leaving she heard a softly spoken, "Thank you, sweetheart."

No one had ever called her sweetheart. No one but her mother. The voice sounded so much like the way she remembered her mother's that she actually turned to look.

She and Anna were alone.

A terrible longing came over Karla. She was again the frightened fourteen—year—old who had lain in bed upstairs and cried silent tears for a mother who could not hear. Why now, when she was grown and strong and independent, had her mother finally answered?

CHAPTER 7

KARLA HATED PUBLIC PHONES. SHE COULD NEVER decide why exactly, only that she felt uncomfortable and transient whenever she used one. The one she'd chosen to finally return Jim's call was located outside at a relatively new Shell station and, as public phones went, was better than most. Still, she didn't like being there any more than she liked having to make the call.

She punched in the numbers to the shop, then her calling card number, and waited to be thanked by the breathy, impersonal voice she mentally answered in an equal breathy, impersonal voice.

Her hand tightened on the receiver when the phone rang at the other end and Jim answered with a cheerful, "Coffee Shop on the Corner—Jim speaking."

"It's Karla."

"It's about time. I was beginning to worry about you."

"I just got here last night and I told you I wouldn't call until I got to Anna's."

"You're usually so hands—on about this place. I don't know, I guess I thought you'd be checking in more often."

"Is that why you tried to reach me at Heather's?"

"So she told you? When I didn't hear, I thought maybe she hadn't."

He would never change. Their whole marriage, whenever there had been something wrong between them, he would wait for her to make the first move, to initiate the conversation, to start the fight. Now he was waiting for her to tell him she knew about the girlfriend.

"Are you there?" he asked.

She stared at a woman dressed in shorts and a T—shirt, pumping gas as she wiped sweat from her forehead. Halloween was less than a week away and it was ninety—one degrees. "How's the shop?" she finally asked, knowing she was only postponing the inevitable. "Any problems?"

"Not so far. Although we're down to our last ten pounds of French roast. When did you say the shipment was due?"

"Friday."

"We may run out before then."

She couldn't ignore the "we" any longer. By the warmth in his voice it was obvious that he meant someone other than the two part—time workers usually there. "Have you hired someone to help you?"

"What makes you think that?" he asked slowly.

"You keep saying 'we' as if you had someone there."

A long pause followed. "Heather didn't tell you?"

70

"What was Heather supposed to tell me, Jim?"

He knew her too well for her to get away with leading him on. "Damn it, Karla, don't make me do this." His voice dropped to a more private level. "I don't want to hurt you."

"Since when?" She lowered her head and saw a penny lying faceup on the asphalt. "Forget I said that. The last thing I want to do is rehash old times. I do think you could have asked before you moved your girlfriend into my house, however. That was a new low, even for you."

"She surprised me. I had no idea she was coming. Say the word and I'll find another place for us to stay."

It wasn't the answer she'd been looking for. She'd wanted him to say he would send the girlfriend back to Los Angeles. "Sounds serious," she said, knowing he would understand.

"I think she's the one, Karla. I know I've said it before, but I haven't even looked at another woman since I met her. What's even more amazing, I haven't wanted to."

If she believed for a second that he had any idea how much his words had hurt, she would be devastated. Instead, she said, "I hope it works out, then."

"Amy's been terrific about helping. She said to tell you what a great place you've got and how much she's enjoying herself."

Karla wasn't sure how much more she could take. "I can't pay her, Jim."

"She knows that. She's doing it for me. You know, learning the ropes and all."

"Why would she care about 'learning the ropes'?" She might not have the right to feel possessive about Jim anymore, but the shop was hers. She shared that with no one.

"I've decided I was an idiot for leaving this place. I love being back. Now don't laugh, but I've been thinking about finding a corner somewhere to set up a shop of my own."

"In Solvang?" She couldn't imagine anything worse.

"I wouldn't do that to you, Kay Bee," he said using his old nickname for her.

He wanted to be her friend. He actually thought he was her friend. She'd been so good at making room for him to be in that position in her life that he didn't have any idea how she really felt about him. "You might want to look into it a little more. With the chains expanding the way they are, a lot of the independent shops are having a hard time staying in business."

"Maybe I'll look into a franchise."

"From what I hear, they're pretty expensive." She meant to be helpful; instead she came across sounding negative even to herself.

He wasn't going to be discouraged. "I guess I forgot to tell you that I came into some money a while back, and for the first time in my life, I didn't immediately run out and spend it all."

"That's wonderful," she said with forced enthusiasm. Now that he was becoming the man she'd always encouraged him to be, he was in love with someone else. "I really should get back to Anna now. You can call me there if something comes up. Otherwise, I'll get back to you in a couple of days."

"Are you sure it's all right for me to call you there? What if she answers the phone? The way she feels about me, it's not going to do that heart of hers any good to hear my voice."

"She has bigger problems than hearing your voice."

"So this whole thing wasn't some ploy to get her wayward granddaughter to come home? She really is dying?"

She didn't want to face the answer by saying it aloud. "I'll tell you about it another time."

His voice serious, he asked, "Is there something I can do?"

"You're doing it." He could have been doing it alone, but it was plain that that bird had left the nest forever. Having Jim show up with a woman in tow was precisely the push she'd needed to get on with her life. "But I appreciate the offer."

"I know this is a crazy time to be saying this, but I never fully appreciated what we had until it was gone. I love you, Karla. I guess in a way I always will. You're the best friend I ever had."

How was she supposed to answer him? What could she possibly say except the obvious? "I'm glad you feel that way. I do, too."

She promised to call and they said good—bye.

Not knowing what else to do, she drove to a park near a new brick church, sat by herself on a bench under a heritage oak as old as the town itself, and cried until all the tissues in her purse were a soggy mess before she got up and went on with her day.

Karla was standing in line at the pharmacy section of the grocery store waiting to turn in Anna's new prescription when she heard someone call her name. She turned and saw Susan headed her way.

"How did the appointment go?" she asked, wheeling her cart closer.

"Fine—as far as I could tell. It was one of those in—and—out things."

Susan eyed Karla. "You look like hell."

She hadn't bothered to repair her makeup before going shopping. "Allergies."

"Doesn't look like allergies to me."

"It's been a rough morning," she admitted.

Susan came around the cart, and before Karla could figure out what she was going to do, put her arms around her in a long, care—giving hug. People turned to stare; even the pharmacist looked up from counting pills. Karla was embarrassed and speechless. She wasn't the kind of person people spontaneously hugged.

"Want something to take your mind off your troubles?" Susan asked.

Karla's first instinct was to say no. She always said no to people like Susan, because she felt out of her element with them. "Why not? I've got an hour or so before Anna said she usually gets up from her nap. What did you have in mind?"

She pointed to the cart. "How does feeding oranges and graham crackers to fifteen preschoolers sound?"

"Like riding a roller coaster through the fires of hell."

Susan laughed. "I like that. Mind if I use it sometime?" Pulling a card out her purse, she handed it to Karla. "There's a map on the back just in case, but you shouldn't need it. We're in the old Hadley house."

Karla looked at the card. "The Kids' Place? What is that?"

"My preschool—we talked about it last night, remember?"

"I remember you saying something about a kids' place, but I thought you were talking about your son and your house."

"I've been in business almost four years now."

"So you weren't kidding about the oranges and

graham crackers," Karla said. "You should know, I'm not very good with children."

Susan laughed. "I don't believe that for a minute. Heather said you're wonderful with hers." She saw that the pharmacist was ready and went to the counter with Karla. "But then, I'm offering you an hour's distraction, not a job."

"I'd love to see the place." When was she going to learn to say no and mean it? "I have one more stop, though. I'm looking for one of those pads that go on the shoulder strap of a seat belt. Any idea where I could find one?"

"Try the Chief Auto Store on Fairway."

"Fairway?"

"I keep forgetting how long you've been away. I'll bet you're glad to be back, though."

Karla didn't know how to answer her, so she just smiled.

Susan was wrong. Karla did have trouble finding the preschool. She circled the block twice before she recognized the old Hadley home. She'd been looking for something stereotypical, a place with cartoons on the walls and sandboxes behind a chain—link fence. Instead, what she found was a meticulously restored Victorian sporting gray and burgundy and cream paint with old—fashioned swings on the porch and flowerpots overflowing with yellow and burgundy and orange chrysanthemums scattered along the railing. An old farm wagon stood in the front yard filled with bales of hay and pumpkins and cornstalks, driven by a life—sized scarecrow.

Karla wasn't absolutely sure she was at the right house until she stepped on the porch and saw a discreet sign that said THE KIDS' PLACE under the doorbell. Susan came to the door before Karla had a chance to knock.

"I saw you pass by—twice," she said with a grin.

"This is not what I expected," Karla said.

"Good. That's the idea." She held the door open. "Come in. I'll show you around."

Susan's pride in what she'd accomplished came through in her voice and stance as they moved from room to room and she told Karla that The Kids' Place wasn't an impersonal baby—sitting service, but as close to a caring home environment as she could provide. There was one teacher for every four children younger than four, and one for every five of the four, and five—year—olds. The waiting list held enough children for two additional schools, but Susan was wary of expansion.

"And this is the dining room," Susan said.

Karla looked at what had once been the back parlor. Five child—size tables were set with plates, napkins, and whimsical Halloween centerpieces. "Nice," she said. "But then I love everything you've done in here, even the wallpaper."

"We got the place so cheap we were able to put more into fixing it up than I'd anticipated. At times looking for just the right knob or faucet was like being on a treasure hunt. I found the wallpaper at a restoration shop on a trip we took to visit Allen's family in Connecticut."

"Excuse me, Mrs. Stephens." A girl with black hair pulled into twin ponytails stood at the doorway.

"What is it, Cindy?"

"Janet wants to talk to you."

"Thank you. Please tell her that I'll be there in a minute."

Karla watched as the girl she guessed to be one of the five—year—olds left. "I'll bet she's a handful."

"Why do you say that?"

"That mischievous twinkle in those big blue eyes."

Susan laughed. "If I allowed gossiping about the children, I could tell you a tale or two about Cindy. But since I don't, about the best I can do is to tell you those twinkling eyes don't lie. There isn't a tree she won't climb or a challenge she won't accept."

The hour that Karla had worried would take forever to pass slipped away without notice. As disconnected as she usually felt around young mothers and their stories about child—rearing, she was fascinated by Susan's philosophy on the subject. She believed that under an umbrella of love should be a lovingly structured environment. Manners and social graces were a given, taught at school by example and expectation and reinforced at home. The hands—on teachers were called by their first names to foster close relationships; Susan was called Mrs. Stephens to show respect for her position. It was assumed every child was brilliant and meant to shine in something and that the joy of accomplishment came from inside. Susan's kids came to the preschool every day knowing they were special, because they were treated that way.

Of all the children she met, Karla was most fascinated by Cindy—her easy laughter, her self—confidence, her fearless climb to the top of monkey bars, and her stoic acceptance of the pain that came with a scraped elbow.

Later that night, while Karla was fixing dinner for herself and Anna, she found herself thinking about Cindy, wondering about her parents and what they had done right that so many others had done wrong.

"I can't remember the last time I slept so long," Anna

said from the doorway to the kitchen. "Or as well."

"I thought about waking you, but then you looked so peaceful I decided to let you sleep." Karla dropped the steamer basket she'd picked up at the store that afternoon into a pot and lit the burner. "I've got a roast and potatoes holding in the oven. The broccoli should be ready in a few minutes."

"Why don't we wait out on the porch? The sun's about to go down and I don't want to miss it."

"You go ahead. I'll set the table."

"That can wait." She waved for Karla to follow. "I can tell this one's going to be a beauty. The kind that should be shared."

Rather than argue, Karla turned the flame as low as it would go and followed Anna outside. "I made an appointment at the bank today," she said settling sideways on the railing while Anna sat in her rocking chair.

"With Mrs. Foster?"

"She's on vacation. Andrew Clark is covering for her."

"I don't like him," Anna said. "He's an overbearing ass and so full of himself his pants have gone up two sizes since he started working there."

"That's called middle—age spread."

"When is Mrs. Foster coming back?"

Karla sighed. Even with their agreement, she should have known Anna would set up roadblocks. "I didn't ask."

"Look at that sky, would you? Did you ever see anything as pretty?"

"I remember Mama telling me that Grandpa never planted anything that would get in the way of you seeing your sunsets." She had no idea where the memory had come from or when the conversation had taken place. It was just there, unbidden, a gift.

"He was a special man. . . . He loved doing things for others more than he ever did for himself. He spoiled me for anyone else."

Karla had always assumed Anna had stayed single because she was too old to be interested in dating after Frank died. But the older she became herself, the more she realized how young Anna had been when she became a widow. She'd lived without her beloved Frank for almost thirty years, learning about the plumbing and mowing and carpentry that were needed to keep the house going in addition to working a forty—hour week at the cleaners. She was a year from retiring when she started her second career—that of being a single parent.

"Was it hard living without Grandpa?"

"The hardest thing I've ever done."

"Even harder than raising three girls by yourself?" In the years she lived with Anna and in the time that had passed since, she'd never once stopped to imagine what having the three of them come to live with her must have been like for a woman alone. Thinking about it now was like being blindsided. The foundation of her long—held resentment cracked and left her as confused and frustrated as a bird trying to fly in a vacuum.

"I must not have told you often enough how much it meant to have the three of you here with me for you to ask that question now."

"But you were getting ready to retire. You could have gone out with your friends, traveled, moved to the coast—a hundred things other than being saddled with us." Anna loved the ocean as much as Karla did, and her mother had loved the mountains. She used to talk about the trips she had taken there as a little girl and how she'd promised herself that when she grew up she would have a house that sat on a cliff far out on a point. Once, after Karla had gone off to school, Anna had rented a house in Santa Cruz for a weekend. It was the only real vacation she ever took with any of them. Karla had said she would try to come up so the family could be together, but she hadn't even asked for the time off from work.

"I can't believe you didn't feel at least a little resentment when we showed up the way we did," Karla added.

"You didn't just show up. You came because I wanted you."

Was it the three of them she'd wanted? Or did the money that came with them provide some of the incentive? "If that's true, why did it take you two years to decide?" She might be confused about other things that had happened back then, but she was on solid ground with this one.

"Where did you hear that? I tried to get custody the week your mother and father died, but your father's family refused to even consider letting you go. They insisted you were better off with them because I was too old to take care of you properly. It was a difficult argument to counter. If you remember, Grace was only four at the time, and I was sixty—four."

Karla forced herself to remember that the robust, healthy woman who had controlled her life as a girl now occupied a frail, easily damaged shell. "You must not have tried very hard. As I remember it, none of the Beckers liked having us around. I find it hard to believe they actually fought to keep us."

"I went so far as to hire a lawyer," she said, indignant. And then, with irony, "But they had the

80

resources to hire someone better—your mother's and father's money. I'd given up hope when I got a phone call from your uncle telling me the family wasn't going to fight me anymore, that I could have all three of you as soon as I sent the money for the plane tickets."

"Why haven't I heard anything about this before now? Those two years we were being shuffled around my dad's family, I don't remember anyone saying anything about you at all—good or bad. I never even heard your name mentioned until the day I overheard Grandma and Grandpa Becker making plans to send us away."

"What about the letters I sent?"

"What letters?"

"I wrote to you every week, sometimes two or three times a week."

"I never got a letter from you—at least, I was never given a letter from you," she conceded.

"And the presents?"

Karla shook her head. Even if missing letters and presents bordered on cliché, she had no more reason not to believe Anna about this than Anna had to lie. "I wondered about our birthdays. You'd always sent us something when Mom and Dad were alive, and I couldn't figure why you'd stopped. I finally decided that with Mom gone, you didn't care anymore."

"No wonder you looked at me the way you did when you got off that plane. I'd never seen such hostility."

"That's not true," she automatically protested. And then, "What makes you think—"

"It's all right, Karla," Anna said gently. "It was a long time ago. You were young and confused about what was happening and how you should feel about it."

Excuse enough for then, but what about now? Finally,

Karla understood that the tone of voice Anna used whenever she talked about the Beckers wasn't neutral to hide her dislike, it was measured to hide her anger. She turned her back to Anna, as much to face the disappearing sun as to close herself off. She needed time to think, to absorb what Anna had told her, to sort through her memories and find the missing pieces that would fit their two versions of the same stories together.

"I still have the letters my lawyer sent and the ones their lawyer sent back if you want to see them," Anna told her. "They're in the bottom drawer of my dresser. I could get them for you now."

"If you don't mind, I think I've had enough for tonight. Could we talk about something else?"

"Certainly. The Beckers aren't my favorite topic either."

She turned back around. "Tell me about Grandpa?"

The runners on Anna's chair gently creaked as she thought and rocked for several seconds before she answered. "Did you know he spoke three languages?"

She hadn't. "Which ones?"

"Finnish for his father, German for his mother, and English for himself. He taught Marie a little German before she started school, but I suspect she lost most of it by the time she was a teenager.

"Frank was the kind of man who got up in the morning convinced the day ahead was full of possibilities. He passed his thinking on to your mother, teaching her how to laugh and take pleasure from the simple things in life. She got the good things from him, the ordinary from me."

In a matter of minutes the sky had changed from a soft pink to marigold orange and then to dark blue. The intense heat of the day settled into the bearable warmth of evening in what passed for autumn in the Central Valley.

"That's not true. . ." Karla said. "When Mama talked about home, she always talked about you. She saved stories about Grandpa for special times when we had company. Or when I wanted something we couldn't afford. Then she'd tell me how Grandpa had told her that the best things in life were created with a little bit of stuff and a whole lot of imagination and I'd appreciate something more if I made it myself."

Anna laughed. "If he told her that once, he told her a hundred times. She used to get so mad at him she'd march off to her room and wouldn't come out for hours."

"There was another one—when Heather or I would complain that we should be allowed to do something because we'd never done it before, Mama would say she wouldn't dream of breaking such a perfect record." Karla smiled wistfully. "I would get furious with her and she would tell me I had my grandfather to thank for that bit of wisdom."

Abruptly, Anna came forward in her chair. "I think I smell the broccoli."

"Damn." Karla jumped up and ran into the house. "It's okay," she called through the window.

Slowly, Anna eased back in the rocker, knowing she had a few minutes before Karla would have dinner on the table. If she'd thought about what she was doing, she would have let the broccoli burn.

Moments like the one they'd been sharing were like cattails that had burst and scattered their seeds in the wind.

If she were keeping score, she would count this first day a success. They still had a long way to go to break down the barrier that had kept them apart for nineteen years, but they'd loosened a brick or two. Not bad, considering that up until then nearly every contact had resulted in a new row added to the wall.

Karla came to the door. "It's ready."

With an effort she worked to keep hidden from her granddaughter, Anna stood. "I'll be there as soon as I wash up."

Karla held the door for her. "I forgot to tell you I ran into Susan at the store today. She invited me over to see her day care, so I stopped by on my way home."

Even if the "home" had been unconscious, a throwaway term, it gave Anna hope. "I haven't been there in weeks. Is the new playroom finished? I've been meaning to ask, but keep forgetting."

"It looked finished to me. The whole house looked great. She and Allen have worked miracles with the place."

Anna moved down the hallway toward the bathroom, concentrating on each step, resisting the urge to put her hand on the wall for support. By the time she joined Karla at the table, she was short of breath, but recovered faster than usual. Which was something that wasn't supposed to happen. Congestive heart failure didn't get better.

"Did Susan tell you she finally got her degree? Not from Stanford, of course, but a degree just the same," Anna said as she sat down at the table. "I don't know what her mother would have done without her during the trial. That's how she met Allen, you know. They had a fire alarm go off in the courtroom one day and he showed up with his fire truck. She tripped going down the stairs, he helped her up, they started dating, and the next year they were married. Heather was her maid of honor and Bill was a groomsman."

"I remember," Karla said. "I was invited to the wedding, but it was on a Friday evening and I couldn't get off work in time to get here."

"And all these years I thought you didn't come because you knew I would be there."

"I don't know that it even occurred to me." Karla mashed her potato with her fork and added a pat of butter. "Makes you wonder, doesn't it? How often do you suppose we look for slights that aren't there?"

"Is that a general question?"

Karla laughed. "Dangerous territory?"

"A battle with no winners." Anna had no appetite for old arguments or for the roast on her plate. Still, to please Karla, she took a bite and was surprised how good it tasted.

"Is the little Taylor girl still with Susan?" Anna asked, steering the conversation in a safer direction. "I can't remember whether she was supposed to start school this fall or had another year to go."

Karla poured herself and Anna a glass of water. "Which one is she?"

"Long black hair . . . blue eyes . . . sharp as a tack."

"You mean Cindy?"

Anna nodded. "Isn't she something?"

"More than I'd want to handle on a daily ·basis. Speaking of kids, what do you want to do· about Halloween this year?"

"The same thing I've always done. I sit out on the porch and hand out the candy as the kids come up. That way I don't have to answer the door a hundred times and I get a better chance to see all the costumes." Anna loved Halloween. She believed it was a holiday more filled with magic for children than any other, even

85

Christmas. She hated that adult parties had become the trend, leaving more and more houses dark to the brightly costumed trick—or—treaters.

"Remember the year Grace insisted she had to have that princess costume and then came home mad after she discovered half the girls in the neighborhood had exactly the same outfit?"

It was a night Anna would never forget. "She's always had a need to feel special."

"Still does," Karla said reaching for a second helping of potatoes. "And she can be just as big a pain about it now as she was then."

Anna was surprised at Karla's seeming criticism. It was the first time she'd ever heard her do anything but defend Grace. If it was a peace offering, she wanted to give something in return. "About Andrew Clark . . . I may not like him, but the bank obviously does. Since you've already made the arrangements, I suppose we should go ahead with them."

"You're too late," Karla said. I already changed the appointment."

Anna took another bite of broccoli. She couldn't remember the last time food had tasted this good or she'd enjoyed a meal more. "Maybe we should try burning something tomorrow night. I haven't had broccoli that tasted this good since . . . since . . . come to think of it, I don't remember broccoli ever tasting this good."

CHAPTER 8

THE NEXT DAY, ON IMPULSE, KARLA STOPPED BY THE Target in Roseville on her way back from getting her hair cut. With the television weatherman's promise of a dry Halloween, she'd picked up orange and black streamers, paper ghosts to hang from the liquidambar trees by the driveway, a monster for the front door, and ten bags of candy, five of which she personally didn't like and promised herself she would tell Anna to hand out last.

She'd hoped to have the decorating finished before Anna got up from her nap, but had barely cut the top off the pumpkin when she heard her coming down the hallway.

"What's this?" Anna asked. She looked pleased at what she'd found.

"I've never actually carved a pumpkin myself and thought it was about time I learned. Dad always did the honors when we were kids, then Heather took over when we moved in with you, then it was Jim." In reality, she'd never had any desire to get involved before now.

"Goodness, what a terrible thing to have to admit." Anna headed for the cupboard that held her medicine, filled her hand with an assortment of multicolored pills and swallowed them with a glass of water. "If you let me help, I promise I won't tell anyone it's your first time."

"The way it's going, you won't have to tell them. They'll be able to see for themselves." Karla frowned at the lopsided circle she'd cut. "This is a lot harder than it looks."

"You need a plan," Anna announced. "Take one of the pens out of the drawer by the sink and draw your pattern before you start cutting the face. And use that skinny knife in the block, the one with the black handle. First, though, we've got to get the inside cleaned out. There's a spoon with a long handle in the second drawer down. I use it for—"

Karla held her hands up in surrender. "I almost forgot how much you like to give orders."

Anna grinned sheepishly. "I guess I do at that: It's been so long since I've had anyone here that I could boss around it appears I may be trying to make up for lost time."

"You said the second drawer down?"

"Next to the grater." Anna peered inside the pumpkin. "I thought we were going to spend the afternoon going over those papers I gave you last night."

"I looked at them before I went to bed and decided they could wait a couple of days." Karla found the spoon and started on the pumpkin, scooping the insides into a bowl.

"Do you want me to separate the seeds?"

"What for?"

"To eat. Once they're cleaned and baked, you eat them like sunflower seeds, only I think they're better. I used to make them for you and your sisters every Halloween. I'm surprised you don't remember."

"Are you sure you're not mixing us up with Mom?"

"Positive. Your mother hated them. Which is probably why she never made them for you."

Karla went back to scooping while Anna got another bowl for the seeds. The ripe, earthy odor reminded her of another kitchen and conversation about pumpkins when she was ten and lived in Nebraska. "I remember one year Mom cooked a pumpkin she'd saved from Halloween and used it to make pies for Thanksgiving."

"I remember that, too," Anna said, her voice animated. "She called me for the recipe. I told her it was far too much work and that canned pumpkin was every bit as good—maybe even better. But she wanted to do something special that year. I don't recall if she said

88

why."

"Grandma and Grandpa Becker were coming, and she wanted to give them an old—fashioned holiday. Grandma Becker used to tell Dad—" Karla glanced at Anna. She looked away, but not before Karla saw a quick flash of pain pass through her eyes.

After several seconds, Karla said, "I don't know how to tell you about Mom without hurting you. My father's family was a big part of our lives. We spent every Christmas and Thanksgiving with them and almost every Mother's Day and Father's Day. Sometimes they showed up for no reason at all, not even letting us know they were coming. Mom wasn't too thrilled when that happened, but Dad was always excited to see them."

"I was such a fool," Anna said. "I like to think I would have realized eventually that caring wasn't the same as interfering, but I don't know that for sure any more than I know if Heather's going to have a boy or girl."

"She's having a girl," Karla said. "And she's going to name her Anna Marie." Heather would be furious when she found out Karla had stolen her surprise. But Heather hadn't talked to Anna's doctor. She still believed there was time to plan ahead for christenings and birthdays and family get—togethers, that the pleasure of anticipation for Anna could outweigh the pleasure of knowing a child was coming that would bear both her and her beloved daughter's names.

Karla would call Heather in a couple of days and explain her reasoning and eventually Heather would forgive her for the breach of confidence, because she would agree that it had been the right thing to do.

"Why are you telling me this now?" Anna asked, her voice bristling with annoyance.

It was not the reaction Karla had expected. "I thought you would like to know."

"But shouldn't Heather and Bill have been the ones to tell me?" The annoyance had become accusation.

Karla dropped the spoon on the table and reached for the towel to wipe her hands. What had been a pleasant, even a happy moment between them had abruptly turned into an argument. "There's no pleasing you. There never has been. There never will be."

"Let's not pretend this is anything but what it is. You told me because you feel sorry for me. I don't need that from you. I may be dying, but that doesn't make me special. It's something that happens to everyone sooner or later. Actually, I've been luckier than most. I've beaten the odds by a dozen years and I'm not through yet. As much as I want you to stop hating me before I die, Karla, I'm not willing to exchange it for your pity. And I can't think of any other reason you would tell me something that should have come from Heather."

"I don't pity you. And I don't hate you. I just don't like you very much. And nothing that's happened between us these past two days has made me change my mind."

"Fair enough. At least I know where I stand. But if it's not too much to ask, would you mind telling me what it is about me that you don't like?"

"I wouldn't know where to begin."

"Anywhere you'd like." Calm again, Anna brought the bowl of pulp to her side of the table and began extracting seeds as if only mildly interested in what Karla might say.

Karla started to leave and then changed her mind. She was through running from Anna. She sat down at the table again, plunged her hand into the bowl with the pulp and began extracting seeds also, as if it were some kind of contest between them. "Did you know Mom liked to read? She always had a stack of books by her nightstand and at least one in her purse."

"What has that got to do with why you don't like me?"

"Nothing. I don't want you to be able to say I didn't keep my end of our bargain."

"Marie learned to read when she was three years old, Anna said. "By the time she was seven, she'd read every children's book in the Rocklin library and we were making weekly trips up to Auburn so she could check books out there. But I didn't know she kept it up when she got married. I guess I thought she'd be too busy being a wife and mother."

"And she liked to sew." Karla looked at the orange goo on her hands, grabbed the towel and wiped them off, and went back to digging out the inside of the pumpkin. "She made a lot of our clothes—hers, too. One Easter she made all of us matching dresses. They were yellow and blue and pink with a white belt."

"She made me a pillow," Anna said. "I think it must have been out of the same material as your dresses." She'd put the ornately constructed pillow with its basket—weave pattern and pink welting on the end of the sofa where no one ever sat, and then, when Marie died, in a plastic bag in the closet away from light or heat or bodies that might cause it damage. She was saving it; she didn't know why or for whom, only that she couldn't bear to have it anywhere else or to see it damaged in any way. "Wait a minute, I'll show you."

Anna didn't have to search her closet; she knew right where to look. Lovingly, knowing she was touching cloth her daughter had touched, looking at stitches her daughter had sewn, holding a gift Marie had made especially for her—the last one she had ever made—Anna took the pillow from its bag and went back to the kitchen.

"Is this it?" she asked.

Karla looked up from the pumpkin. "Oh, my God," she said in a choked whisper. "I'd forgotten all about your pillow. I remember Mom making it. . . . She worked so hard to get all the pieces to fit. . . . She was so proud of the way it turned out."

"Would you like to have it?" Karla would never know how precious the offering or how hard it would be for Anna to let go of this gift from her daughter.

"Yes," Karla said, moisture shimmering in her eyes. She looked from the pillow to Anna. "I'm sorry I told you about the baby. I'll call Heather tonight and tell her what I've done."

"No—don't. I'll act surprised when she tells me and she never needs to know."

"I thought I was doing you a favor, but instead I ruined it for you both."

"No you didn't. You wanted to give me more time to enjoy knowing there would be another Anna in this world. How could I be mad at you for that?"

"Are you sure about the pillow?"

"There isn't anyone else who would understand. You and I are the only ones left who remember the dresses or Marie. We're the ones with the memories, the only ones who really know what a special woman she was. When I die, you'll be alone in this, Karla. Please, don't let us waste this precious time we've been given. You have to think of the things you might someday want to know about your mother and ask me now."

"She left this terrible hole in my heart when she

died." A lone tear rolled down Karla's cheek. "I keep thinking it will close one day, but it never has. I used to be so angry with her for dying, for leaving me alone, for not even saying good—bye, that I would go off by myself and scream as loud as I could that I didn't love her anymore."

"Did it help?"

"Nothing ever helped." She took a tissue from the box on the refrigerator and wiped her eyes. "Did you know I went to Tennessee to see her and Dad's graves when I graduated from college? It was my graduation gift to myself. I was hoping it would make me feel closer to her, but all it did was make me angry all over again that Grandma and Grandpa Becker threw such a fit about not letting Daddy be buried in California." Again, she wiped her eyes, as if stopping the tears before they fell denied she was crying.

"How do you remember that?"

"I don't know. Some things are just there."

"It was so hard for me to leave her in Tennessee," Anna said. "I wanted her to be with Frank, but couldn't bear to think of her separated from your father. Did you ever go again?"

Karla shook her head. "Once was enough. I learned that who she was and what she gave me isn't buried in some cemetery. My mother is as much a part of me as my arm or leg, and she always will be. I accept that now."

"You have your anger," Anna said with sorrow. "I have my regret."

CHAPTER 9

SUSAN STOPPED BY ON HER WAY HOME FROM WORK later that night, Cindy Taylor in tow. "We had some extra decorations left over that we were going to put up for you," she said to Anna. "But I see someone beat me to it. The porch looks great. And I love the ghosts in the trees."

"We brung some cookies, too," Cindy said.

"Brought," Susan automatically corrected.

"*Brought*," Cindy dutifully mimicked.

"Come in," Anna said, holding the door. "I'll trade you pumpkin seeds for the cookies. Fresh—roasted this afternoon."

Susan put her hand on Cindy's shoulder and guided her inside. "Should you be eating all that salt?"

"We made some without." She'd learned to deal passively with all the well—meaning but irritating questions that came with having people know her condition. She looked at Cindy and smiled. "I haven't seen you since summer. How are you doing?"

"Fine."

"And your father?"

"He's working." She followed them into the kitchen. "Somebody's dog got bit by something and he had to operate on it." She perched on the nearest chair. "Mrs. Stephens is going to take me home with her so I can play with Bobby until my daddy can come and get me."

"The woman who usually picks up Cindy is on vacation so I told Mark that she could come home with me." Susan reached into the bag she'd brought and took out a plate of sugar cookies shaped like ghosts and

94

witches and decorated with frosting and sprinkles.

"I fell off the swing today," Cindy announced.

Anna gave what she hoped was a properly concerned look as she offered Cindy the bowl of pumpkin seeds. "Did you get hurt?"

"Just my knee." She lifted her knee up for Anna to see. "But it's better now."

"Where's Karla?" Susan asked.

"At the bank arranging to have my safe—deposit box drilled open."

Susan laughed. "Wait until I tell Allen. He's convinced I'm the only one who ever lost a safe—deposit key. I told him it happens all the time."

"Is he home today?" She and Allen had worked out an arrangement where he took care of the things around the house that Anna couldn't do for herself and she put whatever she thought was fair payment into a college account for Bobby. "I wanted to talk to him about pruning the pyracantha when he has the time."

"He's just starting his four—day—off cycle now. I'll have him call you. Can you believe it, he's finally going to be home to take Bobby trick—or—treating. I think he's more excited about it than Bobby is."

Allen was a firefighter with the Sacramento Fire Department and had a work schedule that confounded Anna. To her it seemed he was either always working or always home. "Did you make Allen a costume?"

"He made his own—Dracula. Pretty original, huh?" Susan looked up at the sound of a car pulling into the driveway. "Oh, good, Karla's back. I wanted to ask the two of you to dinner this Saturday. Allen's father called last night from his fishing trip and said he was bringing back the mother of all salmon and that we were to have the coals fired up and waiting."

95

"I can't answer for Karla, but I'd love to come."

Seconds later Karla came in, spotting Cindy before Susan. Her frustration and anger over banking bureaucracy faded at the smile that lit the little girl's face. "We meet again," she said.

"I'm going to Mrs. Stephens's house. Wanna come? We're going to eat salmon."

"Wrong day, Cindy," Susan said. "We want Karla to come on Saturday."

Karla looked to Anna. "We've been invited to a barbecue at the Stephens'," Anna said.

Karla was rarely spontaneous with invitations or replies, but obviously Susan was expecting an answer right away. "I don't know. . . Anna, what do you think?"

"I already said I was going."

"Then I'd love to come, too. Thank you for including me."

"How does between five and five—thirty sound?"

"Great. What can I bring?"

Susan thought a minute. "I hate making desserts. Would you mind?"

"Cake would be good," Cindy chimed in. "With chocolate frosting."

Cindy was a new experience for Karla—nothing like Jamie and Jason, who were shy around strangers and difficult to get to know. "Then cake it is," Karla told her.

"Allen will be pleased." Susan grabbed her purse. "Gotta run. I still have to stop by the store to pick up dinner."

Cindy climbed down from the chair and joined Susan. "Thank you for the seeds," she said to Anna. "They were really good."

"I'm glad you liked them."

"Wait a minute." Karla took a sandwich bag out of the drawer. "You can take some with you."

Cindy hesitated. She moved close enough to Karla to whisper, "I didn't really like them very much."

Karla put the bag back in the drawer. "Me either," she said softly.

Anna stood on the porch next to Karla and waved as Susan drove away "Shame on you for lying to that child."

"I didn't lie to—"

"How could you tell her you don't like my pumpkin seeds when I could see for myself how much you enjoyed them?"

Karla laughed out loud. "I'm sorry, Anna, but if it was pumpkin seeds or starvation, I'm afraid I'd have to give it serious consideration."

Susan and Allen lived in Stanford Ranch in a house rescued from the normal postage—stamp—sized back yard by being located on a cul—de—sac. Allen had turned the pie—shaped quarter acre into a showplace of planters, walkways, and grass. The trees by the barbecue sported lights shaped like leaves, and the wooden deck held an assortment of chairs and three tables laden with food.

Susan greeted them, added the cake Karla had baked from a mix that afternoon to one of the tables, found a chair for Anna, and then took Karla on the rounds to meet everyone.

"The guy rolling around the grass with the kids is Mark Taylor." Susan had saved him for last.

"Cindy's father," Karla supplied. "Did I meet his wife? I'm usually good with names, but I'm having trouble remembering everyone tonight."

97

"Mark isn't married—at least not anymore. He and Linda divorced about three years ago. She was a singer in a rock band when they met and thought she was ready to give it up for hearth and home but then discovered she didn't just like being on the road, it was the way she defined herself. She was lost staying home and making everyone around her miserable."

"Too bad she didn't figure out how she felt before Cindy was born."

"Don't tell Mark that. He thinks Cindy was the best thing to come out of their marriage. Actually, he and Linda are still good friends. Sometimes when she comes to see Cindy and can only be in town for a couple of days she even stays with them."

Karla dismissed the man wrestling with three energy—filled preschoolers as someone trying to hang on to a woman long gone. She recognized the symptoms; she'd had the disease.

Allen came up to them balancing three glasses of white wine, the stems tucked between the fingers of one hand. "Chardonnay of slightly questionable vintage for the ladies," he announced. "Take a taste and if you think we should save it for salad dressing, I'll pour another round."

Karla took a tentative sip and was surprised at the quality. "It's wonderful," she announced.

Susan agreed. "Where did you get it?"

"Mark. It's part of the case the guy sent him for saving his dog."

Karla tried it again. "He must have been very, very grateful. This stuff wasn't cheap."

"You might tell Mark. The only way he can tell cheap from expensive is if you leave the price on the bottle."

Susan laughed. "That's a terrible thing to say."

"Terrible, maybe, but true."

"Pardon me for intruding," Mark said, draping his arm across Allen's shoulder. "But I could swear I just heard my name mentioned."

"You did, but only in the highest terms," Allen assured him.

Mark looked directly into Karla's eyes. "I don't think we've met—no, I know we haven't met. I would remember."

She tried to break the eye contact but was held by the force of his gaze. "Karla Esterbrook."

He held out his hand. "Of course. I should have known."

"I don't understand." He held her hand as long and confidently as he'd looked into her eyes.

"Cindy told me about you."

"She did?" Knowing that Cindy thought her important enough to talk about to her father pleased Karla. She held up her glass. "Great wine."

He looked confused for a second and then understood. "The man who gave it to me said that it was from one of those wineries in Sonoma that only sells to restaurants and a select list of customers. He told me to save it to share with special friends."

His curiosity getting the better of him, Allen finally took a drink. "My God, have you tasted this stuff?" he asked Mark.

"Not yet."

"It's terrible. I can't imagine what that guy was thinking dumping it on you that way, especially after you saved his dog. Why don't you let me take it off your hands? If nothing else, we can use it to cook with at the fire house."

"It must be even better than I thought," Mark said,

99

reaching for Allen's glass. He held it aloft and tipped it in Karla's direction. "Here's to new friends . . ." He tilted his head to Susan and Allen and smiled. "And to old ones, too."

Mark Taylor was the kind of man who could carry off the disheveled look. She had no doubt he was more handsome when his shirt and hair didn't show the effects of wrestling on the lawn with preschoolers, but then she wouldn't have to fight the urge to finger—comb the strands from his forehead or brush the grass from his shoulder. And she'd never been attracted to the smile or sparkle in the eyes of someone more slickly turned out. Maybe it was that he looked safe. Or maybe it was that he was one of the best looking men she'd ever met.

"Not bad," Mark said after tasting the wine. "Almost as good as that stuff we had the other night at the pizza place."

Allen shook his head. "What a waste."

Cindy came up and leaned against Mark's leg. "I'm hungry, Dad. Would it be okay if I had a cookie?"

"You can have three pieces of celery and two carrot sticks or one cookie."

"Some olives, too?"

"Black or green?"

"Black."

"You can have four."

She took off without saying anything more.

"Was that four olives and a cookie?" Karla asked.

Mark blinked in surprise and then laughed. "Probably."

"How did trick—or—treating go last night?" Susan asked him.

"She came home with a ton of candy. I don't

remember people being that generous when I was a kid."

"Are you from around here?" Karla asked.

"Fresno. My folks have a farm there."

Susan nudged Allen. "Cindy's not the only hungry one. My stomach's growling, too. You start the barbecue and I'll bring out the salads."

The salmon was the best Karla had ever eaten. Even Anna had a second helping but began to fade long before the party was ready to break up.

"I don't know about you, but I'm getting a little tired," Karla said as she sat down next to Anna.

"You're no more tired than Cindy is," Anna gently chided her. "But I appreciate the gesture. Why don't I stay here while you say good—bye for both of us? And be sure to tell Susan I said everything was perfect, as usual."

Karla made the rounds, thanking Susan and Allen for their hospitality, wrapping a piece of cake to take home for Anna to eat later, and retrieving her and Anna's purses from the closet. On her way out she ran into Mark.

"It was nice meeting you," she said politely, adding an equally polite smile.

"Allen said you're going to be in town for a while."

"A couple more weeks at least."

"I have tickets to some kind of concert this Wednesday; how about going with me?"

"Some kind of concert?" she repeated. "Another grateful client, I suppose?"

"Something like that. If you need to know who's going to be there, I'll look and call you when I get home. Otherwise, we could just live dangerously and both be surprised."

101

"I really hate surprises."

"Then I'll call."

"No, don't." She had no business going out with him. She was there to work, not play.

"Decided to be adventurous—I like that. I'll pick you up at six. That way we can grab a hamburger first."

He smiled, and she was tongue—tied, incapable of putting together the words that would get her out of a date she'd had no intention of making. "Do you need directions?"

"To the concert?"

"To my grandmother's house." As soon as she'd said it, she realized she'd been had. "I'll see you Wednesday. If I'm not home, go ahead without me. I'll meet you there."

"But how will you know where to go?" A second later he grinned. "You got me. Nice going."

When Karla came downstairs the next morning, Anna was in the living room waiting for her. She looked up from the book she was reading and motioned for Karla to sit next to her.

"Come see what I found in that box you brought in from the garage yesterday. It's been so long since I looked at what was out there, I'd forgotten most of this stuff existed."

Karla sat on the cushion next to Anna's. "What is it?"

"A scrapbook your mother put together when she was a junior in high school." Anna slid the leather—bound album halfway onto Karla's lap. "This was the program from her first big dance." Something slipped out of the pages. "Oh, and look . . . one of the flowers from her corsage." She gently turned to the next page as if she were afraid it would disintegrate in her hands. "And this

102

is the letter she earned playing varsity tennis."

"She played tennis?"

"All four years." She pointed to a faded color photograph of two young girls standing behind prison bars. "I'd forgotten all about the time we took Marie and her friend Donna to San Francisco for Marie's birthday."

"Where were they when this was taken?"

"Alcatraz. It was the middle of May and bright sunshine outside, and still we almost froze before we got off that island."

"I don't remember Mom ever talking about a Donna. Were they good friends?"

"Best friends—until she stole your mother's first serious boyfriend and dropped out of school six months later to have his baby."

"Mom must have been devastated."

"She was, for about a month or so, but then she met your father."

"Did you like my dad back then?"

"Not one bit. I could see from the first time she brought him home that it was serious between them. She was only sixteen, he was twenty, in the Air Force, and out on his own. They were married the summer she graduated and left for Arkansas a month later. Did you know they stayed here with me and your grandfather when they got back from their honeymoon? It was only a couple of weeks, but I loved every minute they were here."

Karla shook her head. "Maybe she was saving that to tell me when I was older." She picked up a picture of her mother and father that had been tucked behind another program, this one for a school play. They were standing in front of an old car. "She looks so young here."

"She was. They both were."

"She was only a year older than I am right now when she died," Karla said. "I've thought about that a lot lately, about how much she missed. It's hard to imagine her growing old. She'd be a grandmother now—with gray hair and glasses."

"Gray hair, maybe, but not glasses. I can't remember one member of our family ever wearing glasses." Anna turned the page. "Here she is on the homecoming float."

"Where?"

"The one in the lumberjack costume."

Karla opened the dance program for that same homecoming that had been glued to the opposite page. There was writing inside. Her mother's. She leaned forward and read aloud what it said. "Tonight was the best night of my life. I didn't think I was going to get to go to the dance because Dad said we didn't have money for a new dress. But Mom found some material and she made me one that looked like it came from the Weinstocks' downtown. No one could tell it was homemade. None of my friends have mothers like her. She's the best there is. I love her to pieces."

Karla glanced at Anna. "Did you know this was here?"

"I never looked at this without your mother." She read and reread the long—ago written note. "It's almost as if she sent you here to find it for me."

Karla closed the book. "Come with me." She stood and held out her hand to Anna, a gesture that would not have happened just a week ago. "I'm taking you to breakfast."

"Are we celebrating something?"

"Indeed we are. I'm not sure what it is, but I don't

care." She felt wonderful and she felt free and didn't question that she didn't know why.

CHAPTER 10

"SO, HOW'S IT GOING?" HEATHER ASKED. "YOU WERE supposed to call me last weekend."

Karla balanced the phone between her ear and shoulder and opened the closet door. Not knowing how to dress, she'd checked the paper to see what concerts were playing in the Sacramento area and had come up with everything from chamber music to Clint Black. "I forgot."

"How's Grandma?"

"Fine."

"Fine? That's it? You can't elaborate a little?"

"Could I call you back later?" She took a sweater out and studied it. Too bulky. "Tomorrow, maybe? Anna and I just got back from the bank and I'm running late."

"All I want is five minutes."

"I still haven't decided what I'm going to wear and Mark—" She caught herself, but too late.

"Whoa . . . Did I hear you right? Could you possibly have said a man's name in connection with looking for something to wear? Does this mean you actually have a date?"

"It isn't exactly a date."

"Then what is it exactly?"

"He's the father of a friend. He happened to have an extra ticket to a concert and didn't have anyone to go with him. So I said I wasn't doing anything and he asked me if I'd like to come along." The truth, but stretched farther than the old Rubber Man could have

105

managed, even on his most flexible day.

"How disappointing."

Karla pulled out a second sweater, a short—sleeved, burnt orange cashmere more in keeping with the lower temperatures that had moved in on Monday. "How are you feeling? Better yet, how's the baby? Still using your bladder for a trampoline?"

"She's been quieter than usual lately. I have an appointment next week to talk to the doctor about it. Bill thinks it's my imagination. He says I'm anxious for the baby to get here so I can get Anna moved in with us. I don't know, maybe he's right."

Karla started through the limited clothing she'd brought with her all over again. "When was the last time you talked to Anna about moving in with you?"

"I know, she says she doesn't want to, but that's because she's worried about being a burden. As soon as I convince her that it's something Bill and I really want, she'll change her mind."

"She likes living in Rocklin, Heather." Karla added a brown wool skirt and jacket to the growing pile of clothes on the bed. "She doesn't want to give up her home and friends. Susan is wonderful with her, and I have an appointment with an agency that does in—home care. As soon as Anna and Dr. Michaels think it's necessary, she can have someone come and stay at the house with her."

"Why would you do that?" Heather said angrily. "You know how much I've been looking forward to having her stay with me."

"Isn't what she wants more important?"

"Since when do you care what Grandma wants?"

"Can we *please* talk about this later?"

"Promise me you won't do anything more about

hiring someone until we do."

"Okay, I promise."

"How is Susan?"

"*Heather*, I really do have to get ready."

"It would take you less time to tell me than to complain about it."

"She's fine."

"Just like Grandma, huh?"

"The same." Karla kicked off her shoes and unzipped her jeans. "Now I'm going to hang up on you."

"Give Grandma my love."

"Give it to her yourself She's just downstairs—I'll put her on the phone."

"Love you," Heather said.

"Love you, too." Karla opened the door to call to Anna, waited for her to pick up the phone, and said, "Bye . . . talk to you soon."

She glanced out the window as she replaced the receiver and saw a dark green Jeep Grand Cherokee turn into the driveway. "Damn—wouldn't you know it, he's right on time." She raced for the bed and her clothes. "I should have known, he's just the type."

She wiggled out of her jeans, pulled her sweatshirt over her head, grabbed a pair of panty hose and her skirt and sweater, and managed to get everything on except her earrings before the doorbell rang. Stepping into her shoes, she ran a brush through her hair, added spray and a quick spritz of perfume, and was halfway down the stairs by the time Anna had Mark seated in the living room.

"Hi." She actually managed to make it sound casual.

Mark smiled. "Ready?"

"Just have to get my purse and jacket. I'll be right back." This time she took the stairs at a more reasonable pace, pleased that she'd been on time at least once that day and discovering that she was actually looking forward to her night out.

They were on Sunrise Boulevard headed south when Karla crossed her legs and discovered she'd put on her panty hose backward. The heel was on top of her foot, the excess material bunched at her ankle. If she pointed her toes, it didn't look as bad, but she had a feeling Mark might think her a little strange if she tried to walk that way.

"You look great, by the way. I meant to tell you earlier. Whatever color that sweater is, it's become my new favorite."

"Burnt orange. And thank you." Not to be outdone, she gave him a quick once over. "You don't look so bad yourself." He had on tan slacks, a striped shirt open at the collar and a navy blue jacket.

He grinned. "I'm pleased you noticed. It takes a lot of thought to put this stuff together—which is probably why I don't go out very often. Has to be someone or something special."

She was tempted to ask which applied this evening, but thought better of it. He would undoubtedly come up with some outrageous compliment she'd know was a lie but would believe anyway, and where would that get her?

"You haven't asked what we're seeing," Mark said. "Not even a little curious?"

He had the kind of voice that narrated nature shows, deep and empathic, every distinctly spoken word flowing easily into the next. "I'm past caring. After the day I've had, I'm up for anything."

"Good or bad?"

"Both, in a way." She tried tucking her feet to the

side, but the position was so awkward she was afraid her legs would fall asleep and she'd take a nosedive when she got out of the car. "Anna had an appointment with her lawyer to go over some papers this morning and to set up a living will. Then we went through her safe—deposit box this afternoon and found a bunch of things she thought she'd lost, including her wedding ring."

"That must have been hard."

"You'd think so, but she's remarkably accepting of what's happening to her."

"I meant for you. Susan said she was more a mother to you and your sisters than grandmother. It has to be hard to see her purposely tidying her life in preparation for the end."

"Actually, it was my idea." She steeled herself for his disapproval. "I thought it would give her peace of mind to know everything was taken care of. I know it would me."

"I never looked at it that way. I figure as long as I've made sure Cindy is taken care of, the rest can take care of itself."

"Obviously, you've never had to settle anyone's estate. I worked for a CPA who specialized in estate planning, and even when everything is spelled out in a will, people can still go at each other. I saw two brothers almost come to blows over a set of cuff links they both privately admitted they didn't like."

"I've never lost anyone who wanted me to have anything," he admitted as he stopped at a red light and turned to look at her. "I guess that means I should keep my mouth shut until I know what I'm talking about."

It was a good thing he'd given her a wink as he said it or she would have taken him seriously. "Enough about what I'm doing in Rocklin. Since you're plainly not going to volunteer the information, I guess I'm going to have to ask. Whose concert are we attending?"

"It's a sixties revival—one of those Dick Clark kind of things where they gather everyone who had a hit during the decade and is still capable of walking on a stage and send them out on tour."

Somehow she'd missed seeing the notice in the paper. While she'd never purposely choose a revival of anything—short of Shakespeare—as a way to spend an evening, the more she thought about it, the better it sounded. "What fun."

Mark laughed. "You did that really well."

"I'm serious. It does sound like fun. I can see now why you suggested hamburgers. It's a theme thing you've got going. If I'd known, I would have worn a poodle skirt."

"Wrong decade. Poodle skirts were in the fifties. My mom had an original that she wore when she chaperoned my sister's high school dances."

Deciding any man who would take a woman to a sixties revival on their first date wasn't someone who sweated the small stuff, Karla leaned back against the seat and stopped trying to hide her feet. "She saved you the embarrassment of wearing it to your dances, or was the skirt worn out by then?"

"Neither. I skipped my high school dances. I was king of the nerds back then and dead sure no one would go with me, so I wisely decided to save myself the rejection."

Nerds didn't come in Mark Taylor packages. She had no doubt half the women who brought their pets to him did so as much for themselves as for their animals.

"You're kidding, right?" She'd reached the point

110

where she couldn't tell.

"Nope. I was more interested in hanging out with the local vet than I was girls back then, and that kind of thing gets you a reputation."

"I imagine it would. Especially if the vet were female and good—looking."

"Oh, I like that. You catch on quick."

"So do you still have a thing for older women?"

"Now it's the other way around. I like them young. As a matter of fact, I've got a real thing going now for a little charmer who's about to turn five."

Karla smiled. "I can see why."

"She likes you, too. And I've never known Cindy to be wrong about people."

Mark pulled into the turn lane and waited for the traffic to clear. "You were serious about the hamburgers," Karla said as soon as she saw where they were going. "I had no idea In and Out had finally made it to Sacramento. I love this place."

"It was as close to a sixties hamburger joint as I could come up with."

"It's perfect." She didn't know whether it was knowing she would be gone in less than three weeks and would likely never see Mark again or the need for a night that allowed her to escape witnessing Anna's battle with her disease, whatever the reason, she embraced the feeling of freedom and sat back to enjoy the evening.

On the way home they sang songs from the show. Mark led and Karla followed—it was that or sit and listen. Mark's enthusiasm made up for his lack of talent; she worked to keep them in tune.

They reached the house far too soon. Karla wasn't ready for the night to end but said nothing.

Mark had told her earlier that he had surgery first thing in the morning and a full day of appointments.

He opened her door, a politeness she liked and was pleased to see making a return, and walked her to the door.

"I had a lot more fun than I expected," she said, teasing him. "Please thank that 'grateful' client for me."

He laughed. "When did you figure it out?"

"I had a hunch as soon as you told me where we were going. It's hard to imagine anyone giving someone tickets for a sixties revival as a way to show their appreciation."

"I'm wounded. Do you have any idea how hard it was for me to get those tickets?"

She decided to play along. "I can't imagine."

"Damn hard."

"That's it?'"

"All right, if you must know, I had to promise to play golf with one of my partners next week."

"You really did that for me? I'm so impressed."

Grinning, he said, "And I'd do it again."

"Golf or date?"

"Both."

Without giving herself time to think or change her mind, she said, "When?"

"Saturday," he shot back. "Are you up for a day with me and Cindy at the park—weather permitting?"

"Uh . . . I don't—'"

Come on, don't start getting indecisive on me."

"I told Anna I'd take her to get her hair done. And the only appointment her hairdresser had open this week was on Saturday."

He thought a minute. "What time?"

"Eleven—thirty. And afterwards we were going to

lunch."

"Where do you want to meet?"

She wasn't sure she understood. "You want to go to lunch with us? You and Cindy?"

"Is there a problem with that?"

"No. Anna would love it. So would I." They set the time and place. "I'll see you then." Karla extended her hand.

Mark looked at her hand and then at her. "Sorry, I'm not that kind of guy. I never shake hands on a first date." He put his foot on the step where she was standing and came forward. "Now a nice, friendly kiss is another matter altogether."

His lips were on her cheek before she could react. She was both surprised that he'd kissed her and disappointed that his aim hadn't been more accurate.

As if he could read her mind, he said, "Next time." He turned to leave, caught his foot on the bottom step, and had to wave his arms wildly to keep from falling. When he'd regained his balance, he grinned sheepishly, stuffed his hands in his pockets and looked up at her. "Damn—" he said, plainly embarrassed. "All I had to do was make it to the truck and I would have pulled it off."

She laughed. "Don't let it bother you. I like you even better now that I know you're not perfect."

Mark glanced at the dashboard clock as he turned onto Taylor Road and headed for the clinic. He'd promised the sitter he'd be home by midnight which gave him forty—five minutes to check on the Irish setter he'd operated on that afternoon and finish the supply order he'd started two days ago.

The setter was a stray that had been hit and left by the

113

side of the road. A teenage boy had picked it up and delivered it to the clinic. The kid offered to work at the clinic until the bill was paid, but Mark told him they'd get it from the owner, knowing full well it wouldn't happen.

Since Mark was the only one with an opening in his schedule, he took the surgery, doing what he could to repair a severe diaphragmatic hernia. The dog was barely breathing. An X ray showed the intestines, the liver, and the stomach had protruded through a rupture in the diaphragm and depressed the lungs. He went in, repaired the rupture, and shoved everything back into place. After he closed, he sutured several lacerations over the shoulder and hips.

It was the kind of case Mark loved—the lost cause, the one where the spirit of the animal was as important as the skill of the veterinarian. He was attracted to that spirit in animals and humans alike.

Which was undoubtedly the reason he'd been attracted to Karla. She might be the walking billboard of emotional scars Susan had hinted at, but she was also a survivor. He'd sensed in the conversations he and Karla had had about Anna that there was more to Karla's coming home than she realized herself. Karla seemed confused about her and Anna's relationship, talking about her in an almost businesslike manner one minute and then the next with the warmth and caring of a doting child.

He'd asked her out because Cindy liked her so much and Cindy was never wrong about people. Of course it hadn't hurt that Karla had cheekbones you could ski off, possessed a smile to make a dentist proud, and was built the way he liked a woman built, with some flesh on her bones. The really thin ones scared him. There was no way he wanted Cindy around a woman who hyperventilated at the sight of a piece of candy. She would get enough of that kind of thinking at school— she sure as hell didn't need it at home.

But Cindy had nothing to do with the reason he'd asked Karla out the second time. He wanted to see her again for purely selfish reasons. He liked the way she made him feel when she laughed at his jokes and the way she looked at him when they were talking. She was quick and bright and, best of all, not put off by his admittedly dumb idea of a first date. Halfway through ordering their hamburgers it had occurred to Mark that what he'd thought of as clever could just as easily be thought of as cheap. The more he thought about it, the more he wished he'd run the idea past Susan first.

But plainly Karla hadn't been as put off as he'd feared. At least she'd agreed to see him again.

Mark parked at the front of the clinic and rang the bell to get in. Ray, the on—duty emergency vet for the night, opened the door. "How's the setter doing?"

"Hanging on. Her vitals are stable, but her breathing is still labored."

"What about her membrane color?"

"It's good—pink—and capillary refill is normal."

"Maybe she's in pain. Let's give her some butorphenol and see how she does."

"I'll start her on it right away. Unless you want to do it."

"No, go ahead." Mark glanced at the emergency log. So far it had been a quiet night.

"By the way, Linda called right after you left tonight. She said she was coming in sometime after ten and that if she got to the house before you did, she would take care of the sitter."

"They were supposed to be playing Las Vegas this weekend. Did she say what happened?"

"Seems the drummer and bass guitarist got into a fight with a couple of undercover policemen and got the crap beat out of them. They couldn't get two other guys up from L.A. in time to take their place so the manager had to cancel the gig."

Ray had worked his way through school as backup guitarist for a rock band that went on to have several platinum albums and then all died in a private plane crash on the way to the Grammy awards. Mark had always suspected that the stories Ray told Linda about his band's glory days on the road were tantamount to dangling a carrot in front of her. But Mark never tried to stop Ray or to keep Linda from purposely seeking him out for yet more stories.

"I hope she comes up with something better than that to tell Cindy."

"Fights come with the territory," Ray said. "If Linda sticks with the business, Cindy is going to hear a lot worse."

"Oh, she'll stick with it." When Linda had left to join Aderonax, she'd tried to make him understand why she was going by telling him that she felt sorry for Ray, for all that he had missed. In her mind, the band members who'd died in the crash were the ones to be envied. They'd reached the top and died there. Nothing she could have said would have convinced him more that she was never coming back.

"But they may not stick with her. Rock bands at that level come together and break up faster than dogs in heat. It's okay for the guys to get old, but no one in that circle wants to see wrinkles on a chick."

"Why are we talking about this?" Mark went inside

the nursing ward to see the setter. Ray followed.

"I guess it's just a feeling I got when I was talking to Linda. I wouldn't be surprised if she wasn't expercencing some of that ageism stuff already."

"Hell—she's not even thirty."

Ray shrugged. "Could be I'm wrong. I hope so—for your and Cindy's sakes."

He and Ray had been friends since their first year of veterinary school at the University of California Davis. They'd been in each other's weddings and were two of the five partners in the clinic. He was the one Mark had talked to when he saw his and Linda's marriage beginning to disintegrate.

Through it all, Ray had never interfered or given unwanted advice. "If you're going to hope for something, hope for a hit record."

CHAPTER 11

KARLA LICKED HER FINGER AND FLIPPED THROUGH A stack of checks making sure they were in numerical order. In all the years since Frank died, Anna had carefully filed all the canceled checks but never once balanced her checkbook. She'd worked out her own system for keeping track of her money, and for the most part, it had worked. With the exception of $1,826.59 that the bank said she had that Anna insisted she didn't. She'd first noticed the mistake four years ago and called the bank to tell them about it, but they said there was no error, that the money was hers. She'd carried the balance all that time, convinced the bank would figure out where they'd gone wrong one day and ask for the money back.

After three hours of sorting checks, Karla was finally ready to start looking for the eighteen hundred and change. As she marked off each check against the statement and the register, she was surprised to see Grace's name appear. She noticed it again and again until, slowly, a pattern began to emerge. None of the checks were outrageous, all of them between two and four hundred dollars; still, for Anna, it was a large part of her monthly budget. Karla looked at the dates and tried to remember what was going on in Grace's life at that time. She was out of school, working part—time as a page for CBS, going for auditions and landing an occasional job.

Karla remembered it well. She'd paid Grace's rent for two years thinking her sister was living alone. She might never have known any different had she not shown up unannounced to surprise Grace for her birthday and discovered two roommates. Grace had pulled off the deception by keeping a private phone and never meeting Karla at home, and then she'd tried to explain it by saying she was worried Karla would think her a failure and make her give up her dream if she knew how little she was actually earning.

Judging by Anna's canceled checks, Grace had been giving her the same line. Had Heather fallen for it too?

Karla didn't know whether she was more angry or disappointed. What had been going on in Grace's life that had made her so desperate she'd felt she had to lie to both of them to get money? Drugs were an obvious answer, but it just didn't fit. There were no other signs, and Karla had seen plenty of them in her friends when she lived in L.A. If Grace had a drug of choice, it was shopping. She would take money from Karla to feed her habit, but Anna? Of the three of them, Grace had lived

118

with Anna the longest. In every way that counted, Anna had become Grace's mother.

If Karla wanted an answer, she was going to have to ask. All she had to do was decide whether to approach Grace or Anna or neither of them. But what went on between Grace and Anna was really none of Karla's business. What right did she have to get involved, especially now?

Karla shook off her wandering thoughts and got back to the checkbook. When Anna woke up Karla wanted to be able to tell her she'd found the money. After all, she was supposed to be the expert.

A half hour later the one thing she had discovered was that the money appeared the same year Anna started receiving a direct deposit every month from a company called GBI. This, in addition to her Social Security check, appeared to give her enough money to get by every month with a little left over—which, many of those months, had gone to Grace.

Karla glanced up as Anna came into the kitchen. She looked as tired as she had before she'd gone in to take a nap.

"How are you coming?" Anna asked. "Did you find their mistake yet?"

Karla got up and stretched. "Not yet. I'm going to fix a cup of tea. You want some?"

"That sounds lovely. I'll get the cookies Susan brought to go with it."

"Too late," Karla admitted sheepishly. "I ate the last of them while I was working."

"They wouldn't have lasted much longer anyway." Anna sat down and let Karla get the tea. "I can't remember the last time I made a batch of cookies, or baked anything for that matter. I used to make cookies all the time. Frank loved to take them in his lunch box. Did your mother ever make persimmon cookies for you? They were her particular favorite."

"Not that I can remember. But maybe she did and I just didn't like them."

"I never liked them myself, but I must have made enough over the years to feed an army. As soon as the trees started turning color, your mother and grandfather would start in on me. Which means there should be persimmons in the store by now."

"That wouldn't be a hint, would it?"

"I don't know why, but I woke up thinking about persimmon cookies. Even not liking them, I can appreciate how the smell of spices, pecans, and raisins fills the house when they're baking."

"And persimmons, I assume."

"Oh, of course, although I think they add more moisture than flavor or aroma."

"All right, you've convinced me. Tell me what we need, and I'll pick it up when I go out later."

"If you're sure it's not a bother."

Karla laughed. "Of course it's a bother, but you've convinced me I can't go another day without adding a persimmon cookie to each hip."

Anna acknowledged the neatly aligned stacks of checks spread out over the table. "Have you been working on my checkbook all afternoon?"

"Just about."

"I had no idea it would take this long, or I never would have asked for your help. I just don't want to die and leave the problem to you girls to handle when I'm not here to explain everything to you."

Karla dropped tea bags into two mugs and poured boiling water over them. She suddenly wished she'd

120

given Anna's account a quick once—over and made up some mistake to account for the money instead of looking through what amounted to a financial diary. Finding the checks to Grace was like opening the door to a room she didn't want to know existed. Heather would tell her to close the door and walk away, but Karla could no more do that than she could walk by a flower stand and not buy a bouquet.

"Anna, I'm sorry, but I couldn't help looking at the checks as I was going through them. I noticed there were several written to Grace. Would you mind telling me what they were for?"

The question clearly made her uncomfortable. "I promised Grace it would be between us, that I would never tell you or Heather." Her face reflected her turmoil. "But now that you've seen them yourself, it seems foolish not to tell you about them."

She'd been given a way out. All she had to do was tell Anna not to break the confidence. She wouldn't have to confront Grace and would save herself what was sure to be a nasty argument between them. "If you'd rather not, I understand."

"They were to help her with her rent. She was embarrassed that she wasn't doing as well as she'd led you and Heather to believe and afraid you would tell her she had to give up her dream and get a real job."

Karla could hardly blame her for falling for a line she'd fallen for herself. The worst part was seeing how completely Anna had bought into Grace's story and realizing how devastated she would be to know she'd been taken for a ride by her own granddaughter. Somehow it didn't seem so bad that Grace had done the same thing to her. Sisters had a lot of years to work things out between them; they could afford to make mistakes. The kindest thing Grace could do was to let Anna die without trying some last—minute confession.

"She was right," Karla said. "At least about the job part. But then there are a lot of actors waiting to be discovered who manage to work and still get auditions."

"Do you think Grace will make it?"

Karla had been asking herself the same question a lot lately. Grace had the talent, but lately it seemed as if she were more interested in behaving as if she'd already arrived than doing the work to get there. "I don't know. I used to think so, but I'm not so sure anymore."

"It's a difficult business. Or so I've heard."

"Not one I'd want to be involved with."

Anna smiled. "That wouldn't be like you at all."

Despite their truce, Karla felt a familiar stab of resentment that Anna presumed to know what she was like and who she was inside. "And what—in your opinion, of course—would be like me?"

"You were meant to be a mother. I've begun to worry that it might never happen, and that makes me sad. Some people should never have children, you should have a dozen."

Karla couldn't have been more surprised if Anna had told her she was meant to be an alien but had been born human by accident. "I don't like kids."

"What about Cindy?"

"She's different."

"And Jamie and Jason?"

"They're my nephews."

"Surely you must see how children are drawn to you."

"How would you know that?"

"Karla—you used to live here. Did you think I didn't notice?"

"Sometimes."

Anna reacted as if she'd been struck. "Did you really feel that way then, or is it something you feel now?"

"Why did you make me sleep upstairs away from you and Heather and Grace?" The question found its own voice, spoken without conscious thought.

"Because it was the one room in this house where I thought you might find your mother. And I wanted you to feel special, to know that I thought you were special. How could you not have felt that?"

"I only felt lonely."

"I'm sorry. If you had told me I could have—"

"I did tell you."

"I didn't hear what you were saying," Anna said sadly.

Karla was beginning to understand there were ways to listen that she hadn't recognized then. She had heard Anna's words, but they didn't always say what was in her heart. In Anna's mind she had told her granddaughters she loved them a dozen times a day. Karla had only heard silence, needing the words that Anna left unspoken. She didn't recognize what being given the special room meant, or that a special meal had been cooked just for her, or how much thought had gone into a carefully chosen sweater given with the tag still attached so it could be returned without asking where it had been purchased.

"Why is it so hard for our family to say I love you?" Karla asked.

"Not only hard to say, but hard to recognize," Anna told her.

"Why?"

"We never have."

"Why?" Karla persisted.

"I don't know. . . it just wasn't done when Frank and I were growing up. We learned to say things like that in different ways. Ways we all understood."

"Did you ever wonder if the language was being lost from generation to generation?"

"Did your mother not understand?" Anna asked. "Did she not know how to tell you she loved you?"

"She told me she loved me every night, and every morning when I left for school."

"I read your mother a story every night even after she learned to read for herself. And when she went to school, I never made her lunch the night before. I always got up to do it in the morning. Are you telling me she didn't understand why I did this?"

"*She* understood," Karla said. "I didn't." Why was she telling Anna this now when it was too late to make a difference and would only distress her?

Anna seemed to shrink into herself. "I don't know what to say to you."

Karla wasn't surprised. Words, or the lack of them, had always been a problem between them. And, albeit reluctantly, she was beginning to recognize that she was as much to blame as Anna. "I'm sorry if I hurt your feelings. It wasn't what I intended."

"Maybe this is what they mean when they say grandparents make poor parents."

"They?"

"All the experts who write about such things."

"And do they say what should happen to all the kids the grandparents shouldn't raise!"

Anna looked at Karla, puzzled. "What are you saying?"

"You made the best out of a bad situation. I know that now." Karla reached for the forgotten tea, saw that it was cold and started over again. Before she lit the stove, she turned to look at Anna. "I'm wrong. You did more than that. You rescued us from people who didn't care enough to stick it out with us. You may have told me you loved me in a way I didn't understand, but they didn't even try. I made my own lunches when I lived with my father's family. Not only that, I made Heather's and Grace's, too." She went back to the tea.

"Karla . . ."

"Yes?"

"I love you."

Karla didn't turn around. She couldn't. She didn't want Anna to see her cry.

Anna was on the porch—a blanket wrapped around her legs, a shawl across her shoulders, a heating pad at her back—prepared to watch the sunset. Karla had picked up on the nonverbal ways to say I love you as if she'd been born to them. She had stored love her entire life, looking for someone to give it to. Anna was delighted that Karla had decided to practice on her.

"Mom was right," Karla said using her hip to open the screen door, a plate balanced in one hand, two cups in the other.

"These are the best cookies I've ever tasted."

"You think so, huh?"

"Come on, now, you think so too or you never would have told me about them." She set the cups and plate on the wicker table beside Anna's rocking chair.

"The house does smell wonderful," Anna admitted. "I'm always amazed how aromas trigger such strong memories."

Karla sat on the railing and cupped her mug between her hands. "Tell me what you're remembering now."

Anna smiled. "As I recall our bargain, it was supposed to be the other way around. You're the one who should be doing the talking."

"After you."

"First tell me about the lawyer," Anna said. "I saw the note that he called today. Are we ready to see him?"

"We will be by next week."

"And then what?" Anna asked. She was taking a chance, but couldn't let it go.

"I don't understand what you're getting at."

"What you came here to do will be finished. Will you be leaving then?"

"I told Jim I'd be gone four weeks. He made his plans accordingly." She waited and when Anna didn't say anything, she added, "He's staying at my house—with a friend." She took a deep breath. "A woman friend."

Anna's heart went out to Karla. "Did you know he was bringing her?"

"No."

"The bastard."

Karla laughed. "Thanks, Grandma."

Anna felt a warmth go through her that had nothing to do with the Indian summer or the layers of clothing Karla had piled on her. "Anytime, sweetheart."

"You sound just like Mom."

"Do I? That's nice." She saw by the stunned expression on Karla's face that there was more. "What is it?"

"You've never used that word with me before. I've never heard you call anyone sweetheart."

Anna thought about it before she answered. "You're right. I don't know where it came from, but it seemed as familiar as your name. Does it bother you?"

"No . . . it's kind of nice, actually." Karla took a sip

126

of tea. "I wish Heather were here. And Grace."

"Stay for Thanksgiving," Anna said impulsively. "We can ask Heather and Grace. Think how nice it would be to have everyone together again."

Karla hesitated.

"It will be like the old times we never had, all of us in the kitchen cooking, telling stories, laughing. We've been given a chance to make new memories, Karla." She hated sounding needy, but was too old and tired to pretend. "Let's not waste it," she added softly.

"I'll call Jim and see if he can stay another week."

"And I'll call Heather and Grace."

"No—I'll do it."

Anna knew that if she suggested doing the calling, Karla would insist on doing it herself. She'd manipulated her, but for a good reason. Karla needed at least one happy Thanksgiving with all of them together to remember, and she was the only one who could get Grace to come.

To please Karla, she reached for a cookie and took a bite. Her memory hadn't failed her. They were as bad now as they had been then.

"Well?" Karla asked.

"They haven't changed."

"Still hate 'em, huh? Or maybe I didn't make them right. I'm out of my element when I venture past cake mixes and canned frosting."

"They taste exactly the way I remember them, and I dislike them just as much now as I did when I made them for your mother and grandfather."

Karla leaned back against the pillar and looked at the blushing western sky. "It's nice to know that some things don't change."

"And that some do," Anna added.

CHAPTER 12

MARK DROPPED CINDY OFF AT SCHOOL AND remembered the new veterinary journal he'd meant to take to work with him. He made a swing back by the house and found Linda in the kitchen buttering a piece of toast.

"Morning," she said. "Sorry about not getting up in time to take Cindy to school. I'll try harder tomorrow."

She had on one of his white T—shirts with only panties underneath. "I'd appreciate it if you didn't run around like that while you're staying here."

She looked surprised. "Why, Mr. Taylor . . . I thought you were beyond that kind of thing where I'm concerned."

"It's Cindy I'm concerned about." He picked up the journal and tucked it under his arm. "I don't want her thinking we might be getting back together."

"Sorry—you're right. I'll be more careful from now on."

"How long are you staying this time?"

"Until I hear from Gus that the band is ready to go again. Why are you asking?"

"Just wanted a time frame."

"Come on, Mark. I know you better than that." She took another bite of toast. "What are you really asking?"

"If you're going to be in town more than a day or two, I'd prefer you stayed with your mother."

She looked horrified. "You are kidding, aren't you? You don't really expect me to—"

"I don't want Cindy getting the idea you might be back for good."

"If it worries you that much, I'll talk to her and make sure she knows I'm not."

Anyone listening to Linda would think she didn't care about Cindy; they'd be wrong. Linda's love for Cindy, the effort she made to stay in her life, the calls, the letters, the presents, were the reason Mark never objected when she visited and stayed at the house. But only on a short—term basis, and only a few times a year. "You can talk to her. As a matter of fact, I think it's a good idea, but that doesn't change anything. If you're going to be staying in town more than a couple of days, I want you to make it somewhere else."

"I can't."

He looked at his watch. He still had twenty minutes before his first appointment, which gave him ten minutes to finish their conversation. "Why not?"

"I'm broke."

He wasn't surprised. To Linda, credit cards weren't a convenience, they were a way of life. "It's your mother we're talking about, Linda. She may nag but she doesn't charge."

"My aunt and uncle are there. They're using my room."

"Then you can sleep on the couch."

"She won't let me."

The tone of voice more than anything else alerted Mark that Linda wasn't simply being stubborn; she really had nowhere to go. "I'll ask Susan if you can stay at the school. She isn't using the second story. But she's not going to want you hanging around the kids, so you'll have to stay upstairs or find something else to do during the day."

Her eyes flashed anger. "Why are you being such a jerk about this? You always let me stay here before.

129

What's so different this time?"

"Give it up, Linda. You're not going to badger me into changing my mind." He started toward the door.

"Oh, my God. You've got a girlfriend and you don't want me around messing things up for you. After all this time, it finally happened."

He refused to be baited. He turned and gave her a blank look. "I'll let you know what Susan says. If you don't like the idea of staying at the school, start looking for someplace else, because you're not staying with me anymore."

"This is Cindy's house, too. Doesn't she get a vote?"

Mark laughed. "Nice try."

Linda smiled. "Thanks. But not good enough, I take it?"

"Don't unpack your bags," he said by way of good—bye.

He made it to the clinic with a minute to spare. His first case was a long—time client who'd gone to a cat show the weekend before and purchased a kitten that needed an exam and the last of its kitten shots. A good way to start the morning, as long as the kitten was in good health, which he appeared to be.

Before going in to see his next appointment, Mark checked the Irish setter. She'd survived despite her catastrophic injuries, her spirit reaching out to everyone who came in contact with her, compelling the staff to give her the attention and care she needed. Her tail thumped in recognition, and he went down on his haunches to put his hand through the cage to pet her.

The tail thumped faster, and he stole a few minutes he didn't have to talk to her and let her know that she was among friends.

"She's doing unbelievably well," Ray said, bending

down beside Mark. "Especially considering I bet Murray his Saturday shift that she wouldn't make it."

"Murray actually bet that she would?" Of all of the vets at the clinic, Murray was the best surgeon, the one willing to take the toughest cases, the one who witnessed the most miraculous recoveries, yet he was still the one who managed to remain the most pessimistic.

"Well, not exactly."

Murray came up behind them and looked at the setter over their shoulders. "I bet him she'd wake up," he said. "I never said she'd live." He continued on his way to surgery.

They both laughed at his obvious attempt to maintain his position as chief pessimist.

"How's Linda?" Ray asked, taking over stroking the setter's head when Mark stood.

"I'll tell you later. You staying here for lunch?"

He nodded.

"I'll catch you then," Mark said. "As soon as I finish my callbacks."

Ray was pulling a tuna fish sandwich out of a brown paper bag when Mark came into the break room. He took his own lunch out of his computer bag before he sat down beside him. "Linda's doing okay," he said, picking up the conversation where they'd left off. "She isn't sure how long she's staying, said it depends on when the band gets back together, so you were right about that."

"Dr. Taylor?"

Mark glanced at the door and saw Glenda, one of the women who worked the desk looking at him. "Yes?"

"There's a Wanda Jenkins on the phone who wants to know if you'll crop her Great Dane's ears and tail. I told her you don't do cosmetic surgery, but she insisted on talking to you personally."

"Is she a client?"

"No."

He'd fielded calls like this before and wasn't in the mood to argue with someone about the necessity of cutting up dogs if they were to be shown. Mark and his partners had stopped doing the surgery years ago, and none of them were going to change their minds no matter how determined the dog's owner. Glenda had only been working there a week, so she didn't know it was clinic policy to refer such inquiries to a list of other vets automatically without involving any of the partners.

"Is Barbara available?" She was the desk manager.

"I believe so."

"Give it to her to handle. She has the referral list."

When they were alone again, Ray said, "About Linda and her band: It could be weeks, months even, before she hears anything. Sometimes bands never get back together."

"I don't think she'll wait around that long. She's still determined to make it as a singer, whether it's with this band or another one. Hell, I wouldn't put it past her to try to put together a band of her own. She should know enough musicians by now."

"Why do I get the feeling you're not as convinced about what you're saying as you want me to think you are?" He tore open a bag of chips. "Wow, try to say that three times, fast."

"As much as I like that she's worked hard to keep a strong relationship with Cindy, it scares the hell out of me to think of her trying to be a full—time mother again. She doesn't have it in her, Ray. If she tries, Cindy's going to come out the loser."

"What makes you think that's even a possibility? You've got custody. If Linda tries to move in and take over, tell her to take a hike. The law's on your side."

"You're right. I don't know why I'm obsessing on this." At least he'd gotten her out of the house. He'd called Susan between giving a litter of boxers their puppy shots and telling a teenager the dog he'd grown up with had cancer and needed surgery and likely wouldn't live more than six months longer even if everything went well. She'd agreed to let Linda use the second floor of the preschool, but not before he'd told her about his date with Karla.

"You seeing that gal again?" Ray said.

That made twice in one morning that he'd been asked about Karla. "I'm thinking about it."

"You like her, huh?"

"She's all right."

"She's got to be more than all right if you're seeing her again."

"Actually, she's the perfect date. She's here for a couple of weeks and then she's gone for good. We can go out and have a great time and there's no chance it's going to turn into anything serious."

"Famous last words."

"You've already lost one bet this week." Mark took a bite of his peanut butter and jelly sandwich and sat back in his chair.

"Which is why I wouldn't take you on about this unless I thought it was a sure thing."

Mark went back to his sandwich. The way he figured it, he had a lot of years ahead of him listening to his friends try to shuffle him off to the altar. It made no more sense to let them pull his chain about this than it did to let on he knew the difference between red and white wine.

Karla waited for a man wearing a baseball cap to get off the phone before she left her car. Her calling card in hand, she approached the booth, steeling herself for what she knew would be an argument with Grace. She was the last on her list to call. Jim had hardly been able to contain his excitement at being asked to stay on at the shop another week and a half, even promising to send a fresh supply of coffee for their Thanksgiving dinner. Heather was so happy she'd started crying the minute Karla told her why she was calling.

While she'd made the other two calls from the house, this one she didn't want Anna to overhear. Before picking up the receiver, she spotted the penny she'd seen sitting on the asphalt three weeks before. This time she bent to pick it up and stuck it in her pocket. She'd take her luck anywhere she could find it.

Grace answered on the first ring. "I'm on my way out, so make it fast," she said breezily.

"It's Karla."

"She died," Grace said dramatically.

The statement threw her. "Who died?"

"Grandma. Isn't that why you're calling?"

"Grandma's fine. I'm calling because I want you to come up for Thanksgiving dinner."

Grace laughed. "You can't be serious. You know I always have Thanksgiving with my friends. Grandma gets Christmas—at least she does when I can get the time off."

"Time off? From what?"

"That was mean."

After finding the canceled checks, Karla was feeling mean. "I want you to make an exception this year.

134

Heather is coming and I'll be here. Anna would like all of us together." It was tempting to add "this one last time" but she didn't want to use emotional blackmail on Grace. She wanted her to come because she recognized it was the right thing to do.

"We've already made plans," Grace insisted. "Everyone is counting on me, I can't let them down."

"Bullshit," Karla said, losing the temper she'd sworn she would keep. Going all the way, she threw out a threat. "You either change your plans or I call my credit card company and cancel your insurance."

"You wouldn't do that."

"The hell I wouldn't. I'm tired of everything going your way. It's time you started giving a little in return."

"I'll see what I can do."

Euphemism for "give me some time to come up with a better excuse for doing what I want to do." "That's not good enough."

"What is it you want?"

"Your body at Anna's dinner table on Thanksgiving day."

"Jesus, what did she do, promise you the house?"

"Don't mess with me on this, Grace."

"All right, all right. You win. Satisfied?"

"I'll send you a plane ticket." She wasn't going to let Grace back out at the last minute because it was too dangerous to drive in valley fog—the excuse she'd used when Heather had tried to have a family Christmas at her house six years ago. Of course the fog could ground flights, too, but at least she'd know the excuse was genuine.

"Do you have any idea what a zoo the airport is on holidays?"

"No. And I can't imagine why you would either."

135

A long silence followed. "You know, there are times you can be a real bitch."

She'd long suspected the circle of friends Grace used for an excuse to get out of things was no more real than an unpaid rent bill. "Unless you're through asking me for favors, I'd be careful what I say if I were you."

"Don't you think it's a little late to be playing the tough big sister role? I know exactly what's happened. You went up there to tell Grandma you weren't interested in her money and then you saw how much it was and changed your mind. You screwed up and stayed away from her all this time and now you're in a panic because you think she's not going to leave any of it to you. Well, I'm not going to let you take your mistakes out on me. I'll be there for Thanksgiving, but I'm not coming because you asked me to, I'll be there for Grandma."

How was it Grace could put on a performance like that and not get a job acting? "You can look for the ticket in a couple of days," she said with finality.

"And money for a rental car," Grace added hastily. "If I have to come up, I might as well visit some of my friends while I'm there."

"I'll pick you up at the airport, and if any of your friends are still around and available, you can use my car to see them."

"You're treating me like a little kid."

Finally, something Karla could laugh about. Grace had demanded her way, thrown a tantrum when she didn't get it, whined that she wasn't being treated fairly, and insisted Karla foot the bill.

"What's so funny?" Grace demanded.

"It's not worth talking about. I have to go. If you haven't gotten the tickets in a couple of days, call me.

Otherwise I'll see you in two weeks." She hung up before Grace had a chance to answer.

"Did you find the money?" Anna asked, patting her freshly coiffed hair for the third time since leaving the shop. "I saw that you'd put the canceled check box back in the closet."

She'd heard what Anna said, but it took a second to connect. The traffic on Douglas Boulevard was even heavier on Saturday than it had been in the middle of the week when Karla had had her hair done, and she was having a hard time with landmarks. "Oh, yeah— I've been meaning to tell you about it."

"I'm sure the bank will be happy when—"

"It isn't the bank's money, Anna, it's yours. Or I guess you could say it's mine, depending on how you want to look at it. I never cashed the checks you sent to me that year for Christmas and my birthday. I didn't even look at them, so I had no idea the one was for as much as it was." Normally, when Anna couldn't get out or couldn't think of something to send for a present, she sent a check—for twenty or twenty—five dollars. While the birthday check that year had been the standard twenty—five dollars, she'd sent two that Christmas: one to repay the six hundred dollars Karla had given Grace for books for school, the other for $1,201.59.

"Where did you get that kind of money?" Karla had told herself she wouldn't ask because it was none of her business, and there it was, almost the first thing out of her mouth.

"I sold the house. It was to one of those companies that doesn't take possession until you die or until you have to move into a nursing home. I took some of it in cash to pay for Grace's last two years in school and the

137

rest in monthly payments for as long as I live. School didn't turn out be as much as I thought it was going to be, so I divided what was left between you three girls for Christmas that year."

"You mean you took a reverse mortgage?"

"That's it."

No wonder she hadn't found the deed. It hadn't even occurred to her that the house could have been sold. She knew what that place meant to Anna, what it had always meant. "You love your house. How could you have sold it?"

"It seemed like the most reasonable thing to do at the time. I could have taken a loan against the house, of course, but there was no way I could make the payments. I figured one way or another, I was going to lose the place—this way, at least, I got to stay."

As frugally as they'd lived at Anna's, there should have been more than enough money from their parents' estate to see all three of them through college. Month to month they'd lived on Social Security, both Anna's and their parents'.

"You need to get in the other lane," Anna announced. "The restaurant is coming up."

At Anna's request, they were going back to Macaroni's, the Italian restaurant where they'd eaten with Susan. Mark and Cindy met them at the door. Karla tried to blame the warm flush of pleasure she felt at seeing Mark again on the unseasonably hot day, but then he looked into her eyes and smiled, and it was useless to try to pretend what she was feeling was anything but what it was.

"I'm glad we're finally getting a chance to visit," Mark said to Anna when they were seated at the table. "It seems like all we ever do is exchange a few words in passing. You may not know this, but you're one of Cindy's favorite people. She's talked about you since she started going to Susan's."

Anna smiled at Cindy. "I talk about you, too."

"What do you say?"

"That you can climb a tree faster than any little girl I've ever known and that you make beautiful pictures."

"Do you tell people I can read?"

Anna's eyes widened in surprise. "You can? I didn't know. When did this wonderful thing happen?"

"I dunno." She looked at Mark. "When did it happen, Dad?"

"She's been reading for about a year now," Mark said. "I'm not sure when she started, it just seemed to happen. Susan's been working with her the last few months, and she's really started to take off."

"My mom's home," Cindy announced, ready to move on to something else. "She's staying at my school, so I get to see her every day. Sometimes she even sleeps with us."

Mark let out a mental groan. To explain would give the living arrangements too much importance, but letting it go would give Karla the wrong impression. "Linda's in town while her band is working out some problems. Since she didn't know how long it would take, Susan offered to let her stay upstairs at the school."

"We met," Karla said. "In passing, that is. She was on her way out the door when I dropped by yesterday afternoon."

"She didn't say anything." Unusual for Linda; she didn't miss much. But then how could she have known that Karla was the one he'd taken out? Cindy didn't know, and Susan was the last person to tell Linda

139

something like that.

Karla smiled. "I must not have made much of an impression."

"Impossible." He'd meant the flattery to be exaggerated but the inflection was all wrong. Instead it came out sounding sincere, spoken the way he felt, rather than the teasing way he'd intended.

"We didn't spend much time together, but Linda seems very nice," Karla said.

There was an implied question in the statement—why would two nice people who obviously still liked each other, who were the parents of a wonderful child, choose not to raise that child together? "She's an incredible woman." He turned to Cindy, caught her chin in his hand, looked her directly in the eye, and said, "Who just happens to be the mother of an incredible little girl."

Cindy had been drawing on the paper tablecloth with the assortment of crayons left by the waiter and was impatient at being disturbed. "You say that all the time."

"Only because it's true," Anna told her.

The waiter came for their order. When he returned an hour later to ask if anyone wanted dessert, Anna's lack of interest in her food was obvious by her barely disturbed lunch. Mark surreptitiously noted the effort she made to hide how tired she was and came up with an excuse to leave long before he would have liked.

He and Cindy waited with Anna while Karla got the car.

"Thank you for lunch," she said. "I hope we can do it again before Karla has to leave. She's staying longer than she first planned, you know. Until after Thanksgiving."

It was everything Mark could do to keep a straight

140

face. The old gal might be on her way down for the count, but she wasn't past a little matchmaking. "No, I didn't know. I'm glad you told me."

Karla pulled up in front of them. Mark helped Anna into the car, bent down to say good—bye to Karla, and took Cindy's hand before crossing the parking lot to his Jeep. "Well, what do you think?" he asked Cindy when he had her belted into the car.

"We should get some ice cream."

He grabbed her leg and gave it a shake as if checking to see if it were hollow. "About Karla."

"She's funny."

"Funny how?"

"The way she looks at you—like she likes you a lot."

"You think so, huh?"

"*Daaaad,*" she said in a singsong, impatient voice. "Can we please get our ice cream now?"

Mark got in the car and took Sierra College Boulevard to the Dairy Queen. Two dates and he was still interested—a first since his divorce. No, it was more than interest he felt for Karla. He was intrigued. Her words, her actions, her silences were like a trail of bread crumbs in the forest, impossible not to follow. The farther he went, the more he wanted to go.

CHAPTER 13

"I'M FINE," HEATHER SAID TO BILL AS SHE ROLLED TO her side. Not being able to sleep any way she wanted was the one thing that truly annoyed her about being pregnant. The rest—the morning sickness, the heartburn, the backaches—were reminders of the life growing inside her. Her precious little girl. The baby she'd been told not to have.

"I talked to Dr. Agostini yesterday," she added. "He said that as long as I don't overdo it, there isn't any reason I can't go to Grandma's for Thanksgiving." Not the exact words, but close enough. She'd finagled his permission by promising she wouldn't be gone more than a day and that she would rest and let everyone else prepare the meal. What she hadn't told him was how long a day that would make, which was why she'd decided that as long as she scheduled plenty of down time, it actually would be better if she stayed a couple of days instead of just one.

Bill snuggled against her back spoon fashion, his hand splayed on her belly. After several seconds, he adjusted his hand to better feel the baby's movement. "She's up already."

"She's been up since four." After almost two weeks of little movement, Anna Marie had finally decided to make her presence felt again—big time. She woke Heather out of a sound sleep two or three times a night now, a clear preview of things to come when she finally made her appearance.

"I'll be glad when she's here. It seems like you've been pregnant forever with this one."

Heather put her hand over his and curled her fingers into his palm. He'd fought having this baby, terrified he would lose them both after the warnings the doctor had given them about having other children when Jason was born. He rarely talked to her about it, but she could see the fear in his eyes in unguarded moments when he didn't know she was watching. He'd stopped trying to hide how he felt at obvious times—when she was slow getting up or slept a little later than usual or put her hand to her back to ease an ache. "Three more months

142

. . . fourteen weeks. . ." She turned and gave him a kiss. "Ninety—eight days. . ."

"But then who's counting?" He smiled tenderly as he brushed the hair from her forehead. "I love you, Heather."

"I know you do. And I expect you to worry, but not all the time. I swear I'm all right." She loved the way he looked in the morning, his hair disheveled from sleep, the shadow of a beard, his eyes soft and lazy. This was her time; no one else saw him this way. To the rest of the world he was the crisp, efficient lawyer—from his hair to the shine on his shoes. And handsome, the kind of man women turned to look at again. He had liquid blue eyes, an anomaly with black hair, startling in their intensity, made more so by the unconscious way he used them. He could grill a witness with a look or, with a conspiratorial wink, persuade a clerk to work after hours to find an obscure bit of information.

She touched his lower lip with the tip of her finger. "And I promise you nothing is going to happen to me or the baby." After giving him a long kiss, she added, "Once she's here and tearing through the house, you're going to shake your head in wonder that you ever thought she wouldn't make it."

"Right now I don't care if she turns my office into her own personal toy box. I'll even let her play in the closet if she wants."

She widened her eyes in disbelief. "Not the *closet*. What if she discovers the hidden body?"

He laughed. "Okay, you made your point." He looked past her at the clock on the night stand. "I gotta get out of here. I'm due in court in an hour."

"I thought the trial didn't start until Wednesday."

"We have a meeting with the judge. It shouldn't take

143

more than an hour or two, but something tells me we're going to be there all day."

"Do me a favor?"

"Anything."

"Oh, you should be more careful with your answers, Mr. Johnson." She smiled seductively. "I just might take you up on one like that someday." Not any day soon, regretfully. Sex was a dangerous activity with this pregnancy, a forbidden, and therefore desperately desired, need.

"You've got a three—month window to take advantage of me. After that I go back to being the hard—nosed bastard you fell in love with."

When she'd married Bill, she'd thought love was the excitement she felt in just being with him and the sense of loss that came when he was gone. Now she knew it was so much more. Love was getting up in the middle of the night with a sick child, a flower picked on the way into the house, a Sunday drive to Monterey to see the sea lions when a Forty—niner game was on television, and driving a Volvo station wagon instead of a sports car. Love was a series of small moments that made up her days. She was convinced that it was her guardian angel who'd put her foot on the accelerator instead of the brake pedal that summer day nine years ago and let her car plow into the back of Bill's. They'd lived such different lives back then, she was convinced it was the only way they could have met. She never failed to say a little prayer of thanks to her winged protector when she went to bed at night.

"Well? What's the favor?"

"If you have a break. . . and can't find anything else to fill the time . . . would you mind looking to see if you can find some stollen?"

144

He groaned. "I should have known. Which bakery this time?"

She didn't expect him to understand; it was enough that he went along with her crazy craving. She was trying to duplicate the special holiday bread she'd first had with Anna in San Francisco. They'd gone by bus that year to see the Christmas decorations, and in her mind everything about that day had been magical. Stollen was only available a few months every year, and she'd already tried the bakeries she knew in Carmel and Monterey. Most of them simply stuffed a few raisins and nuts and citron into a loaf of sweet bread, put some frosting or powered sugar on the top, and passed it off as stollen. "I don't know. Pick one at random. You can't do any worse than I've been doing."

He got out of bed, dropped his shorts, kicked them up to his hand, and tossed them in the hamper. "By the way," he called from the bathroom, "I'll probably be late tonight, so go ahead and have dinner without me."

"Do you want leftovers or are you going to pick up something?"

"I'll pick up something."

"Maybe I'll take Jason and Jamie out for pizza. I promised them we could go to the park today and we could go from there." She'd started detailing her days for him when he'd tried calling her several months ago and had panicked when he couldn't reach her. The cell phone he'd insisted she carry was still so new she'd accidentally left it in the car when she went shopping. Thankfully she'd been found by an understanding policeman whose wife was also pregnant.

"There's supposed to be a storm moving in tomorrow, so it may be a while before we can go again," she said.

"Don't—"

"—overdo it," she finished for him. The phrase had become a mantra between them.

Heather sat on a hard metal bench and watched Jason climb to the top of the tube slide. Her heart in her throat, she waited until he was seated and came out the other end. It was everything she could do not to hover. Only knowing her fears would become theirs kept her from shouting warnings to be careful every time one of them climbed to the top of anything.

When the baby was born and Anna came to live with them, Heather planned to take them to the park whenever possible. She believed in sunshine and vitamin D and singing birds—all the good things that came with being outside. She knew Anna couldn't live forever, but she also knew that under the right care she would live longer than she would if she stayed by herself, maybe even long enough to see her namesake take her first step and speak her first words. Heather refused to think it was unreasonable to believe Anna might even be there for Anna Marie's first day of school.

Even though she knew it was something that had to be done, she was angry with Karla for insisting that Anna put her estate in order. She didn't want Anna to spend time thinking about dying; she wanted her to concentrate on living.

She shifted position on the bench, making a mental note to put the pillow she normally brought with her to the park back in the car. She wasn't a "sitting" kind of person, so even with the baby as a constant reminder, it was hard to remember she was under doctor's orders to do so as much as possible. The sitting was a compromise. The doctor would prefer she was in bed.

Heather didn't know what she would do without Anna in her life. Who would she call to share the intimate joys that came from a day no different from any other but made special because Jamie had scored his first soccer goal, or Jason had said something funny, or Bill had sent her a bouquet of flowers for no reason except he'd seen them and thought of her? Anna cared in a way no one else did, not even Karla. When Anna died, she would take a part of Heather with her, a part so special Heather was afraid she would never be whole again.

The ten—year—old girl she'd been when she first came to Anna had been in desperate need of love and attention. Karla had drawn fire from their father's family for her stubbornness, Grace had charmed them all with her smile, no one had bothered with Heather at all. She'd been lost in the middle, left behind by her mother and father, left alone by everyone else.

Somehow, Anna saw this in her and found a way to make her feel special. In time she actually grew to believe she was.

Bill thought she was paranoid the first time they made plans to go somewhere without the boys and she refused to fly in the same plane with him. He quoted statistics proving it was safer to fly than to drive to the local grocery store, but she was adamant and told him they either went separately or not at all. She lived with the fear that something would happen to her and Bill and that Jamie and Jason would be left without anyone to raise them. There were no other Annas in their lives. Bill's parents would never let themselves be tied down with children again, his brother had sent his own children off to boarding school, Karla was too busy figuring out who she was to be much good to two little

147

boys who needed help finding out who they were, and Grace couldn't take care of herself, let alone anyone else.

"Mom. Look how high I'm going," Jamie shouted from the swings.

"Be—" The "careful" caught in her throat. Not even for her own peace of mind could she steal his pride in his accomplishment. "Wow," she said instead. "You're almost to the top of the bar."

"Look at me, Mommy," Jason called from the slide.

"I see you, Jason."

"Watch what I can do." He went into the tube backwards and slid down on his belly.

The competition had begun. It was time to go for pizza.

"What is that fantastic smell?" Bill asked. He went to the chair where Heather sat, her feet propped up on the coffee table, and gave her a kiss.

"Applesauce cake. It's Anna's favorite. I thought I'd take one for Thanksgiving." She smiled at his look of disappointment. "Don't worry, I made one for us, too. I thought you were going to be later than this. I would have held supper if you'd called."

"I decided what I had left to do could wait until tomorrow. Where are the boys?"

"Cleaning up their rooms. I told them we could go out for ice cream when you got home if it was before their bedtime."

"If they cleaned their rooms!"

"I know, I swore I'd never use bribery, but damn it, it works."

"Hmmmm. . . . if that's the case, what are a couple of stollens worth to you?" He held two bags aloft.

She put her feet on the floor and sat up straight. "You got them. I knew you would. How do they look?"

"I'll let you be the judge of that. Frankly, I still can't see what's so great about a wannabe fruitcake."

Taking the bags from him, she headed for the kitchen and the cutting board. "Just wait. When I find one that tastes the way it's supposed to taste, you'll understand."

"Hey, don't I even get a thank you?"

"Oh, you'll get a lot more than that as soon as I'm through with these."

"Now that sounds promising." He leaned against the doorframe and watched her cut into the loaves.

She tasted one slice and then the other and went back for another bit of the first. She crossed the room to give him a kiss. Holding a square out for him to take a bite of the first slice she'd cut, she said, "Your turn."

He did as instructed. "Hey, that's not bad."

"See, I was right." She could hardly wait to tell Anna what they'd found. What had been a memory between just the two of them had grown to include Bill. Someday, she would find a way to make Jamie and Jason and Anna Marie a part of the memory, too.

CHAPTER 14

MARK SLID THE KEY INTO THE IGNITION AND BACKED out of Anna's driveway. "Be prepared to eat your way into another size. The food at this place is incredible."

"This place being . . ."

"Slocum House. It's in the old part of Fair Oaks, across the street from the park."

"Sounds nice." The windshield wipers thumped in quiet rhythm as they moved across the window, clearing

149

the mist that had followed an earlier downpour. The second storm of the season had moved in the night before, dumping six inches of snow in the Sierras with the promise of more. The local news was filled with reporters calling in their satellite stories of snow falling at Blue Canyon, interviewing ski resort workers about the possibility of the lifts being open for Thanksgiving weekend, and skycam shots of Lake Tahoe and Truckee.

"You sound a little down. Are you all right?"

"I'm fine." Karla gave him a smile to reassure him, but couldn't pull it off. "No I'm not. Anna and I went to the lawyer this afternoon. It was hard seeing her try to divide the little she has left into three equal parts." She put her head back and stared at the ceiling. "She's never owned anything of value, nothing that anyone would want. At least that's what I thought until I came up here to help her parcel everything out. Now I know what she has is priceless. There are linens that her mother and grandmother made that she's put in a cupboard and stacked in three neat little piles for me and Heather and Grace. She saved the strangest things. I found a cardboard box that used to hold marshmallows. . . . Did you know marshmallows came in boxes?"

"In my lifetime?"

"I have no idea whose lifetime it was." She turned her head to the side to look at him. She desperately needed someone to talk to about what she was going through, someone who could listen without judging and without feeling the need to find answers where there weren't any. She would be taking a chance if she tried to make Mark that person. They were barely past the polite—conversation stage in their relationship. In their dance of getting to know each other, his hand was still at the small of her back, hers was on his shoulder. Still, she plunged ahead. "What am I going to do with all that stuff?"

"Throw it away after she's gone?"

The question almost sounded like a test. "I couldn't. She saved what she did thinking she would pass them on to her daughter. They would have meant something to my mother because they came from memories she shared with Anna, but most of what Anna has is meaningless to me. She showed me an old black hat with a pearl stickpin the other day. She said it was the hat her mother wore to her father's funeral. I never met my great—grandparents. The hat is a curiosity to me, not what Anna wants it to be."

"She didn't save anything that belonged to your mother?"

"A couple of things from when she was a little girl. My mother was eighteen when she and my father got married. She took most of what she had then with her when she left."

"I suppose a lot of the stuff that would have been important to you and your sisters got lost when she died."

"My father's family has never been caught up in sentimentality. After the funeral they came in and took what they thought they could use and sold the rest. No one thought to save anything for us." She sat up straight again and mentally shook herself. "I don't know why I'm telling you all this. You must be bored out of your mind."

Instead of answering her right away, Mark slowed and waited for the traffic to clear then changed into the right lane. As soon as he found a parking lot he turned in and shut off the engine. "Would you be disappointed if we saved Slocum House for another night? I know a great omelet place—that is if you don't mind something a little more casual and don't object to having breakfast for dinner."

She must not have been as successful at hiding her neediness as she'd thought. They hadn't known each other long enough for him to pick up on the fact she didn't want to be around a lot of other people. "I'll go anywhere I don't have to cook."

"What if I told you that you might have to help with the dishes?"

"Forget your wallet?"

"Don't need it. I was thinking we could have dinner at my place. You happen to be in the presence of a man who went grocery shopping today. For the first time in weeks I can put together an omelet that has something in it besides eggs and cheese. I'm afraid if child welfare ever finds out the weird way Cindy and I eat sometimes, they'll start a file on us."

"I love omelets. But wouldn't pizza or hamburgers be more to Cindy's liking?" When he gave her a puzzled look she added, "I assume she'll be eating with us."

"She's gone for the weekend. Linda went to see her mom and took Cindy with her." He waited for her to say something and when she didn't, added, "Is that a problem?"

She didn't know him well enough to know if it was a problem or not. Some men regarded being alone with them at their house or apartment as tacit agreement for sex. She wasn't good at game playing and didn't know how to broach the subject except to deal with it straight on. "It's just omelets, right? We're not going to let anything happen that would complicate things between us. That's the last thing I need right now."

"Then it's not going to happen." He picked up his car

152

phone. But before hitting any numbers, he said, "We still have time to make it to the restaurant if you'd prefer. It's an experience not to be missed."

"I believe you. But I think I'd rather save it for another time." Realizing the statement made it sound as if she assumed there would be another time, she quickly added, "Not that I think there will be another time, mind you." That sounded even worse, as if she were fishing for a commitment the way people did compliments. "What I meant to say is that I appreciate that you wanted to take me to a wonderful restaurant, but—"

"You'd just as soon not be around a lot of people tonight."

"Yes. Thank you for understanding. And for helping me take my foot out of my mouth."

He looked at her for a long time before he said, "I feel the same way, you know. This isn't so much a date for me as a progression of our relationship." He paused. "I suppose I should add that I like knowing you're thinking along the same lines. It means I'm right about what I'm feeling."

She waited for the self—conscious panic that invariably came with finding out someone was interested in her. Instead there was a sense of anticipation nudged by excitement. "And just what is it that you're feeling?"

He grinned. "It sounds clichéd, but I have this sense that we're like connecting pieces to a puzzle. I have no idea what it means yet, but I'm looking forward to finding out."

She took the safest path and decided she and Mark were destined to become really good friends. "Me, too."

Mark canceled the reservation, and they headed back to Rocklin.

Karla wasn't sure what she'd expected Mark's home to look like but was pleasantly surprised when they pulled up to a small, brick ranch—style house on a large lot in Loomis, not more than three miles from Anna's. They were greeted at the door by two cats and the ugliest dog Karla had ever seen.

"What kind of dog is that?" she asked Mark as he hung up her coat.

"Loving." He bent, ran his hand over the dog's head, and scratched its ears. "Aren't you, fella?" The dog's tail wagged in agreement. "The people who owned him were moving to an apartment that didn't allow pets, so they brought him to the clinic to be put down. I talked them into letting me try to find him another home." He shrugged. "You see where he wound up."

"How long ago was that?"

"Three years."

"Does he have a name?"

"Old Blue Eye." Mark turned the dog's head for her to see the dog's eyes. One was blue, the other brown. "I call him Blue for short."

"And the cats?"

"Strays dumped by stupid people who think they're doing the animal a favor. We get them out here all the time. Mostly they wind up eaten by coyotes or hit by cars, but their lives are pure hell before that happens." As if realizing he'd answered more than she'd asked, he added, "Sorry, it's a sore spot with me."

Mark walked over to the fireplace and flipped a switch. Flame instantly leaped over logs carefully stacked behind glass. When a fan came on minutes later she realized she was standing in front of a gas furnace made to look like a fireplace. Form, function, and environmentally sound, an interesting statement for the man as well as the appliance. "Does it put out much heat?"

"The only room in the house it doesn't reach is my bedroom, but I like it cool in there."

She looked around. The room was done in browns and greens and yellows. An overstuffed sofa sat against one wall; bookshelves filled with books and mementos framed the fireplace. There was a small table under the window with a chair on either side. Two watercolors hung behind the sofa, both original and both more evocative than literal in the interpretation of their nature scenes. The floor was oak, worn to a scuffed and polished patina and half—covered with an Oriental carpet in burgundy, blue, and rose.

"Nice," Karla said. "Did Linda do the decorating?"

"Linda has never lived in this house."

"You did this yourself?"

"Now why would you say that in that tone of voice?" He motioned for her to sit on the sofa.

"Not for the reason you're undoubtedly thinking. I've been working on furnishing my house for years, and it's still not finished." The sofa felt like it was filled with feathers. She had the urge to kick off her shoes and curl up in the corner. "I never seem to find the time to look for things, let alone coordinate them, and I don't have a five—year—old taking up my free time."

"The trick is to buy the furniture from someone who'll do all that stuff for you." The dog left Mark to lie down by the fire. "Would you like a glass of wine before I start dinner?"

"If you have some cheese and crackers to go with it, I'd be willing to skip dinner. I'm not very hungry tonight."

"I think I can manage that."

155

"Do you want some help?"

"Your job is to entertain Francis." He pointed to the blue tabby. "He hasn't had a lap to sit in for a couple of days."

Karla patted her lap. "Looks like it's just you and me, Francis." As if they were old friends, the cat jumped up and settled in. Karla ran her hand over the soft fur and felt a powerful sense of having done so before. But it was another cat, another time. She closed her eyes and concentrated. Nothing. She was used to the feeling. Her life was a series of free—floating thoughts and ideas and sensations; the smell of cinnamon made her happy, discarded shoes made her sad. The real reason she'd left her therapist was that he'd started adding obscure meaning to her triggers, telling her they represented repressed sexual fantasies.

She knew what they represented. They were the memories of a child not observant enough to give meaning to action but aware enough to capture the feeling and hold it for the waiting adult. Hummingbirds held special meaning, as did putting her head back and letting snowflakes fall on her face. Her heart filled her throat when she saw a little girl sitting on her father's shoulders. In her mind's eye she knew exactly what the world looked like from that lofty position. Whenever she ate fast food she was compelled to fold the empty straw wrapper into accordion pleats; she felt a terrible longing when she passed a moving van on the highway.

"I can see you really had to work to get him on your lap." Mark set a tray filled with three kinds of cheese, red and green grapes, and an assortment of crackers on the coffee table. Francis looked up and sniffed the air, decided there was nothing worth losing his lap over, and stayed where he was.

"I've thought about getting a cat," Karla said, "but I'm home so little it would be alone most of the time and that doesn't seem fair."

"Maybe you should start staying home more." He poured a glass of wine and handed it to her.

"I have no reason to stay home." For once she didn't care if someone knew she was lonely. Despite the exchange in the car earlier, her gut instinct told her that Mark was a finite friend—someone to talk to and enjoy and leave. That meant she could tell him things she couldn't tell a steady friend, about all the hurt and emptiness and longing that she carried around as compulsively and comfortably as her purse. Mark would listen, maybe even sympathize, and be glad when she and her troubles returned to Solvang.

"If our generation has a tag, I think it has to be that we bought into the lie that you can't be truly free unless you're single." He sat facing her, his arm across the back of the sofa. "All those people roaming the bars on Friday and Saturday nights are looking for the kick they think comes with the freedom. The only people who end the night happy are the bartenders."

Karla worked her fingers into Francis's fur as she moved her hand down his spine. "I tried that scene for a while. God, it was so depressing. All those desperate smiles and shopworn lines."

"What about the coffee business? I would think it was a great place to meet people."

"It is a great place to meet people—joggers, retired couples, tourists. They're one of the reasons I love what I do."

"And the other reasons?"

"What do you mean?"

"You said one of the reasons."

157

"Oh, I like being my own boss, knowing that I succeed or fail on my own initiative." She thought about what she'd said. "That's not right. It's more than initiative. If that was all it took, no small business would ever fail. There's a lot of luck and timing involved, too. Jim and I started the shop before the chains expanded. Now it seems they're in every other strip mall. To stay in business I paid attention to what they were offering and matched them latte for latte."

"Smart."

"The coffee shop is more than a business to me, it's my passion, my . . . family." A chill crawled up her spine. She'd almost said child. How sick was that?

"You must be anxious to get back."

"I am. At least I was in the beginning." When, how, had the transition taken place? "I guess I've been so preoccupied lately, I've put it to the back of my mind."

Mark tipped his glass and absently noted the beautiful golden color of the chardonnay. It really was a fine wine and, as his client had said, one meant to be shared with someone special. "I'm not surprised. What you're doing for Anna must leave you drained at the end of the day."

"Don't feel sorry for me, Mark. I don't deserve it."

"Can I admire what you're doing?" She obviously didn't realize what a gift it was for Anna to be able to talk to someone about what she was going through. Dying was a lonely business.

For most people, their friends and relatives felt it their duty to offer hopeful platitudes rather than practical help. Karla saw what needed to be done and did it.

"Admire me for what? Altruism had nothing to do with my being here. I came here because I have this compulsive need for order. You can throw selfishness in there, too. I wanted to make sure Anna didn't leave a

158

mess behind when she died because I knew I would be the one who'd have to clean it up."

"Jesus, is that what you're hiding behind?" Did she really not see the bond she had with Anna, the one that was so clear to everyone else?

Karla reached forward to put her empty glass on the table. Disturbed by the movement, Francis left her lap to curl up by the fireplace next to the dog. "I don't run from the truth, Mark. I learned a long time ago that it only catches up with you sooner or later."

"If you leave before you figure out the real reason you're here, one day that truth is going to knock you on your ass." Now he'd done it. She was mad and had every right to be. He had stepped way over the boundaries of a casual friendship. "I'm sorry. I had no right to say that."

She put her elbows on her knees and held her head between her hands. "Somehow you've gotten the idea that Anna and I are close. We're not. We never have been. Luckily, we've managed a truce that's made my time here a lot easier than I thought it was going to be, but that's all it is. Scratch the surface and we'd be at each other again the same way we always were."

He reached over to pull her hair back so that he could see her face. With her profile backlit by the fire, she looked fragile and vulnerable and he was caught up in wanting to make her world good and whole again. "If you really believed what you just said, you wouldn't be crying."

She sat up and ran her hands over her cheeks. "I'm not crying. What a stupid thing to say."

He touched his fingertip to the tender skin below her lashes and showed her the moisture. "What's this?"

"I'm tired."

"And you always cry when you're tired, I suppose."

She turned on him. "What business is this of yours?"

"None. Which is why it's been so easy for me to get sucked in, I guess." He sat back and opened his arms. He wanted her to come to him, sensing she would resist if he tried to comfort her openly.

She hesitated.

"I just want to hold you. This isn't the kind of conversation two people should have from opposite ends of the couch." He moved to let her squeeze in beside him and put her head on his shoulder. "Now, isn't that better?"

"I suppose this is what you do with Cindy?"

"She sits on my lap." He moved so that his chin rested on the top of her head. "Do you want to sit on my lap, too?"

She laughed, relaxing finally. "I'm just fine where I am, thank you."

"Now tell me why you think you don't like Anna." He liked the way she felt next to him, as if she belonged there.

"First tell me why you care."

"Because I let my father die without telling him I loved him and I've never forgiven myself." He'd never told anyone how he felt about his father, not even Linda. "You're luckier than I was; you have time to say good—bye. My dad went out for the morning paper and died before he could get back in the house, leaving a hundred things unsaid between us. He knew how much I appreciated the money he spent to get me through school, or at least I hope he did, because I never got around to saying it out loud. I was going to show him how much I learned about being a father by being the same kind of father to my children. He died before

160

Cindy was born. My mother remarried, and I've grown to like her husband a lot. He's a terrific grandfather to Cindy. But I'll never think of him as anything but my mother's new husband."

"It's not the same thing, Mark. You loved your father, and even if you didn't get a chance to tell him in some carefully composed speech, he knew how you felt. It's different with me and Anna. There's the love that comes because we're family, but we skipped the love that comes with actually knowing each other. I can't change that just because she's dying. It's too dishonest. And besides, she'd never believe me."

"All right. I've said my piece. We can move on to something else."

"Like?"

"Your choice."

She suddenly realized she was hungry after all. But she didn't want to move. She hadn't been in a man's arms this way for so long she'd almost forgotten how wonderful it could feel to be comforted. She chose to ignore the voice that told her it was as much who the man was as the comfort he gave. "Seen any good movies lately?"

"Sure—now you're going to ask me to tell you what it was, aren't you?"

"Give me the plot, I'll do the rest."

"There's these baby dinosaurs that have lost their parents and they have to find a place with big leaves."

"*Land Before Time.*"

"Hey, you're good."

She put her hand on his chest and pushed herself up to look at him. "Damn right I'm good. Want to try another one?"

He stared into her eyes. "A guy brought a girl home

161

to feed her, only it turned out she was afraid to try his cooking and said she wanted cheese and crackers instead."

"I must have missed that one."

He touched her face, running his fingertips along her jaw, his thumb across her lips. Slowly, deliberately, he came forward and kissed her. "It's still in production," he murmured against her mouth.

"The kiss or the movie?"

"Both." His mouth opened and covered hers.

She didn't want to stop and yet still pulled away. "I'm not sure this is such a good idea." She didn't sleep around, telling herself it was as much for conscience as health—a noble principle, easy to follow without temptation, a hell of a lot harder when she felt herself responding in places she'd purposely tried to forget responded to such things.

"You're probably right, but I'm not sure I care." He kissed her again, longer and deeper this time.

She kissed him back, swept along on a wave of need and awakened longings. "It can't mean anything," she said, her hand at his waist.

"What don't you want it to mean?" Mark asked, stopping to look at her.

"Promises, commitments, that kind of thing."

"So what you're suggesting is casual sex?"

"Yes, basically. I'm not sure I would have said it exactly that way, but that's good enough." She didn't like the way this was going.

He smiled sadly. "Sorry, that's not what I'm about."

He might as well have hit her. "I don't understand."

"I can make love to you without loving you, Karla, but it's not something I can toss off as meaningless. I wouldn't do that to myself or to a friend, and I consider

162

you my friend."

"And how would that change if we made love? What would you expect from me?"

"Nothing. It's what I would expect from myself." He kissed her tenderly on the forehead and sat up straight. "You were right, it would be stupid to do anything to complicate our lives any more than they already are."

She adjusted her sweater. "Does that mean you're not going to feed me either?"

"I thought you weren't hungry."

"Changed my mind."

He stood and reached for her hand. "I have to warn you. Once you taste one of my omelets it will spoil you for any other."

"So from now on I either give up omelets or drop by when I'm feeling the need for one, is that it?" She shouldn't feel this disappointed. He hadn't rejected her, he'd rejected using her. Wasn't that the kind of friend she needed?

"How else am I going to get you back here?"

Pillow talk without the pillow. He was flirting with her, making her feel good about herself, worthy. Was it something he did with women in general, or just her?

What an idiotic question. She really needed to get out more.

CHAPTER 15

KARLA SET THE IRON ON THE END OF THE IRONING board and moved the tablecloth to the next section. She couldn't remember the last time she'd ironed anything herself; she sent her clothes to a laundry, and the few tablecloths she owned were permanent press. The mindlessness of the work and the instant gratification brought a peculiar satisfaction, one she certainly hadn't expected.

She did housework because she didn't like the way her house looked when she didn't, not out of any sense of accomplishment or pleasure. Given the option, she would have put the tablecloth on the way it was, figuring the table settings and food dishes would cover most of the wrinkles. But Anna wouldn't hear of it. Everything had to be perfect for their Thanksgiving dinner, which was why she'd started preparing three days ago.

She'd had Karla pick the mums that were salvageable from the garden and they'd made arrangements for every room in the house, including the bathroom. Cindy made her a paper turkey at school that Anna put on the front—door window. Susan brought Indian corn and gourds and miniature pumpkins, extras from the decorations she'd bought for school. Anna gathered colored leaves to add to the flower arrangements and scatter amongst the gourds and pumpkins.

The orange candles that Anna had Karla dig out of a drawer were bent from the heat of a dozen Sacramento Valley summers. Karla bought new ones the next time she went to the store.

She hadn't wanted to stay for Thanksgiving, doing it as a favor for Anna, but now, seeing the house decorated and Anna excited and happy and full of anticipation, she was glad that she had.

"That was my mother's tablecloth," Anna said as she came into the room with a handful of matching napkins, freshly laundered. "I don't think she ever used it, because it was in perfect condition when it came to me."

"I noticed there's a stain on one of the corners now."

She gave a final swipe with the iron and gently folded the cloth in half before laying it on the back of a chair.

"Your grandfather had a little too much eggnog one Christmas and knocked over the gravy boat during one of his stories. I managed to get most of it out, but that one little spot never would come clean."

"Grandpa was a drinker?"

"Lord, no—which is why it didn't take much to get him going when he did. He was a quiet man most of the time, but then he'd get a couple of beers in him and started telling stories and people would be rolling on the floor. I wonder sometimes if Grace didn't get her gift for acting from him."

"She got her blond hair from him. I don't see why she couldn't have gotten that, too." Karla had no idea whether that kind of thing was passed from one generation to another, but if Anna wanted to believe it was possible, what harm was there in agreeing?

Anna folded each napkin into a bishop's hat as Karla finished ironing it. "I can hardly wait for everyone to get here. Did I tell you I ordered a fresh turkey from Bel Air? I told them we'd pick it up Wednesday—I guess that's tomorrow, isn't it? I can't believe how fast the days have disappeared."

"I'll stop by the store on the way home from the airport. Is there anything else we need?"

"Did you get the cornmeal?"

Karla nodded.

"What about the mincemeat?"

"Yes, but I was hoping you'd forget about it."

"I couldn't forget. Heather loves mincemeat pie."

"I still think we should buy the pies. You're going to wear yourself out cooking and be too tired to visit. It's not the food that's important, Anna, it's the company.

I'm sure everyone would be just as happy if we forgot all about cooking and ordered takeout."

"You don't believe that business about the pizza any more than I do. Thanksgiving is a time for tradition. Or at least that's what it used to be. More and more it's becoming a placeholder to mark the official beginning of the Christmas shopping season. Think about it, Karla. There are no presents to exchange, no candy to hide or give away, nothing but sharing a traditional meal with the people you love."

"Not much profit in being a placeholder for Christmas. I'm not surprised the holiday gets less and less attention every year."

Anna stopped folding to look up and smile. "Besides, I'm not making the pies—you are."

Karla laughed. "I've never made a pie in my life."

"Then it's time you learned, don't you think?"

"Why? There are wonderful bakeries in this world, and I believe in supporting small businesses."

"Your mother made pies," she said pointedly.

Karla bristled at the obvious attempt at manipulation. "What has that got to do with anything?"

"I think it's time you realized why you came. Helping me was a nice gesture, and a convenient excuse, but you're really here because somewhere in the back of your mind you knew it was your last chance to find your mother. If you can't admit why you're here, Karla, you can't succeed."

"In case you haven't noticed, Anna, my mother's dead. If I want to find her I know where to look—in a cemetery in Tennessee." She instantly regretted what she'd said and the way she'd said it. Meanness wasn't a natural part of her, any more than spitefulness. "I'm sorry. I shouldn't have said that."

166

Karla chanced a look into Anna's eyes, expecting pain or at the least rebuke. Instead she found sorrow and understanding. "I told you the first day I came why I was here and that it was too late for things to change between us. The only thing I can say now that I couldn't then is that I wish it could be different."

"But it is different," Anna insisted. "You just haven't recognized it yet."

"I'll make the pies."

Anna got up from the chair she'd been sitting in. Thinking she was headed for the kitchen, Karla moved aside to let her pass. Instead she stopped in front of Karla and, with the force of her gaze, made Karla look at her. "I know this is something you don't want to hear, but I'm going to tell you anyway."

Karla had already lost her temper that morning after promising herself it wouldn't happen again. She would not let it happen twice no matter what the provocation.

"You want to think you are your mother's daughter, that you have her traits, that you love what she did, and find fault where she did. But it isn't true. We are the ones alike, Karla. You and I. I see myself reflected in you, in the way you guard yourself against pain, the way you love, and the depth of your loyalty. If you want to see your mother, look at Heather."

"How can you say that? You have no idea what my mother was like. You hardly ever saw her after she left here."

"Do you really think the miles kept us from loving or knowing each other? She was my daughter. We could have gone the rest of our lives hardly seeing each other and the bond would have still been there."

"I suppose you think I don't have that bond with her because we were only together twelve years."

"You're wrong. I know you do. That same bond is what ties us together, and it's what keeps us together through all the arguments and anger." She put her hand on Karla's elbow. "Now come with me. We have pies to bake."

Two hours later the house was filled with the spicy smells of pumpkin and mincemeat pies. A plate sat in the middle of the kitchen table, a pyramid of piecrust cookies. Made from dough scraps and dusted with sugar and cinnamon before being baked, the cookies were a holiday treat she'd almost forgotten, and she had a hard time staying away from them. Finally, after giving into temptation one too many times, she covered the plate and put it in the cupboard.

Watching her, Anna said, "They're good, aren't they? And so simple."

Karla looked around the kitchen, at the dishes she still had to wash, at the spilled flour on the floor. "Good, yes. Simple, no."

"They'll disappear in another generation. You have to make piecrust from scratch to have leftover dough, and hardly anyone does that anymore."

"Then why did we?"

"Tradition. Just like the meal itself. There are some things it's all right to let go of, others. you should do what you can to keep. We had the time to bake pies today, so we did. I know you find it hard to believe, but someday you will pass this on to your daughter."

"If that's what you're after, you'd be better off teaching these things to Heather. I don't know that I'll ever get married again, let alone have children."

"You know what a shame I think that would be. But you don't have to *have* children to be a mother. Take

168

Cindy, for instance. I've seen how you are with Cindy. If any little girl ever needed a mother, that one does. She's desperate for a woman's attention."

"Linda was supposed to be here for Thanksgiving." She'd run into Mark as he was picking up Cindy from school. He was clearly upset, and she'd offered to listen while he waited for Cindy to gather her jacket and project of the day. "She promised Cindy she'd take her to see Santa the day after, but then she got a call that her group was hired to do some big television thing in L.A. and she left without even telling Cindy good—bye."

"Promises mean more to some people than others."

"If they're between, adults, it's one thing. But when you make a promise to a child, it should come before anything else." Karla put water and the freshly ground coffee Jim had sent for them into Anna's ancient pot and wiped the counters while she waited for it to brew.

"How does Mark feel about Linda leaving so abruptly?"

"He was worried how Cindy would take the news, but I don't know how it turned out. The only times I've talked to him in the past week were when he called to cancel our dates."

"I thought you went to a movie with him Monday night."

"I was supposed to meet him at the clinic, but he had an emergency and was in surgery when I got there. He left word that he didn't know how long it would take and that I should go on without him. I stopped by Susan's instead. Allen was working, so we decided to rent a couple of movies and made popcorn. After that I came home."

"That's too bad. When are you going to see him again?"

"I'm not." Karla prepared Anna's coffee—a slightly mounded teaspoon of sugar and just enough milk to turn the liquid a creamy brown—and gave it to her. "I didn't think there was time between now and Sunday with shuffling Grace around and Heather and Bill being here. And I still have to pack." Somehow she'd managed to say the words without showing how disappointed she felt.

"I'm going to miss you." She took a sip of the still—steaming liquid. As if purposely trying to keep the conversation light, she added, "And I'm going to miss your coffee."

"I'll send you your own supply as soon as I get back to the shop." She still thought of the shop as hers, but knowing Jim had been living and loving and laughing in her house with his new girlfriend made it hard to think of the house as her home anymore. She should have taken Jim up on his offer to find somewhere else to stay, but at the time, it had been more important to make him think she didn't care.

"What time does Grace's plane get in tomorrow?"

"Twelve-thirty. I have a feeling it's going to be a zoo out there, so I'm going to leave here early enough to find a parking place and wait for her inside the terminal so we don't miss each other."

"I'm so glad she's coming." Anna's voice was filled with a mixture of excitement and anticipation, a child waiting for her parents to go to bed on Christmas Eve. "I was worried she might have already made other plans."

As much as Karla liked seeing Anna happy, she worried about her heart's bearing the extra load of having everyone there. Even if Thanksgiving turned out exactly the way she imagined, all the turmoil that went with a house full of people was bound to be hard on her. She might lie down in the afternoons, but Karla doubted that she would get any real rest.

"Grace did have other plans," Karla said, "but she changed them to be here with us."

Grace checked her side and rearview mirrors, then glanced overhead for a helicopter. I—5 was notorious for speed traps, and she couldn't afford a ticket.

"You know, you could slow down a little and you wouldn't have to worry so much about getting caught," the woman next to her said. "You're driving like you've got someone chasing you."

"I hate this road," Grace told her. "It's so damn boring that if I don't drive fast, I fall asleep."

"Yeah, maybe—but I'd like to get where I'm going, so I'd appreciate it if you took it a little easier."

Reluctantly, Grace dropped from eighty to seventy. It was on the tip of her tongue to tell Holly that the thirty dollars she was paying for the ride didn't cover bitching rights, but knew it would only make things even worse between them. They'd already gone at it about the music Grace wanted on the radio, the place she wanted to stop to eat, and what kind of gas to buy. Thank God Holly was only going as far as Tracy. Much farther and Grace would have dumped her alongside the road even if she never got paid.

It was Karla's fault Grace found herself stuck in the car with Holly. Her gas credit card was maxed out and she'd been forced to go to the college to look for people who wanted rides north for the holiday. Karla had a knack for picking the worst times to make one of her points, which inevitably left Grace scrambling to work things out. If she'd just sent the money for a rental car,

Grace wouldn't have had to turn in the ticket for Sacramento to one for Phoenix, where Cliff was filming his new movie. He'd asked her to spend Thanksgiving with him, and if Grace had had the money to get there on her own, she would never have agreed to go to Anna's.

She was so damn tired of being broke all the time.

Too bad there weren't any career opportunities in juggling money; she'd be head of her own company by now.

"You're doing it again," Holly said.

"Oh, fuck off," Grace snapped. "This is my car, I'll drive it any way I want."

"Well, you can damn well do it without me. Anderson's is at the next off ramp, you can drop me there."

"You don't have to do that." Grace needed the thirty dollars she was charging Holly. If she didn't make the minimum payment on her Visa, she couldn't charge that dress she'd found at Nordstrom. "I'll slow down."

"That's what you've been saying since we left L.A. I'm not buying it anymore. I want out of this car and I want out now."

"All right, but you still owe me for the trip."

"If you think I'm going—"

Grace shot her an angry look. "Pay or jump."

"I can't believe your family actually wants to see you." Holly dug for her wallet and threw the money at Grace. "You're such a bitch."

The words hit home. "Look, I'm sorry. I've been under a lot of pressure lately and you just happened to have the bad luck to be with me when I had to let off a little steam." She pulled to a stop in the restaurant's parking lot. "If I could, I'd give you back your money,

172

but it's all I have to get home."

"You need to see someone." Holly opened the door and reached in the back seat for her suitcase. "You're a real nut case."

"Thanks, I loved meeting you, too." She rolled down her window as she drove away. "Happy Thanksgiving. I hope you put on five pounds."

CHAPTER 16

KARLA HEARD THE KNOCK ON THE FRONT DOOR FROM upstairs in her bedroom. She waited to see if Anna would answer but then remembered she'd decided to take her shower that night instead of in the morning. Grabbing her robe, she shoved her arms in the sleeves as she descended the stairs. Another loud knock, the third, sounded before she was halfway down the hall. "I'm coming, I'm coming," Karla called with equal impatience.

Before opening the door, she turned on the porch light and looked through the curtain. She should have been surprised to see Grace standing there, but it took a lot anymore to surprise her where Grace was concerned.

"You weren't supposed to be here until tomorrow," she said as she let Grace in.

"I know, but I couldn't wait." She dropped her suitcase and gave Karla a warm hug. "So I decided to drive up today."

"It's good to see you, too." No one hugged her the way Grace did—all out and with an enthusiasm that left Karla feeling special that she was the recipient of something so wonderful.

"This place never changes." Grace looked around.

"Where's Grandma?"

"In the shower." Karla was always a little taken aback when she saw Grace after they'd been away from each other for a while. She was so beautiful she was an anomaly. Everyone arrived in the world with the same basic features—hair, eyes, nose, mouth—but with some people they came arranged in a way that left the rest of the world awestruck. She and Heather had the same genetic makeup, but their eyes were either a fraction of an inch too close or too far apart, their lips not as full, their noses not upturned. Whatever the reason, no one turned to look at them when they passed, or singled them out at a party, or hated them on sight for the way they looked the way people did Grace.

"Should she be taking a shower by herself?"

"If you called to check on her once in a while you'd know the answer." Karla found it harder and harder to make excuses for Grace.

"What's that all about? I just get here and you're already on my case? You could at least give me time to get unpacked."

Just like that, Karla was ready to apologize. "All I'm saying is that you owe her a phone call once in a while. And not just when you need money."

The confident smile left Grace's face. "What's that supposed to mean?"

"You're forgetting why I came here. I've spent the past five weeks going over Grandma's finances."

"She told you I asked her for money? What else did she say?"

"She didn't say anything. You know her better than that." But then maybe Grace didn't. Karla couldn't remember one time during her and Jim's breakup and divorce that Grace had called to ask how she was doing

174

or offered a shoulder to lean on. At the time Karla had put it off to Grace's age and the eight years between them. Now she couldn't remember why she'd thought that it should make a difference.

If it would change anything she would tell Grace about the checks she'd found, but the confrontation wasn't worth the fight that was sure to follow. Anna had never asked for much from them, not even a peaceful Thanksgiving. But Karla would see that she had one if she had to choke on words left unspoken.

"I'm starved," Grace announced, her smile returning now that the threat of discovery had apparently disappeared. "What's there to eat?" She started for the kitchen. "I was going to call Grandma and put in my requests—especially for that fresh cranberry stuff she always makes—but I was afraid I'd trip myself up and say something about coming early."

"You're surprised Grandma can take a shower by herself and yet you expected her to make your favorite foods?" Karla took out the soup left over from her and Anna's dinner from the refrigerator and handed it to Grace.

"Jesus, there's no pleasing you. First you make this big deal about me being here for Thanksgiving, then I bust my butt getting here and now you're acting like you wish I'd stayed home."

"Which reminds me, why did you drive when I sent you a plane ticket? The real reason."

"First criticism and now inquisition?" Grace ladled the soup into a bowl and put it in the microwave.

"Answer me before Grandma gets in here."

"I told you, I wanted to surprise you. Of course, that was when I thought you'd be happy to see me." She punched in two minutes and waited.

"What did you do with the ticket?"

"I don't know. It's at home somewhere."

"I want it back," Karla said. "Or I want the money."

Grace braced her hands behind her and hopped up to sit on the counter. "All right, it's obvious there's something going on here, and that you're not going to stop harassing me until you get it out. But before you say anything, I want you to remember that you screwed up my plans for Thanksgiving by insisting I come up here for this big family get—together. I missed an audition, a really important one, so I could get here early, thinking it would please you. The least you could do is show a little appreciation that I not only did what you asked, I went out of my way to try to make you happy."

Karla didn't know whether to laugh or cry. How many times in the past had she actually fallen for one of Grace's impassioned speeches? She was a master at turning a weak defense into a powerful offense. Had Karla been gullible up to now, or had she heard what she wanted to hear because it was so much easier to travel the road that held no curves or bumps?

"The ticket or the money, Grace," Karla said evenly. "I want it waiting for me when I get home."

"When are you going home?"

"Sunday."

"How am I supposed to get something to you by then?"

"All right, Monday then."

"You're being unreasonable, Karla. I'm leaving for Phoenix as soon as I get back on Saturday."

Anna came to the door wrapped in an oversize terry cloth robe, her face an uncustomary pink from the heat of the shower. "I thought I heard voices out here."

176

Grace let out a squeal. "Grandma." She jumped from the counter and went to Anna, her arms outstretched. Wrapping her in a long, rocking hug, she said, "There aren't enough words in that big, fat dictionary you gave me for Christmas to tell you how much I've missed you."

Anna took Grace's face between her hands. "You just keep getting more and more beautiful."

"You say that because you love me."

"Yes, I do. But I also say it because it's true." The microwave made a beeping sound. "What's that?"

"Your leftover soup. I didn't want to chance stopping anywhere for something to eat for fear you'd already be in bed and I wouldn't get to see you until morning."

Karla almost gagged.

"There has to be more here than soup for you to eat. Let me see what I can find."

"I can't tell you how hungry I am," Grace told her.

"And I can't tell you how tired Grandma is after the day she just put in," Karla said pleasantly. "But then I'm sure you remember where everything is, so if soup isn't enough, we'll just sit here and keep you company while you find something else to eat."

Grace looked at Anna as if expecting her to contradict Karla. "Do you want me to fix you something, too?" she asked.

"I'll make tea," Karla said to Anna. They'd missed their tea on the porch that night, caught up in looking at a photo album Karla had found on a back shelf when she was looking for the silver. "Chamomile okay?"

"It is for me. What about you, Grace?"

"I'd rather have coffee—as long as it's not decaf. I can't stand the taste of that stuff."

Karla handed Grace the special decaf blend she'd had

Jim make for her and Anna. "How was the trip? Run into any fog?"

"No fog, but the trip itself was pure hell. I made the mistake of bringing someone with me for company. She did nothing but complain from the minute she got in the car."

"Wouldn't have been about your driving, would it?" Karla asked innocently.

"That's mean, Karla. You know I'm a good driver."

"No you're not, you're a lucky driver. There's a big difference." Karla reached for the cookies she'd made that afternoon and froze at the soft sounds of Anna trying to catch her breath. "Are you all right?"

She tried to smile a reassurance. "Just . . . give . . . me . . . a minute."

"Did you take your pill?"

Anna shook her head.

"What's happening?" Grace demanded.

Karla turned to Grace, keeping her back to Anna, and mouthed, "Shut up."

Grace ignored her. "Are you okay, Grandma? Should we call an ambulance?"

This time Anna shook her head more forcefully.

"Really . . . I'm fine." She reached for the pill case in her pocket. "I just need a minute."

Karla crouched down in front of Anna, gently took the case from her trembling hand, and gave her one of the nitroglycerin tablets. She'd watched Anna go through this a half dozen times and it still left her shaken. The rest of what she'd seen since she'd been there—the slow movements, the easy fatigue, the long naps—she could pass off as reasonable for an eighty—five—year—old woman. This, however, was an in—your—face reminder of the disease that was slowly,

178

relentlessly destroying Anna's fragile heart.

The microwave beeped, again announcing the soup was finished. Grace tested it and added another thirty seconds. She looked at Karla nervously. "Shouldn't we be doing something?"

Karla matched her breathing to Anna's, the one sure way she'd come up with to tell whether or not the pill was working. "Like?"

"Call the doctor, take her to a hospital . . . I don't know. There has to be something we can do besides just stand around waiting for her to stop breathing."

"I may not . . . be able to breathe . . . as well as I'd like, but there's nothing wrong with my hearing," Anna told her.

Grace teared at Anna's gentle chiding. "I'm sorry, Grandma, but you scared me. You know I'm not very good with things like this." She stopped to take a deep breath and then another. "I fall apart when people are sick, especially when they're people I love."

Karla frowned, confused. Was Grace making a plea for understanding, or did she expect Anna to feel sorry for her? Either way, she'd skillfully managed to shift the focus from Anna to herself. Satisfied the pill was working, Karla got up to finish the tea. "I think you should go to bed when you finish this, don't you?" she said to Anna. "We've got a big day ahead of us tomorrow."

"What time are Heather and Bill getting here?"

"She said if they didn't get caught in traffic in San Jose, they should be here around noon."

"They'll be hungry when they get here, too," she said and smiled at Grace. "We should think of something to feed them for lunch."

Grace broke off a corner of one of the piecrust

179

cookies and popped it into her mouth. "I'd almost forgotten about these, Grandma. But I should have known you wouldn't."

"Karla made them."

Grace laughed. "Don't tell me you're turning domestic on us." She took another bite. "Oh, my God, you've got a man in your life again. Who is he? Come on now, don't make me drag it out of you."

"There is no man," Karla said. "Grandma thought it was time I learned to make pies, so she had me in the kitchen all afternoon trying to teach me."

"How disappointing." She made a pouting face and then laughed out loud again. "I see now why she's so tired. Teaching you to make pies must be like teaching a man how to ask for directions."

Anna looked from one to the other granddaughter. "It's so good to have you home again. I can hardly wait for Heather to get here tomorrow."

True to her word, Heather arrived at a few minutes past noon the next day. The boys beat her to the house, calling for Anna as Karla opened the front door for them. "Grandma Anna—we're here."

"So you are," she said from her chair in the living room. "I've been sitting right here by the window so I could see your car as soon as it pulled into the driveway."

They tumbled into her lap, each fighting to be the first to get their arms around her.

"Boys—take it easy," Heather said, following them in. She stopped to give Karla a quick hug.

"Where's Bill?" Karla asked looking past her to the car.

"Getting the food. I made a casserole for tonight."

"No wonder Grandma loves you the best." Karla had meant it as a joke but could see that Heather took her seriously.

"That's not true. She loves you—" Realizing she'd been had, she lightly punched Karla's arm. "I'm so damned easy. It's like I've got a sign taped to my back saying 'You Can Tell This One Anything.' "

Karla took Heather's sweater and hung it in the closet. "How was the drive?"

"Fine. More important, how's Grandma?"

"Why don't you come in here and see for yourself," Anna said.

"I guess that tells me all I need to know."

Anna met Heather at the doorway. Karla felt like an outsider as she watched them embrace and fall into easy, familiar conversation. The love and caring was unmistakable; Karla had expected as much. What surprised her was the instant connection. Over a half century separated them and yet they had formed a bond of friendship as well as family.

Karla and Anna had shared some special moments the past five weeks, especially when they'd found common ground talking about Marie, but there had been nothing like this. Anna had not smiled the way she did when she looked at Heather, nor had her eyes lit up with happiness the way they did when Heather told her she'd baked her an applesauce cake.

A cake? Was that what it took to make Anna happy? Had she known, she could have signed her up for the dessert—of—the—month club.

The thought brought Karla up short and left her confused. She sounded jealous, but that was crazy. There was no way she could be jealous of Anna and Heather's relationship. They had nothing she wanted or needed.

"What time does Grace's plane get in?" Heather asked.

"She got here last night." Karla worked to keep her voice neutral.

"Well, where is she? Don't tell me she's still asleep."

"She's visiting a friend," Anna said. "But she'll be back soon, I'm sure."

Heather gave Karla a questioning look. Karla shrugged. "I don't know where she is. I was in the shower when she left."

"Where do you want me to put this?" Bill asked. He leaned over to kiss Anna's cheek. "Hi, good—looking. You still playing the field and breaking hearts?"

The pocket of love that surrounded Heather and her boys and Anna had grown to include Bill, nudging Karla even farther to the outside. "I'll take that," she said to Bill. "Sit down and visit for a while and I'll fix lunch."

"I'll help," Heather said.

"No, that's okay. You haven't seen Anna in a couple of months. I'm sure you have things you want to talk about."

"We talk to each other all the time." Heather put her arm around Karla's waist. "It's you I hardly ever get to see."

Heather had given her a sense of belonging, of being wanted, and Karla reacted with a spontaneous hug. "I've missed you, too."

"How is Grandma really?" Heather asked when they were alone in the kitchen. "And have you talked to her again about coming to live with me?"

"She's better than I expected in some ways and worse in others. And I did tell her that I thought she should

182

give more thought to moving in with you, but I don't think it did any good. I don't think you're going to win this one, Heather."

"I'll just keep at her until I wear her down. There's no way I'm going to let her die alone."

"She wouldn't be alone."

"Then with some stranger."

Karla gave up. "I'm going to pick up the turkey after lunch. You want to come with me? We could stop by to say hi to Susan on the way."

"As long as we're not gone too long." Heather moved things around in the refrigerator to make room for the food she'd brought with her. She gave Karla a cat—that—ate—the—canary took. "While we're fixing lunch, why don't you tell me about Mark?"

"How—Never mind, I know. Anna told you about him."

"Nope. Susan did."

"Well, sorry to disappoint you, but there's nothing to tell. He's a nice guy. We went out a couple of times. That's it."

"That's not what Susan says."

Karla hated knowing she was being talked about. "All right, I'll bite. What did Susan say?"

"That sparks flew the minute you met and that you're perfect for each other."

"I know you would like nothing better than to see me safely married off, but saying it doesn't make it so, Heather. There were no sparks before, during, or after." Not exactly the truth, but better than fueling her sister's matchmaking fire.

"You're telling me you feel nothing for this guy and you still went to bed with him?"

Karla let out a gasp of protest. "Who said anything

183

about going to bed?"

"You did. Isn't that what you meant about the before, during, after part?"

"Wrong interpretation. I meant when we met." Karla took plates out of the cupboard, added silverware and napkins, and headed for the dining room.

Heather followed with bread and the deli platter she'd found in the refrigerator. "Should we set a place for Grace?"

"She can take care of herself when she comes in. I don't want Anna to have to look at an empty seat all through lunch."

"I take it you two have already had a run—in? Isn't that my job?"

"When did she become so self—centered?"

Heather gave Karla a disbelieving look. "When wasn't she? What surprises me is that you've finally noticed."

"I'm back," came a call from the hallway. "Where is everybody?"

"Speak of the devil," Heather said. To Grace she called, "We're in here."

Grace appeared in the arched doorway. "Oh, my God, you look wonderful," she squealed. "You should stay pregnant all the time." She rounded the table and threw her arms around Heather. "Where's Bill? And those incredible nephews of mine? I can't wait to see them."

Grace's enthusiasm was contagious. "You're looking pretty good yourself. I love that sweater. Where did you get it?"

"At this fabulous little shop on Rodeo Drive. It's my favorite place in the whole world." She caught Karla staring at her. "Of course I mostly just look. The only time I get to buy anything is if it's on sale."

184

"Nice save," Karla said.

"Would you tell her to stop being such a grump?" Grace said to Heather. "I thought we came here to have fun."

"Karla," Heather said, "stop being such a grump."

Karla laughed despite herself. If she didn't snap out of her foul mood, she was going to ruin the holiday for everyone, Anna included. "Tell us one of your stories, Grace."

She needed no further encouragement and clapped her hands the way she had since she was a little girl and too excited about something to hold it inside. "You're not going to believe this one. It's soooo wonderful. You both know Robert Sandkey, right?"

Karla nodded, Heather didn't.

"He's the one who starred in *Westerley's Companion*? Ring a bell?" She waited. "*Stalker Past Midnight*?"

"Okay, I got him. He's the short guy that looks seven feet tall on the screen."

"That's him. Anyway, he's been making this movie in New Mexico, and you probably don't know this, but he has this huge reputation for joking around on the set, always pulling pranks on people, and no one has ever been able to get him back because he figures out what they're up to before they even get started. He also has this huge appetite for women, has a new one every day like dessert after dinner. So the crew hired this absolutely gorgeous female impersonator and had him change places with the woman who was supposed to show up at Bob's trailer for 'lunch,' so to speak. Anyway, they all stood around waiting for Bob to come unglued when he found out the woman was a man, but nothing happened. An hour later Bob is standing at his door dressed in nothing but his shorts telling the guy good—bye. It turns out he didn't find out it was a guy because he hasn't been having sex with the women who come there, he's been having them help him with his lines. He didn't want any one to know he's dyslexic."

"That's such a sad story," Heather said. "I feel sorry for him."

"Wait, wait—I've got another one. It's even better."

Karla felt herself being pulled in by Grace's infectious charm. Perhaps it wasn't possible for any one person to have it all. Maybe to captivate people you gave up being responsible, to exhibit startling beauty in its best light required a self—awareness that forced you to give up being aware of others. And maybe, instead of trying to make Grace into something she wasn't or could never be, Karla would have to learn to appreciate her for what she was.

CHAPTER 17

KARLA RESISTED THE TEMPTATION TO TELL GRACE TO turn down the radio that she'd brought into the kitchen from the bedroom. Twice already that morning Karla had been accused of relapsing into her bossy older sister routine, and it was only nine—thirty. She told herself she was only looking out for Anna, trying to keep a modicum of control over the bedlam that surrounded them, but Anna seemed more rejuvenated than exhausted by all the activity. Up since seven, she'd divided her time between the kitchen, where Karla, Heather, and Grace were preparing Thanksgiving dinner, and the living room, where Bill and Jason and Jamie were making table decorations.

186

"How small do you want these pieces of corn bread?" Grace asked Karla.

"I don't know. Ask Grandma." Karla finished dicing the onions and added them to the celery and butter and spices already bubbling in the heavy skillet on the stove.

Heather finished cleaning the turkey and put it on the counter to stuff. "If we don't get the dressing in this bird pretty soon, it's not going to be ready until tomorrow."

Karla scraped the last of the onions from the cutting board into the pan and took it to the sink to wash. She had on yesterday's clothes, her hair was held back with a plastic clip, and she smelled like an onion. "As soon as we get this thing into the oven, I'm staking claim to the bathroom."

"Would you mind if I go first?" Grace said. "I'll be quick."

"That'll be a first," Heather said. She noticed something outside and leaned as far forward as her stomach would allow to look out the window. "Someone's here."

Grace and Karla looked, too. Grace let out an appreciative whistle, Karla groaned.

"Oh, no . . ." Karla grabbed the clip in her hair and tossed it on the counter. "What's he doing here?" She wiped her hands on her jeans and tucked in her shirt. By then Mark and Cindy were on the front porch.

Heather's eyes widened. *That's* Mark Taylor? He's really cute, Karla."

"Cute, hell," Grace said. "He's gorgeous."

"Shut up," Karla said, her voice low. "He'll hear you."

Heather eased open the window to listen when Bill answered Mark's knock.

"Hi, I'm Mark Taylor. Is Karla here?"

"Yeah, hang on a minute," Bill said. The screen door squeaked as it opened. "Come on inside. I'll get her for you."

Grace reached over to finger—comb Karla's hair. She made several attempts before she frowned and shrugged and pinched Karla's cheeks. "Sorry, it's the best I can do."

"He's just a friend," Karla insisted, trying to make her voice casual.

"And Tom Cruise is just an actor," Grace fired back.

"Karla . . ." Bill appeared in the doorway. "There's someone here to see you."

"Go for it," Heather whispered, putting her hand at the small of Karla's back and giving her a nudge forward.

"If you don't, I will," Grace added.

Karla sent them both threatening looks. "Thanks," she said to Bill. "I'll be right there."

"This reminds me of the time we waited up to see if that guy who took Karla to the prom was going to kiss her good night," Heather said to Grace.

"What a loser he was," Grace added. "The creep didn't even walk her to the door."

"Thanks for reminding me." Karla tucked a loose strand of hair behind her ear, took a deep breath, and put on a smile that she hoped would convince him she was glad he'd come.

His eyes lit up with their own smile when he saw her. "Cindy made something for Anna at school yesterday and I told her we could stop by to drop it off."

"I think she's in the living room," Karla said to Cindy. "Should I get her for you, or would you like to take it to her in there?"

"In there," Cindy said.

Cindy hesitated when she saw Jamie and Jason. Karla introduced them and watched as the boys took this stranger's measure. Whatever their criteria, Cindy met it. In less than a minute Karla saw the fundamental basics of friendship form as the boys openly included Cindy in their circle.

Anna took her time looking at her present, examining it carefully, noting the careful construction, the colorful patterns, until finally she announced with obvious pleasure at her discovery that the papier—mâché turkey was the perfect decoration for the table. She had Cindy put the lopsided piece of art in front of the flower arrangement. "So I can look at it while I'm eating," she said.

"We're making napkin rings," Jamie said. "Wanna help?"

"Can I, Dad?" Cindy asked.

"For a few minutes. That is, if it's all right with Mrs. Olsen."

"We could use your help with the leaves," she said to Cindy. "We were just getting ready to glue them on."

When Cindy was settled at the table, Mark turned to Karla.

"Come outside with me for a minute?"

Because she couldn't think of a reason not to, she went with him. They walked across the yard, their feet rustling the leaves Karla had meant to rake before everyone came. Finches abandoned the feeders at the sounds they made and took refuge in the trees where they watched and waited until the bravest or most foolish returned and the others followed.

The cool morning would soon yield to the sun. Sweaters and jackets would be discarded and children would be sent outside to play. But for now they were alone.

"I wasn't expecting you," Karla said, consciously keeping herself from reaching up to adjust hair that only a shower and blow—dryer would help.

"I wanted to apologize in person for canceling out on you all week and to find out when you're leaving."

"Sunday——and no apology needed." Heather and Grace were right. Mark was an amazing—looking man. His hair fell across his forehead in the way that made advertising models look sexy and a little wild. Only with Mark it wasn't from the artifice of hours in front of a mirror—he drove with his window down and used his fingers for a comb. His lean build she credited more to missed meals than diet, his muscles from wrestling eighty—pound dogs off and on examining tables. His incredible blue eyes, like Grace's, were genetic. But his personality, the part that most appealed to her, was all his own.

"What about Saturday evening? Have any plans?"

"No—but I think I should spend my last night here with Anna."

"Friday?"

"Heather and Bill will still be here."

"Well, when are you coming back, then?"

"I don't know."

He reached for her hand. "I want to see you again. If not here, then in Solvang."

"To what point, Mark? We're really better off leaving things the way they are."

"I've thought about this—a lot, as a matter of fact. And I've decided complications don't bother me."

"They do me." She eased her hand out of his. "As much as I like you, anything more is impossible."

"Anna warned me you were stubborn."

190

"You've been talking to Anna about me?"

"Only in the most general terms." He smiled ruefully. "I must have impressed her with my winning ways, because she's given me a hell of a lot more encouragement than you are now."

"Then I guess the only thing left for me to do is step out of the way and leave the path open for you two."

"Nice comeback. But it's going to take a hell of a lot more than that to dissuade me."

"You just found your answer, Mark. No relationship can survive with two stubborn people. One of them has to be willing to give a little."

"Okay, you're elected. When you get home, figure out when you can clear your schedule for a couple of days and I'll do what I can to clear mine. We'll go somewhere and see if there's any reason to think we might have a chance. If it doesn't work, it doesn't work, but there's no way I'm letting go until I know for sure."

No man had ever pursued her this way, and it made her more suspicious than pleased. She had no doubt it happened to Grace all the time, but then all anyone had to do was look at Grace to understand why men would be falling all over themselves to go out with her. With Heather and Bill, even with a smashed car between them, the attraction had been instant and mutual.

She and Jim had eased into their relationship so slowly that getting married had seemed the next logical step rather than a romantic conclusion to an almost nonexistent courtship.

Mark could break her heart as easily as he flattered her now and never know it had happened. He was attracted to her veneer of strength, believing her capable of taking chances with her emotions. And why not? With Anna, she'd handled what to others would be a crushing experience and done it with little outward effect. She'd let him in for a little while the other night, but he didn't really know what was going on inside her, what she kept hidden from everyone, what she even tried to keep from herself.

Continuing the argument was fruitless. She'd let him call and then find reasons she couldn't see him until he gave up and stopped trying. "I'll send you my number."

"Don't bother, I'll get it from Anna."

God, how she wished he were as sincere as he sounded. "I should get back. There are a couple of empty cavities in our turkey that need filling, and I'm in charge of the operation." She didn't wait for an answer before starting back to the house.

Mark took her hand and turned her toward him. "Give me one more minute."

"All right, but then I've really got to get back."

"Promise you'll at least think about what I said."

"What good would it do? Your life is here, mine is in Solvang." She could see that she hadn't convinced him. "Let's say we did pursue this and it started to get serious. What then?"

He didn't answer.

"See?" she said softly.

"Just because I don't have a ready answer doesn't mean there isn't one." He smiled. "Now shut up and kiss me good—bye. You've got a turkey waiting, and I told Susan I'd baby—sit Bobby while she and Allen did the cooking."

What the hell—it was a kiss, not a commitment. She put her arms around his neck, fit her hips into his, and tilted her chin up to give him a kiss, intending it to be one they'd both remember.

But he refused to yield the lead and hesitated a

moment when she came forward, looking deeply into her eyes. Slowly, with calm deliberation, he covered her mouth with his, coaxing hers open, touching her lips and then her teeth and finally her tongue with his own.

Involuntarily, she let out a low moan and drew closer still, her arms around his neck. She'd read about a kiss leaving a person shaken, but never experienced the effect. Now she was left wondering if her leg would hold her when she let go, if she could let go at all.

"I'll see you in Solvang," he said, his voice low and determined.

She could only nod.

"Wow. . ." Grace said softly. "Would you look at that. Big sister's found herself a man who knows how to turn her on."

"We shouldn't be watching this," Heather said, frustrated that her belly kept her from getting closer to the window.

"I'll leave when you do."

"She'll kill us if she finds out."

"Me maybe, but not you." She fingered the curtain open a fraction of an inch farther. "What exactly do we know about this guy?"

Heather searched her memory for something she might have forgotten. She and Susan had talked about a dozen things that day on the phone. At the time Mark had been a footnote to a conversation about Karla visiting the day—care center. "He likes kids and animals."

"He has a little girl and is a vet—what a surprise," Grace said sarcastically.

Heather ignored her. "His ex—wife is a singer for a rock band, and—"

"Now *that's* interesting. Which band?"

"I don't know."

"Well, what's her name?"

"I don't know that either."

"You're useless. Go call Susan and tell her we want to know everything she knows about this guy."

"Right now?" Heather asked. "She's probably up to her armpits stuffing her own turkey."

"We only have today to work on Karla—we need facts. We have to know whether we should be encouraging her or discouraging her about this guy."

"You know it's really none of our business who she goes out with."

"The hell it isn't. You want her hooked up with another Jim?"

"She's not going to listen to us." Heather didn't know whether she was more afraid of Grace's fury or Karla's.

"Give me the number, I'll call myself."

"Wait . . . they're coming back." Heather dropped her corner of the curtain and stepped away from the window.

"Do you think she saw us?" Grace said, hurriedly picking up a spoon and giving the onion and celery mixture on the stove a quick stir.

"I don't know." Heather glanced at Grace and was hit with how ludicrous they looked in their effort to appear normal. "We're acting just like we did on Karla's prom night."

Grace laughed. "Yeah, but this was a whole lot better. I could feel that kiss all the way in here."

Heather felt the goose bumps on her arms. "Me, too. Bill's in for a real surprise tonight."

"Shhh, here she comes."

The warning struck Heather as funny, making it seem

even more like the nights they used to spy on Karla. She tried to keep from laughing, but the effort only fueled the need. She grabbed a dishtowel and put it over her mouth.

"Stop that," Grace hissed and turned so that she couldn't see Heather.

"I'm trying," Heather barely managed to get out before she broke down again, muffling her laughter in the towel. Grace clamped her hand over her mouth but it didn't help.

She and Heather managed to regain control by the time Karla saw Mark and Cindy off and returned to the kitchen.

Karla went back to work as if Mark had been an ordinary deliveryman, not worth mentioning. She dumped the crumbled cornbread into the bowl with the bread cubes, added chicken broth, and then the onion—and—celery mixture. The silence became impossible to ignore. A wooden spoon in one hand, the other on her hip, she looked from Heather to Grace and back again. "Whatever you're thinking, keep it to yourselves."

Grace put her hand to her chest, a wronged expression on her face. "I can't imagine what you mean."

Heather bit her lip, her eyes filled with laughter.

"Don't start with me," Karla warned.

Heather and Grace looked at each other. They exchanged a spontaneous high five. "It's true," Grace called out.

"Karla's got a boyfriend," Heather said in a singsong voice.

For an instant Karla was furious that they'd been watching her, and then she could think of nothing but getting even. Feigning a headache, she took two aspirin

195

out of the bottle in the cupboard, picked up a glass, filled it with water, then with swiftness and accuracy, dumped half over Grace's head and tossed the rest at Heather. "I've wanted to do that for years—ever since the first time I saw you two spying on me."

Heather started to reach for a towel, but at the last second grabbed Karla in a bear hug, making sure she got as much water on her as possible. Grace joined in and hugged Karla from behind. She felt like the cream filling in a soggy cookie.

"What's going on in here?" Bill asked. "Are you three okay?"

Karla looked at Heather as she put it her hand over Grace's on her shoulder. "We're better than we've been in a long, long time."

Jamie and Jason hopped up from the table and headed for the kitchen to see what was going on. Anna stayed where she was, holding a paper napkin ring closed as she waited for the glue to dry. She didn't have to see what was happening—she knew. Given the circumstance and opportunity, Marie's girls had found each other again. She couldn't have asked for a better Thanksgiving.

"My work is about over, Marie," she said softly. "It's time you and your grandmother got started on that peanut butter fudge."

CHAPTER 18

"OH, AND REMEMBER THE TIME GRANDMA LEFT HER purse on top of the car and it didn't fall off until we got on the freeway?" Heather passed the bowl of mashed potatoes to Bill.

"And the highway patrol guy had to put out flares and stop traffic to get it back?" Grace added. "He wasn't too happy about it, either."

Anna chuckled. "Well, the way you girls were carrying on, who could blame him?"

Another memory Karla didn't share, a tie that bound Heather and Grace and Anna that she had missed when she left for school and only returned for short visits. While she was gone, she'd imagined herself missed; instead they'd built a family unit without her.

Heather reached for Anna's hand and gave it a gentle, loving squeeze, the gesture as natural and comfortable as if it were one of her children. There were no barriers to break down with Anna for Heather or Grace, no longing for another mother. That burden was Karla's.

And *Anna's*, Karla suddenly realized with startling clarity. Finally, everything that Anna had been trying to tell her the past five weeks made sense. She and Anna shared a bond that Anna had with no one else. The hurt, the longing, the loneliness for a woman gone almost a quarter of a century were theirs alone.

And when Anna was gone, it would be Karla's. There would be no one left to remember the woman with the magical laugh and loving arms. No one who knew that Marie had once had a crush on Ricky Nelson and that she'd stuffed socks in her bra in eighth grade. Only Karla had seen her mother eat the carrots left out for the reindeer as she danced with her father on Christmas Eve, and only Karla truly remembered the mother who had made them matching dresses and sung lullabies to daughters who could no longer recall the sound of her voice.

"Karla? Are you crying?" Heather asked.

"What?" She wiped her hands across her cheeks. "No, I was just thinking how Grandma used to burn the popcorn every time we went to the drive—in movie."

"I did not," Anna protested.

"Yes, you did," Grace said.

"It must not have been burned too badly. You all ate it."

"I'm ready for dessert," Bill announced, leaning back and rubbing his stomach.

An anticipation she hadn't expected came over Karla at the thought of having the focus on her pies. She glanced at Anna and saw that she understood. Karla started to get up.

"I made a surprise," Heather announced, standing up first. "Well, I made one and found one."

With fanfare suitable for a birthday party, Heather brought in the applesauce cake she'd made and put it in front of Anna. Bill followed with the stollen.

"My goodness, all of this for me?"

"Better tell her you remember the stollen the two of you had in San Francisco, or you're going to break her heart," Bill said.

"Of course I remember. It was at Christmas, a little bakery we found off Union Square."

Heather beamed. "I have to admit, the cake was as much for me as you. I was digging through a bunch of your old recipes and happened across it a couple of weeks ago."

Karla looked at the ring cake with only a sprinkle of powdered sugar for icing and knew exactly what it would taste like. It had been her mother's favorite cake, one she rarely made because her father didn't like nuts or raisins. "That was Mom's favorite cake, too."

Anna smiled. "Yes, it was. She asked for it every

birthday. I gave her the recipe, but she swore that hers never tasted as good as mine."

"I didn't know that," Heather said, as if she'd been left out of a secret.

"So what?" Grace said impatiently. "What possible difference does it make who loved what as long as someone is still making the cake? Now are you going to sit around talking about it all evening or are you going to cut the damn thing and let us find out for ourselves what's so wonderful?"

Anna took the knife from Heather, cut a piece of cake, and passed it to Grace. "Don't keep us waiting. We all want to know if you've inherited the Olsen women's gene for applesauce cake."

Grace took a bite. "It's okay, but I'd really prefer a piece of that pumpkin pie Karla has been guarding since I got here."

Karla could have kissed her. "I'll get it for you."

"I thought the line was—if I wanted it, I could get it for myself."

"You made pies?" Heather said to Anna. "You were supposed to leave everything to us."

"I didn't make them, Karla did."

"Karla? You're kidding. This I have to see." Heather followed Karla into the kitchen.

"Don't worry," Karla said. "They're just pies. I'm not after your home economics crown."

"My, my, aren't we touchy. I was just surprised, that's all. I know you don't like to cook, let alone bake."

"It's not as if it were hard. Anyone can make a pie."

"You bought them, didn't you?"

Grace came up behind then and put an arm around each of their shoulders. "I believe in sibling rivalry, but over a pie? Why don't you save it for something important—like which of us is the prettiest or who Grandma loves best."

The fight abandoned Karla. "This is really embarrassing."

"Do you think Grandma and Bill could hear us?"

"They're too busy talking about who the Republicans are going to run for president to pay any attention to us," Grace said.

Heather made a face. "Politics—ugh. I'm not sure I want to go back. Anyone for pie in the kitchen?"

"*Homemade* pie in the kitchen," Karla said as she got them out of the refrigerator.

"I have to admit, they look pretty good for store—bought," Heather said, looking over her shoulder.

"You know, I never understood the humor in pie throwing. Until now."

Heather put up her hand to ward off the blow. "I'll tell Grandma."

Grace protested, "That's my line."

For the next five minutes they laughed and bumped and jostled and teased and became the grown—up family they'd never been. As much joy as the moment brought, the poignancy of knowing it would likely never happen again hung like a thick blanket of fog ready to envelop each of them. "We should do this again for Christmas," Karla said surprising herself as much as her sisters.

"Only let's do it at my house," Heather said.

"No, it has to be here." Anna's house was a part of their history, the knot that held them together. If they were to become a real family again, the seeds had to be planted and nurtured here.

"I can't," Heather said. "My doctor won't let me travel anymore after this."

"That's crazy," Grace told her. "I have a lot of friends who've traveled right up to their due date. And a lot farther than between here and Salinas."

"Unless there was something wrong in the pregnancy." Karla studied Heather. "Is there?"

"After that little problem I had with Jason, my doctor is being cautious that's all. He doesn't want me going into labor anywhere but at home, where he can be at the delivery."

Grace dumped the whipping cream into a bowl. "Then I don't see the problem."

Of the three of them, Karla had expected Grace would be the most difficult to convince, especially after the battle she'd had getting her to come for Thanksgiving.

"Grandma always comes to our house for Christmas. She loves watching the boys open their presents."

"Well, far be it from me and Karla to mess up your little tradition." Grace turned on the mixer, effectively ending the conversation and giving herself the last word.

Karla folded the dishtowel and hung it over the stove handle, then reached for a canister under the sink. "I'm going to feed the birds."

Heather finished wiping the counter. "Wait a minute and I'll go with you."

Karla had come up with the idea because she needed a few minutes alone. The constant shifting from near—euphoria to battle between the three of them had finally worn her down. "You've hardly had any time with Anna. Why don't you visit with her awhile?"

"Shouldn't she be getting ready for bed soon?" Grace asked. "I thought she'd reached the point where she slept most of the time."

Karla frowned. "What point is that?"

"I don't know, I just remember reading somewhere that the worse her heart gets, the less energy she'll have, and that eventually she'll be spending more and more time in bed until she doesn't get up anymore." She worked the broom into a corner. "You went to one of her appointments, didn't you?" she asked Karla. "What did the doctor say?"

Grace had tried too hard to sound casual when she should have sounded concerned. Karla wondered if it was bad acting or bad mental directing. "He's encouraged by how well Anna is doing." When that didn't get a response, she added, "He said if she continues to take care of herself the way she has, there's no reason she couldn't live several more years."

Grace wasn't a good enough actor to hide the fact that the news upset her. What she didn't reveal was why, and Karla couldn't come up with an answer that made sense. "I'll be outside if anyone needs me."

She stopped to put on a jacket, the old one Anna kept in the front closet and saved for working in the yard. The sky was clear, the temperature crisp. She took a minute to look at the stars, spotted the Big and Little Dippers, but not the Milky Way she'd seen as a teenager from Anna's backyard. During dinner Grace and Heather had talked about the campouts they'd had in the backyard, about hearing coyotes during the night and waking to find a skunk eating one of their sandwiches. All Karla could do was listen. She'd always believed herself an important part of her sisters' childhoods. During the past two days she'd learned that in her rush to get away from Anna, she'd left before the truly memorable times had occurred.

Karla opened the can and scooped the shelled sunflower seeds into the measuring cup, allocating a half cup to each feeder. The tube style she had to take down to fill; one required her to sit on the ground with the feeder balanced between her legs. She tried to imagine how Anna accomplished the task.

As she hung the feeder back on its hook, she looked up and saw Grace coming toward her.

"I need to talk to you," she said, hugging herself against the cold.

"I'll be through in a minute. I just have the one by the fence left to fill."

Grace followed her across the yard. "I'm in trouble."

Karla was stopped as much by the frightened tone she detected in Grace's voice as her words. She put the can and feeder on the ground and gave Grace her full attention. "What kind of trouble?"

"I owe a lot of people a lot of money and I can't put them off much longer."

"I don't understand. We just went over your bills a month ago and you were doing all right. At least well enough to buy a new car."

"I didn't show you everything. I knew it would upset you if you found out how much I really owe, and it didn't seem necessary at the time."

"Something's changed since then, I take it?"

"I thought Grandma was a lot sicker than she is."

It took a second for what Grace was telling her to sink in. When it did, Karla was so angry she had to shove her hands into her pockets to keep them still. "Precisely how much money were you counting on her leaving you?"

"I talked to a real—estate agent, and he told me the house should be worth a minimum of two hundred and

203

fifty thousand, considering how much land goes with it. I don't know for sure how much Mom and Dad left us, but there had to be life insurance policies, and that guy who hit them was rich, so there had to be a settlement there. As tight as Grandma has been with that money all these years, even if she's only had it earning minimum interest, the way I figured it with the house and everything else divided three ways, we should each have around a hundred and fifty, maybe even two hundred thousand coming to us."

"How long have you been counting on this money?"

"Don't make me out to be some ghoul, Karla. It's not as if the same thing hasn't occurred to you and Heather. I'm just more honest. Grandma is eighty—five. She can't live forever. Besides, that money is ours. Mom and Dad left it to us, not her."

"I had no idea a will had been found. When did this happen?"

"All right, I accept that you're upset with me. I should have told you I was having problems, but that's no reason to act like a jerk about this."

Usually Karla was caught off guard when Grace maneuvered her into a defensive position; this time she was prepared. "You haven't seen anything yet."

With that, Grace started to cry. "I'm saying this all wrong. I came to you for help. You know I wouldn't ask if I weren't desperate. You're the only one I can turn to. My life is collapsing around me." She made a hiccuping sound that turned into a sob. "And just when I'm on the verge of getting my big break."

To an outsider, Grace's speech would be laughable. Karla felt sick to her stomach. "I'm curious—what do you expect me to do?"

"Loan me enough to get by until . . ." She let the rest

hang, unspoken.

"Grandma dies?" Karla finished for her.

"Yes. Are you satisfied?" Fresh tears spilled onto her cheeks. "And you don't have to tell me how bad this sounds. I already know. I feel terrible about this. There's nothing you can say that I haven't already said to myself. But that doesn't change a thing. I need you, Karla. You have to help me."

"I can't."

"Can't or won't?" Grace shot back, angry now. "Wait—forget I said that. I'm taking this out on you and I shouldn't. It's just that I'm so scared I don't know what I'm saying half the time anymore." She sent Karla a pleading look. "I'll never ask you for another thing as long as I live."

"Who do you owe money to that has you so scared?"

"I haven't paid my share of the rent in three months. Judy said, if I didn't come back with the money, she was going to throw me out and dump all my things on the sidewalk. I have thirty—two credit cards maxed out and can't even make minimum payments on half of them. I had to borrow the gas money to come up here. If you don't help me, I don't know what I'll do."

"File for bankruptcy."

Finally, Karla had said something that reached her. "Do you know what that would mean? I'd have to give up my charge cards. They're the only thing that gets me through some months. How would I live?"

Karla had never felt so tired. "I don't want to talk about this anymore. You're on your own this time, Grace. I'm not going to bail you out. As a matter of fact, I'm going to have the bank take back the car now that I know you never had any intention of making the payments."

"You can't do that. How will I get to my auditions?"

"I don't know. And, what's more, I don't care anymore. If it's something you want, you'll find a way."

"I only came to you because I knew you wouldn't want me going to Grandma. But now I have to. I've worked too hard to get where I am to give up on my dream now. You have no idea what it is to want something so badly you're willing to sacrifice anything to get it."

"I'd be more impressed if you were the one making the sacrifices, but it's me you come to when you're in trouble. Me and Grandma. And for all I know, you've sucked Heather into your problems, too."

"So Grandma has been talking about me." Again the pleading look turned to anger.

"Be careful, Grace. If you have a champion, it's Anna. If anyone has sacrificed themselves for something they believed in, she did. Only it wasn't for herself, it was for us."

"She got paid."

Karla had never hit one of her sisters and was as surprised as Grace when she slapped her across the face. "You ungrateful little bitch."

"That's our money," Grace shouted as she backed away. "She had no right to keep it from us."

"*There is no money*," Karla said. The words hit Grace as hard as Karla's hand. "Not a dime. Anna doesn't even own the house anymore. She sold it to pay your college tuition."

"You're lying." Her eyes pleaded with Karla to tell her it was so. "She's still here." A glimmer of hope surfaced. "You have to be lying."

"She took a reverse mortgage that lets her stay here until she dies or moves to a full—time nursing facility."

"What about our money?"

"I told you, there is no money. As far as I could see, there never was."

"She's got it hidden somewhere. She has to. You said yourself that you heard her talking about it to her friends that day when they were playing cards."

"Why would I lie to you about this now, Grace?"

"Because you hate me. You're jealous. You always have been."

"And that's why I've been supporting you all these years?"

"You feet guilty."

Karla almost laughed. "Jealous and guilty, huh? What about love?"

"If you loved me, you'd help me."

"This is where I came in." Karla headed back toward the house.

"What am I going to do?" Grace wailed.

If ever there was an appropriate moment to quote Rhett Butler's final line in *Gone with the Wind,* this was it. She refrained, knowing the irony would be wasted on Grace.

With every step her legs grew heavier. She didn't want to go back inside. She couldn't face her grandmother, not yet. She wasn't the actress Grace was. Anna would know something was wrong.

She put the seed can on the porch and started walking, not knowing where she was going, only that she had to get away.

CHAPTER 19

MARK'S HEADLIGHTS ILLUMINATED THE FRONT OF HIS house as he made the turn into his driveway. For an instant he was sure he'd seen someone sitting on the porch but decided it was a shadow from one of the bushes. He either had to hire someone to do some pruning around the place or take time off to do it himself. Another six months and he'd have to use a machete to hack his way to the front door.

He stepped from the warm jeep into the coldest night of the year so far—at least according to the radio station he'd been listening to on the way home. He was ready for winter. His and Cindy's skis were waxed, adjusted, and ready to go, propane and wood had been delivered to the cabin, the leak on the roof had been—

The shadow on the porch moved. "What the hell?"

"I'm sorry, I thought you saw me."

"Karla?" He took a closer look. His heart slammed against his ribs in a sudden surge of fear. "What are you doing out here in the dark? And where's your car?"

"I walked." She was curled into herself, her arms folded tightly across her chest, her shoulders rounded.

A dozen questions hit at once, but instead of asking them, Mark took off his coat, wrapped it around her, and opened the door. He led her to the gas fireplace and flipped the switch.

"What's this all about, Karla? You decided to go for a stroll and just happened to wind up here?" The fear became a cold hand pressed to his spine. She knew he was at Susan's. If she'd wanted to see him, she would have looked there.

"Kinda."

Her ears and the tip of her nose were bright red. He cupped her face in his hands, warming her cheeks with his palms and wrapping his fingers over her ears. "Where were you really going?"

"Nowhere. I was just walking."

There was only one thing he could think of that would put her in this state. "Is Anna all right?"

She nodded.

"Then I don't understand."

She came forward, laying her head on his shoulder and tucking her face into his neck. "You know how in every family there's one person who sets the rules, and fields the problems—the responsible one whose existence allows everyone else the freedom to be irresponsible?"

"Yes." In his family it had been his sister. He'd always felt a little sorry for her even though she'd fought hard to win the role over their brother.

"I've always taken the responsible role in our family, whether I needed to or not. I'm tired of the role. I want to stop but I don't know how."

Once acquired, the position was almost impossible to abdicate. "Not everything today turned out as planned, I take it."

"As far as Anna's concerned, everything turned out perfect. We had exactly the Thanksgiving she wanted us to have, from the four of us in the kitchen preparing the meal to me making the pies." She tapped his shoulder with her fist. "I should be happy, since she's the only one who counts in all of this."

"There you go, acting responsible again." He pulled her tighter into his arms. She belonged there. He was convinced of it. Now if he could just get her to see it, too.

"I came here to talk to you," she said. "But I want you to know things without my having to tell you." She looked up at him. "Does that make any sense at all?"

"Is it anything like me wanting you to know how I feel about Linda breaking her promise to Cindy to take her to see Santa Claus but not wanting to say the words?"

"How do you do that? How do you understand these things when no one else does?"

"It isn't me, Karla, it's us. Remember when I told you we're like puzzle pieces? We connected from the beginning. From the moment Susan introduced us, I had the feeling I'd always known you, that we simply needed to catch up on a few things to get back to where we once were." The fan came on. He removed his jacket from her shoulders and tossed it on the sofa.

"I don't believe in psychic connections, or karma, or any of that stuff, any more than I believe in love at first sight." She was lying. If she hadn't felt a connection, why would she tell him things she told no one else?

"Too pragmatic?"

"I guess." She left his arms to stand closer to the fireplace. "Although I prefer to think of myself as a realist."

He smiled knowingly. "That way, whenever something bad happens you can always convince yourself you were expecting it all along."

"Is there something wrong with that?"

"A lot. But we'll save it for another time."

They might be connected, but they couldn't be more different. Mark blithely assumed there would be another time, while Karla was convinced there wouldn't be. A thought abruptly stuck. "Where's Cindy? Why isn't she with you?"

"She and Bobby are in the middle of a movie. I came back to take care of the animals. Which I'd better do before they start looking for another home." He started to leave, then turned, his eyes alive with discovery. "See what I mean? I knew there was a reason I had to come back to the house. I assumed it was Blue and the cats, but they could have waited. They were just an excuse to get me here."

He spoke with a quiet belief that she didn't try to counter. If nothing else, she liked that he wanted to believe they were connected. "I have to admit, I'm glad you didn't wait for the end of the movie. It's a long walk back, and I don't think I could have lasted outside much longer." She could have added how much she needed to be with him tonight, but the words frightened her.

"Do you want me to get you something hot to drink while I'm in the kitchen?"

She shook her head. "I'm doing better now."

When he came back she was curled in the corner of the sofa, her shoes on the floor, Anna's jacket on her lap, her feet tucked under her legs. "I hope you don't mind."

"What?"

"That I've made myself to home, that I've intruded on your Thanksgiving, that I'm about to dump even more of my problems on you."

He sat at the other end of the sofa and reached for her feet, holding them between his hands to warm them. "Dump away. I'm ready for anything you want to send in my direction."

By the time she finished telling him about Grace, her feet were warm and she was snuggled into his side, where she'd wanted to be all along. "I can't stand knowing she's been sitting around waiting for Anna to die. If Anna ever found out—I don't want to think what it would do to her."

"Anna's a pretty sharp old gal. I'll bet she knows more than you think she does. Have you considered talking to her about Grace?"

"I couldn't." She found a snag in his sweater and absently began working on it until it was gone, taking pleasure in doing something for him, wishing it could be more. He'd exposed a domestic side to her she'd tried to deny existed. Something else she would have to deal with when she went home and was alone again.

"Then it will become a secret, and I don't know one secret that didn't wind up hurting someone in the end. I'm not saying you have to give Anna all the details, just enough to keep her from wondering why Grace isn't coming back."

"Were there secrets between you and Linda?"

"Lots of them—hers, not mine. She had a need for a private life away from ours. I have no idea where the need came from or what it included, only that it crippled our marriage when it spilled over into areas of trust. I didn't like the people she saw or brought home, but I looked the other way until I found them using drugs with Cindy in the house."

"Linda's an addict?"

"She's a free spirit. At least that's how she explains herself. If she's held to the same pedestrian standards as the rest of us her talent will stagnate and she will never fulfill the promise of her God—given gift."

"I've heard that speech from Grace. Or at least one close to it. I thought it was the artists who were supposed to suffer for their art, not everyone around them."

He touched his lips to the top of her head and softly asked, "Are you suffering?"

She thought about his question. "I'm confused. I've always seen Grace the way I wanted to see her. And I'm just beginning to realize that I didn't help her because I'm such a kindhearted person, I did it because it made me feel needed. Now that she really needs me, I told her it's time she took care of herself. She doesn't know where to begin. No wonder she's angry."

"You're doing the right thing, but she's going to be a long time thanking you for it."

"I don't care about being thanked. I'd settle for having her speak to me again before I die."

"How is her relationship with Heather?"

"All right, I guess. I don't really know."

"Will Grace go to her for help?"

"She might, but she'd have to be pretty desperate. Heather isn't as easy to manipulate as I've been and she doesn't hesitate telling Grace what she thinks." Karla sat up reluctantly. She didn't want to leave him. "I should get back. I didn't tell anyone where I was going and I've been gone a long time."

"Do you want to call first?" He stood and offered his hand.

She shook her head. "I don't want to try to explain over the phone." Standing next to him she saw another snag, this time in the sleeve. She fought an urge to fix it for him. "Thanks for listening, for being here." She smiled. "For paying attention to the voice that told you to come home to feed the cats. I owe you. If there's ever anything I can—"

"There is. Come with me tomorrow. I'm delivering the setter to his new home in Grass Valley and Cindy

213

decided she'd rather go to a friend's birthday party than come with me."

"I don't know, Mark. . . . I promised Heather I'd go through some boxes we found out in the garage." *If there's ever anything I can do for you?* Did she mean it, or didn't she? "What time?"

"I told Tony I'd be there by noon."

They could be up and back in a couple of hours. "I'd love to go."

Grace's car was gone when Karla got back to Anna's. She thanked Mark again, kissed him and said good night, then went inside, hoping Heather was still up and they could talk. Instead, she found Anna dressed in her old bathrobe, sitting alone in the living room, a book by her side.

"Come in," Anna said softly. "I've been waiting for you."

Karla took off Anna's jacket and hung it on the back of a chair. "Where is everyone?"

"In bed—except for Grace, of course. She left about an hour ago."

The look on Anna's face told Karla it was useless to act surprised. "What excuse did she give?"

"An early—morning audition."

"I didn't expect her to hang around long. With all the excitement she has in her life in L.A., we must be a pretty boring group by comparison." Karla sat next to Anna on the sofa. She felt emotionally and physically drained, her mind too filled with questions of her own to successfully field them from Anna.

"I've been sitting here thinking about all the mistakes I made with you girls, and I'm afraid I've gotten myself in a melancholy mood. So bear with me." She gave

214

Karla a quick, self—effacing smile. "It's not something I expect you to do anything about—you couldn't if you tried—it's only background."

The profound sorrow in Anna's voice was like a hand squeezing Karla's heart. She wanted to take the sadness onto herself, but didn't know how. Heather could heal with touch, Grace with openness and humor; Karla simply sat there and waited for Anna to go on.

"There isn't any money. There never has been. When you and your sisters came to me, it was with broken hearts and half—empty suitcases. We lived on your grandfather's pension and my Social Security. I put every dime of you girls' Social Security into the bank for college. Even that and your grandfather's insurance money wasn't enough, which was why I sold the house. But then we talked about that before."

"Why are you telling me this?" She had a sinking feeling she already knew, but couldn't let go of the small sliver of hope that she was wrong.

"I was in the garage when you were talking to Grace. I heard everything."

"I'm sorry."

"You have nothing to be sorry for. I should have told you how I managed a long time ago. You had a right to know why there wasn't money for your high school graduation trip and why your clothes came from thrift stores."

"Why didn't you tell us about this then? You had to have a reason."

"You'd already had so much taken away from you, I didn't want to take your father's family, too. I knew I could never tell you how that money disappeared without letting you see how angry it made me. I hated those people, and I've always blamed them for stealing

215

whatever chance you and I might have had to work things out between us."

Anna twisted the tie to her robe around her finger over and over again as she talked. "If I'd thought for a minute any of what they did was planned, I would have gone after them to recover the money for you. But they're stupid people who never had their hands on more than a hundred dollars at a time, and they had no idea what to do with that money when it came to them. They don't deserve you, but they're your family, too. I never tried to stop them from being a part of your life when you moved here, and I never understood why they didn't try harder to keep in touch."

The loyalty was all on Anna's side. Karla had attempted to reestablish contact with her father's family when she went away to college. Only her grandmother had responded, and that was to tell Karla how financially strapped they all were, that there was no way any of the Beckers could help her or her sisters with their college expenses, then or in the future. Karla wrote back to tell her she didn't want or expect money from them. She never received an answer.

She'd driven past her grandparents' house when she went to visit her parents' graves, more out of curiosity than longing. Their home was smaller than she'd remembered, and in a poorer part of town. The pickup truck in the driveway had rusted fenders and a gun rack; a chain—link compound in the backyard held three barking dogs. Plainly they hadn't used the insurance money to better their lives in any substantial way. More likely, whatever they kept for themselves had simply slipped through their fingers in a rush of foolish spending.

"They must have assumed you told us about them,"

Karla said. "It's something they would have done in your place."

"I should have found a way to tell you what you needed to know that wouldn't have hurt you."

"This isn't your fault," Karla said. "It's mine." She told Anna about the conversations she'd eavesdropped on and the conclusions she'd drawn and how she'd been the one who kept the myth about their parents' money alive by passing on what she thought she knew as fact to her sisters.

"Thank you for telling me. I understand now why Grace feels the way she does." Anna released the tie and smoothed it with her hand. "If I'd only known."

"How much of the money do you suppose was spent just trying to keep us from coming to live with you?"

"I don't know, maybe the majority. The lawyer they hired didn't come cheap. But that was a lump in my throat I swallowed a long time ago. I was so happy to see the three of you get off that plane and so scared something was going to get in the way of my keeping you that I wasn't taking any chances. I figured I could provide whatever you needed one way or another."

"There must have been times you wished you could have sent me back." Karla didn't have to reach for memories of how she'd been then; they were as fresh and troubling as her fight with Grace.

"Not one."

"I was terrible to you."

"You hurt yourself more than you ever hurt me. My pain comes from all the years we missed. How am I going to explain those years to your mother?"

"She'll understand. Remember, I'm my mother's daughter." Karla wept inside for the lonely child and the woman who'd so desperately wanted to love her.

217

"And my grandmother's soul mate," she offered softly.

Anna looked at her with tears in her eyes. "My dear, sweet Karla, you can never know what those words mean to me. Thank you."

"We can't be what we should have been, but we can be friends."

"Yes . . . I would like that. I know your mother would, too."

Karla saw someone come into the room and looked up.

"What are you doing out here?" Heather said to Anna in a proprietary tone. "It's almost midnight." To Karla she said, "And where have you been all this time? Did you know Grace took off? I tried to stop her, but she said she had to get back for some audition or something."

"Karla went to see her fella," Anna said.

As easily as that, Anna took the focus off the conversation they'd been having and protected Karla from Heather's curiosity. Grateful, she went along. "*Please,* not you, too. What do I have to do to convince you people that Mark is just a friend?"

"If he's your 'friend,' then Bill's my UPS driver." Heather ran her hand over her belly. "There's something going on between you two that's as obvious as Rudolph's nose. Why don't you just admit it? What's the big deal?"

"Since you brought it up, I told Mark I'd go with him tomorrow to deliver a dog to a friend in Grass Valley. I'll only be gone a couple of hours. Is that going to cause a problem with anyone?"

"Bill is taking the boys to Arden Fair to see Santa Claus, and I was hoping the three of us could do

218

something fun together—the way we used to. Of course, at the time I thought Grace would be here, too, but I'm sure we can struggle along without her." Again, Heather's selective memory had put Karla in a scenario where she didn't belong. "I'll try to be back by one."

"That's when Grandma takes her nap. If we're going to do something, it has to be in the morning."

"I promised Mark I would go with him," Karla said. "I'm not going to back out on him now."

Anna leaned her elbow into the arm of the sofa, pushed herself up, and put her hand out to Heather. "Stop making such a fuss. With everyone gone we'll have the house to ourselves. Think how nice and relaxing that will be. We can go through my catalogs and you can help me pick out Christmas presents for everyone."

Anna was providing a way out for Karla, and Heather acted as if she'd won the coveted best—student award at school. Karla felt like thumping her on the back of the head the way she had when they were kids. The thought brought her up short and she almost laughed out loud. "This is perfect," she said to Heather. "I've been trying to figure out a way for you and Grandma to have some time alone together. I've had her all to myself for over a month—it's only fair that you have your turn."

Anna's eyes narrowed in amusement as she looked at Karla. "That's very thoughtful of you."

Karla picked up Anna's jacket and hung it in the closet. Before closing the door, she ran her hand along the worn sleeve. She hoped she aged as well as her grandmother. Anna's body might have betrayed her, but her mind was as sharp as her three granddaughters' combined.

She waited to hear the sounds that let her know Anna

219

had settled in for the night, turned out the porch light, and went to her room. She looked for a note from Grace, but wasn't surprised when she didn't find one. The hours since the confrontation had given her enough distance that she was no longer sure she'd made the right decision about cutting Grace off financially. She was convinced it had to be done, but worried about doing it so abruptly that Grace wound up with nowhere to live.

She wanted her sister responsible, not desperate. Grace was a survivor, but desperate people took desperate measures. If she was telling the truth, which, considering the circumstances and their result, seemed pretty certain, she was in too deep to charm her way out this time. She needed help, but Karla wasn't sure yet how she was going to give it to her. The one thing she did know was that this had to be the last time, and it wouldn't come easy. Grace was going to find out what "struggling actress" really meant.

Karla crawled into bed, put her hands behind her head, and stared up at the shadows playing across the ceiling. "If you just happen to be listening, Mom," she whispered. "I could really use your help."

She closed her eyes, expecting to see the image of her mother that had come to her for twenty—two years. Instead, this time, she saw Anna. And she was smiling.

CHAPTER 20

"SHE'S SO BEAUTIFUL. AND SO SWEET," KARLA SAID, passing a dog biscuit through the cage to the Irish setter as they pulled onto the freeway. "If she were mine, I'd have notices posted everywhere looking for her."

"She hadn't been out on her own for long," Mark said. "She was well cared for—and obviously well loved."

"Then why do you suppose the owners didn't try harder to find her?"

"I'm only guessing, but I suspect whoever they are discovered we had her and were afraid to come forward because they couldn't afford to pay the bill. Which is too bad, because we could have worked it out. We always do."

She took a second to study him while he concentrated on traffic. He was a man whose passion and compassion were such an integral part of his nature that what he'd done for a stranger's pet was no more extraordinary than breathing. If she wasn't very careful, Mark would become her standard, spoiling her for any other man. "I've never even owned a goldfish, so I have no idea how much something like this would cost."

"I didn't bother adding it up, but it probably ran a thousand dollars or so."

"You're kidding."

"There isn't anything cheap about medical care for animals or humans anymore. We use the same supplies and no one gives us discounts. About the only place we can save money is on equipment that we sterilize and use again and hospitals for humans throw away."

She stuck her fingers through the cage to scratch the setter's ear. "After all you went through to save her, I'm surprised you didn't want to keep her for yourself."

"I would have if I hadn't found someone else who clicked with her. Then this thing happened between her and this friend of mine and I knew she'd found a new home. He and his wife own their own business and work out of their home a lot, so they'll be around to

221

make sure everything continues to heal the way it's supposed to." They had reached Auburn, and Mark changed lanes to take the Highway 49 exit.

The setter curled up and closed her eyes. "She's obviously been in a car before."

"I think she might have belonged to someone who worked construction. Of course that's only a guess. I've taken her for walks around Rocklin and Loomis and she didn't show any sign that she was in familiar territory."

Karla turned back around in her seat. "I like that you're the kind of man who takes on hopeless cases and looks for happy endings."

"And I like that you're the kind of woman who leaves her life and business to take care of a woman she feels more loyalty to than love."

"I got more out of coming than Anna did having me here." She'd been slow reaching that conclusion, but when it came, it was as clear as a freshly cleaned window, as obvious as Mark's love for his daughter.

"It must be hard knowing you're leaving in a couple of days."

"Harder than I thought it was going to be," she acknowledged. "If I didn't have to get back to the shop, I'd probably stay another week or two." She'd talked to Jim that morning, and he was anxious to get going on his search for his own place.

"Where do you see yourself twenty years from now?"

She thought about her answer. "That's an odd question. Why do you ask?"

"I was curious about your dreams—your ambitions."

"I see myself still running the coffee shop, only twenty years closer to retirement and financially secure. That's a big thing with me. I don't ever want to be dependent on anyone." She'd almost added "again," but

222

that would lead to other questions she didn't want to answer. All of her and Jim's friends, even their families, believed she'd wound up with everything of value after the divorce, because she ended up with the shop and the house. What they didn't know was that Jim had taken the cash while she assumed the debts. She drove an old car and bought her clothes in the discount stores and ran the shop six days a week with only part—time help because she was determined to be debt—free one day. Another year like the last one and she would reach her goal.

"And your dreams?"

"I've been too busy with the ambition part to have time to dream."

"Then you need to slow down. Dreams are what put the silver linings in those clouds that come along and dump on us every now and then."

"Tell me yours."

He didn't hesitate. "I want someone to share my life with. The problem is, I won't settle. I'd rather be alone than do that. And I want more kids. Every day I'm with Cindy she manages to make the world new for me again. Life through her eyes is pure and basic and full of promise."

"I envy the two of you that. It's been a long time since I've looked at anything that seemed full of promise." She sounded pathetic, even to herself.

"It's there, you're just not seeing it. You have to find the kid in you again and take another look." He groaned. "Did that sound as corny as I think it did?"

"Well, now that you mention it . . . But then, I gave you the lead and that cancels my right to complain."

"I'm glad you came." He glanced her way and gave her a wink. "You're my new best friend."

If it was true that inside every man was a little boy, Mark represented the best part of childhood. He still looked at the world in wonder, believed only good waited for him around the corner, and had room in his life for all strays, whether human or animal. "I guess that means you're my new best friend, too."

"Want to come over to my house and play later?"

"I can't. I told Heather I'd be back for this family thing she's planned." She was more tempted than she sounded. But it wasn't Heather she was worried about disappointing, it was Anna, and that made the deciding difference.

"Does she know what happened with Grace?"

"No, and I'm not going to tell her."

"For her sake or Grace's?"

"I'm not sure. Maybe even mine. Grace is a sore point between us."

"Now that you've had a night to sleep on it, are you still thinking about helping her out after all?"

"I really am afraid to push her too far," she admitted.

"Why? What do you think will happen?"

She hated considering the possibilities, let alone saying them out loud. But the need for someone to talk to was more powerful than her fear. "I've read about girls who turn to drugs and prostitution when they have nowhere else to go."

"And you think that supporting Grace's spending habits will keep her on the straight and narrow? Do you really make that much money?"

"You're leading up to something—why don't you just say it?"

"Grace is twenty—five—"

"Almost twenty—six," Karla said.

"What were you doing at that age?"

224

She'd been on her own for four years by then, paying for her own graduate degree by working two jobs. "That's beside the point. Grace and I are nothing alike."

"What about Heather?"

"You can't compare any of us to each other. We're nothing alike."

"All right—there's Susan and Allen and your ex—husband, Jim and a hundred other people I can name who are nothing like each other either. But most of them were their own people by the time they were Grace's age. When is Grace going to grow up?"

Karla didn't have an answer. She put her head back and looked at the passing countryside. They'd left Auburn and moved deeper into the foothills. Here the earth was red, the forests pine, and the hamlets named by gold prospectors instead of conquering Spaniards. She was a Californian by choice rather than birth and couldn't imagine herself living anywhere else. Not until she'd come north again, however, had she realized how deeply this part of the state, the valley and foothills, were imbedded in her mind. Even scarred from development, this was the land her mother had loved, the place she would talk about with longing in her voice, the place of the dry heat, an expression and reality Karla couldn't understand until she'd lived here herself.

"Why did you settle in Loomis?"

He followed her lead, never questioning the abrupt change in conversation. "You mean rather than Fresno, or anywhere in general?"

"Anywhere."

"I knew I wanted to stay in California, so that narrowed it down some. I did some part—time work at the clinic and got to know and respect the people there.

Then, when the partners invited me to join them and I took a harder look at the area I found I particularly liked the semirural setting and the militant attitude of the longtime residents against wholesale development. By then Cindy was on the way and I couldn't think of a better place for her to grow up, so I said yes."

"And this is where you intend to raise those other kids you'll have someday?"

"Why do I get the feeling there's more to this than idle conversation?"

The question threw her. "I don't know. Am I prying? I didn't mean to."

He let it go. "We've talked about me enough. Tell me something about you."

She tried to think of something interesting. "I'm a movie buff."

"I already knew that. Anyone who knows the plot of *Land Before Time* either has kids or ran out of movies to rent at their local video store."

"When I wear out a pair of socks, it's at the heel, not the toe."

"Hey, that's pretty good. Certainly not something I would have figured out for myself. Now tell me something else."

She dropped her voice to a sexy purr. "I like long walks on the beach, curling up by the fireplace with my well—read copy of the complete works of Dostoyevsky, bubble baths by candlelight, and Sunday afternoon football in the park."

"You read my singles ad. And here I was wondering whether it ever made it in the paper."

He not only kept up with her, he was a step ahead. She liked that. "There was one part I didn't understand, though."

226

"And what was that?"

"Why you said no one under sixty—five should reply."

He grinned. "I thought you'd have it figured out by now—I've only been going after you to get to Anna."

She put her hand to her forehead. "I feel so used."

"I have to admit I've enjoyed our time together more than I thought I would."

"I can't tell you how much that means to me."

"I really have, Karla," he said, serious again. "I'm sorry it's coming to an end."

"I thought the weeks would seem like months before I came," she said. "I dreaded every day I would be here. And now it seems as if I just arrived and I'm leaving."

"And I'm sitting here trying to come up with the words that will get you to stay even knowing there aren't any."

"I know. I feel the same way." She smiled. "It's hard to say good—bye to a new best friend." They hit a pothole and she turned to check on the setter. The dog opened one eye, then settled back into sleep.

Facing forward again, she said, "I go back and forth between wanting to be with Anna and wanting to get back to work. Maybe if I didn't like what I do so much it would be easier to stay away, but the shop is my life, it's my identity."

"You're a hell of a lot more than a coffee shop, Karla." Mark slowed the car to make a left—hand turn. He drove another half mile and then turned left again into a long driveway. A classic brick colonial sat at the top of the hill surrounded by heritage oaks, a gray Mercedes in the circle driveway. Mark stopped behind the Mercedes as a tall man came out to greet them.

"You just missed Melinda. She took the boys to

basketball practice." He held out his hand to Karla. "I'm Darren. And you must be Karla. I told Mark he didn't have to drag you all the way up here, that I was perfectly willing to come down there to pick up Tammy, but he insisted."

Mark looked at Karla and shrugged. "I figured it was the only way I could get you to see me again. Of course I wasn't figuring on Darren shooting off his mouth about it."

Darren laughed. "Anytime I can be of service. Now let me see that dog of mine."

"You named her Tammy?" Karla said.

"My oldest boy came up with it," Darren told her. "Melinda and I just went with it, no questions asked. But I have a feeling it has something to do with a girl he met last summer at camp."

They went around to the back of the jeep. Tammy was up and waiting to be let out of the cage. Her tail thumped loudly against the plastic sides when she saw Darren. He grinned and held out his hand for her to smell.

"How you doing, girl?" She came into his arms as soon as Mark opened the cage, licking his chin and whining in excitement. He put her down and she followed them into the house. She moved with the grace and confidence of a dog in a show ring, her head and tail high, unaware how peculiar she looked with a belly of soft fuzz where there had once been glorious, silky feathering.

"We can't stay," Mark said, giving Tammy's ears a loving, final scratch.

"Melinda's going to be real unhappy to hear that," Darren told him. "She made your favorite casserole for lunch."

228

"It's my fault," Karla said. "I'm the one who has to get back."

"Maybe next time, then," he said graciously. The setter leaned possessively against his leg and gave him a doe—eyed look. She almost missed the appearance of a small black cat as it wandered into the room, its tail riding high. The cat spotted the setter, made a high—pitched sound, and tensed. "Mess with her and she'll put you right back in that hospital," Darren told the adoring dog.

Mark chuckled. "I'm sorry I'm going to miss this. Call me if you need help."

Darren and a distracted Tammy walked them to the door. "Are you and Cindy still planning to come up for the tournament next week?"

"She wouldn't let me miss it," Mark said. "Tell Melinda and the boys we're sorry we had to take off before they got back."

"It was nice meeting you, Karla. Come back when you can stay awhile."

Darren was the kind of man who made the ordinary sound sincere. Karla had no doubt she would be as welcome as Mark should she come again.

"I like Darren," she said as Mark drove away. "How did you two meet?"

"We've been friends since high school. I talked him into taking a job up here when he finished college, and now he owns his own software business."

"And how did he and Tammy get together?"

"He stopped by the clinic to pick up some medicine for the black cat. I had Tammy in the break room with me, and it was love at first sight for them both."

"Just like in one of my movies. I hope they have a happy ending, too."

"What's this—sloppy sentimentality?"

"I've been known to indulge once in a while. It's not something I spread around, so you should know I'll be forced to take extreme measures should it get out."

"A sense of humor, too? Now I really am impressed."

"You've hardly scratched the surface where I'm concerned, Mr. Taylor." Was this really her? Somewhere there was a memory of a teasing, carefree girl, but she'd been gone so long, Karla hardly recognized her anymore. How had Mark found her so easily?

When she glanced in his direction she saw that he was looking at her. Before he turned to look at the road again, she said, "Thank you."

"You're welcome. I assume you're going to tell me what for?"

This time, for the first time, she was the one who reached out to touch him. She wasn't usually a tactile person, having learned to stop wanting the hugs that stopped coming. "For being my new best friend. I'm really sorry I'm leaving," she admitted.

"And not just because of Anna. I'm going to miss you, too." She saw the beginning of a smile. "Okay, I said it. Satisfied?"

"More than you can imagine. It's the most encouraging thing you've said all morning."

"How's this—I wish . . ." She stared out the window. "Never mind."

"Tell me what you wish."

She hesitated, took a deep breath, and plunged forward before she could change her mind again. "I wish I lived here or you lived in Solvang, that we'd met before or never at all, that I knew what I wanted and had the guts to go after it, that you would let me see the side

230

of you that you keep hidden, especially if it's a side that would let me walk away without regret."

"Sorry, Karla. There is no hidden side. With me, it's what you see is what you get."

"I know . . ."

"Well, there's something you don't know that I need to tell you."

She looked at him.

"There's no way I'm going to let you walk out of my life. There's more, but I don't think you're ready to hear it yet."

Her heart swelled until it filled her chest. As much as she wanted to know what he would say next, she didn't want to spoil the moment by asking him to explain. For now, this was enough.

"I had a bet with Grandma that you wouldn't be back until tonight," Heather said as she gently rocked in Anna's chair and watched Karla rake leaves.

"For the third time—we're just friends. Saying it's something else isn't going to make it so." She finished one section and moved to the next. "When I leave on Sunday I doubt we'll ever see each other again."

"Real friends stay in contact."

"You know, you can be a real pain sometimes."

"I'm supposed to be. It says so in my little sister contract." She stood and stretched. "What do you suppose got into Grace?"

"What do you mean?"

"Leaving the way she did. And where were you? Did the two of you have a fight?"

"We had a discussion." Heather would find out what happened sooner or later and would have her feelings hurt if she thought she'd been lied to.

231

"About?" she prompted.

"Her finances."

"God damn it, Karla. You're not giving her more money, are you?"

"Think about it Heather. If I'd given Grace money, we wouldn't have had a fight."

"Don't tell me you finally stood up to her."

"You might say that."

"And?"

"And she wasn't happy."

Heather left the porch and crossed the lawn. "I want details."

"Later." She was talked out where Grace was concerned. And she was tired of worrying about her, which was just about all the control she'd ever had over their situation. "I think I see Bill and the boys coming."

As if on cue, they drove up. Jamie tumbled out of the car and into Heather's arms. "Look what I got." He held a plastic car aloft.

"I got one, too," Jason told her when Bill released him from his car seat. "Mine's blue."

Karla leaned into the rake and watched the reunion. She tried to picture herself in Heather's role, wondering what kind of mother she would make. She had a hundred ideas about being a good mother, some intractable, others open to change. There would always be a bedtime story and never a time when she was too busy to pay attention to a small need. Hands were meant to hold and laps to sit on and cheeks and foreheads and chins and noses were to kiss.

"She's good with them, isn't she?" Bill said coming to stand beside Karla.

"Wonderful. She was born to be a mother."

"Are these nephews of yours—and the soon—to—be

niece—ever going to have any cousins to play with?"

Her immediate thought was to give him a flippant answer about Grace being a long way from motherhood, but the question hit too close to home not to be taken seriously. "Not from me. I've had to face some uncomfortable truths this past month, and one of them is that I'm not mother material. I have a lot of ideas, but not the dedication it takes to do the job right."

"You're selling yourself short, Karla."

"Maybe. But if you listen closely, you'll hear my biological clock ticking its final hour. The timing is wrong for me to do anything about it now, and there's nothing I can do to change it."

He slipped his arm around her shoulder and gave her a hug. "I'm sorry to hear that."

"Me, too." One of the things she liked best about Bill was that he never argued with her about her feelings. He acknowledged she knew herself better than he possibly could by taking the effort to really listen to what she said. She wondered about his choice of professions; to her law seemed a place where nothing was ever accepted at face value.

"I have a favor to ask." He lowered his voice but kept a show of casualness. "I need your help talking Heather into leaving this afternoon instead of tomorrow."

"All right. Can I ask why?"

"She's putting up a good front, but she's exhausted, and that's not good for her or the baby."

A warning chill went through Karla. "I thought everything was all right with this pregnancy."

"That's what Heather wanted you to think. She didn't see any sense in having the whole family worried over something they couldn't do anything about."

"Is it the same thing she had last time?"

"Yes."

"Then she lied to me." Karla had asked Heather the result of her ultrasounds, and Heather had told her that the placenta was where it should be with this pregnancy. With Jason it had been low, between him and the birth canal. She'd damn near died before they could get Jason delivered by cesarean section and stop her hemorrhaging. Another few minutes and they would have had to perform a hysterectomy. Now Karla wondered if that wouldn't have been better. No pregnancy was worth her sister's life.

Karla didn't look at Bill. If she saw confirmation of the fear she heard in his voice, she wouldn't be able to keep up the pretense if Heather happened to look their way. "I can't believe the doctor let her come. Or that *you* did."

"She'll be furious if she finds out I told you."

"I won't say anything," she reluctantly promised. What she'd like to do was give them both hell for taking such a foolish chance with Heather's life.

"I don't understand why she put herself at risk again when she knows how much you and Jason and Jamie need her. It doesn't make sense."

"I've said the same thing to myself a hundred times. I can't believe I agreed to have another child, but you know how persuasive Heather can be when she wants something. At the time it made a crazy kind of sense, now I can't imagine that I fell for it."

"What could possibly matter more than her health?"

Bill rubbed the back of his neck as he considered how to answer her. "Heather heard about a DNA strand, or something like that. Only women have it, and it's passed from mother to daughter. If the link is broken, it's gone forever. She became obsessed with not letting that happen. She talked to the doctor and convinced him—and me, I should add—that she could manage one more pregnancy. If it was a boy, she promised she wouldn't try again, but she wanted this one chance for a daughter. She kept reminding me that it wasn't a hundred percent that she would have the placenta previa again."

As much as Karla wanted to vent her frustration over the risk they'd taken, in the end, it was their decision. She had no right to tell them they were wrong. "And one of the things she's not supposed to do is get overly tired."

"She's actually supposed to be in bed as much as possible," Bill said, relief heavy in his voice.

"Give me a few minutes to come up with something."

"Thanks, Karla. I owe you one."

"If there's a debt to be paid, it's mine." Heather was carrying the baby she so desperately wanted. The deed was done. She and Bill needed her support, not her criticism. "I couldn't ask for anyone better to love my sister. You've given her everything I could wish for her, and a love I never imagined." She desperately wanted to tell him to take care of Heather and to keep her safe, but knew the words were unnecessary. Heather couldn't be in better hands.

CHAPTER 21

"YOU WANT TO TELL ME WHAT WE'RE REALLY DOING on this trip?" Anna said, her hand resting on the padded shoulder strap.

Karla wasn't surprised at the question, only that it hadn't come sooner. "I told you, I wanted to give you an

235

early Christmas present."

"The real reason."

Anna wasn't going to let go, nor would she accept a pat answer. "Bill thought Heather was overdoing it and figured the only way to get her to rest was to take her home."

"Now that makes sense." Anna's fingers moved in a waving motion to the child in the car next to theirs. The little boy giggled and ducked out of sight, then popped up again, his tongue stuck out. Anna stuck her tongue out, too.

"Whatever the reason we're here, it's nice to get away for a while."

Karla had packed a lunch and brought a blanket and pillow for Anna's afternoon nap, planning to bed her down in the back seat if she refused to fall asleep sitting up. She'd never intended for her and Anna to actually take the trip over to the ocean, it was simply a way to get Heather to leave. But once set in motion, the idea had taken on a life of its own. Anna had been up and ready to leave that morning before Karla had poured her first cup of coffee.

"You do realize your sister is a little put out with you," Anna said. "She had a whole list of plans for today."

"I expected as much." Heather's possessiveness where Anna was concerned would have been laughable if she weren't so serious. "She'll get over it."

"Have you heard from Grace?"

Karla was tempted to lie, nothing big, just enough to ease Anna's mind. "No, but then I really didn't expect to. She knows the one sure way to get to me is with silence. She's probably sitting there waiting for me to call."

"Can you just cut her off like that?"

"I don't know." Karla glanced in the rearview mirror to check traffic before exiting for Petaluma. "I feel like I'm caught in one of those damned—if—you—do, damned—if—you—don't situations. No answer feels like the right one." She glanced at Anna. "What do you think?"

"Remember, I'm the one who sent Grace all those rent checks. I helped create the problem."

"What is it with us? I don't think anyone would ever consider either one of us a soft touch, and look what we did."

In spite of the context, the "us" pleased Anna. It was another example of the small, daily gifts Karla unknowingly gave her. Like this trip. She didn't mind in the least how it had come about. Karla could have found a dozen different ways to accomplish her goal of getting Heather to go home. Instead she chose one that meant something special to Anna. She would see her ocean one last time. She would feel the wind against her face and smell the salty air. And she would create a memory with her beloved first granddaughter that maybe someday Karla would look back on as a gift in return.

She'd taken this drive a hundred times and never tired of the journey. The coastal mountains between Sacramento and Bodega Bay were benign cousins of the Sierra, no more than softly rolling hills by comparison. But they provided the valleys and slopes that produced the grapes made into wines known around the world.

A thick carpet of green grew beneath the brown of last summer's grasses. By February, the hills would be on their way to spring, the mustard showing promise of the brilliant yellow soon to take over the fields and vineyards. As they neared the coast, the grapes gave way to pastures and dairy farms, the sunshine to fog.

"You may not get to see the ocean after all," Karla said.

"We'll find a clear place. And if not, we'll enjoy the fog. I'm content just to be here. I don't need vistas." She reached up to touch the soft pad that rested on her shoulder, not because it was in the way, but because she liked knowing why it was there. "Did I remember to thank you for buying this for me?"

"You did."

"There's something I wanted to talk to you about before everyone got to the house, but it never seemed the right time." What she would say was hard because it would put Karla in an awkward position, but she'd told the lawyer that she had one more part of the will to finish and it couldn't be completed until she talked to Karla. "I know you started out telling me you didn't want to be in my will." She chuckled softly. "Of course that was back when you thought I had something of value to leave."

"I'm sorry you had to sell your house, but you have no idea how much easier that makes all of this for me. I only wish you'd told me a long time ago."

"For Grace, you mean?"

"For me. Mom used to say there were two kinds of people in the world, givers and takers, and that they both needed each other to survive. A marriage worked best if there was one of each. It could survive with two givers, but was doomed with two takers. You're a giver, and I've decided I am, too. I've taken the long road to a short point, but if I'd known you were going to sell the house, I would have stopped you. More important than that, even, I would have known about the money and I like to think I wouldn't have wasted all this time being angry." She glanced at Anna. "Does that make sense?"

"I thought we decided we weren't going to dwell on the past."

"See, there you go, giving your forgiveness before I'm done with my apology."

"There's a way you can make everything up to me."

"I'm almost afraid to ask."

"There are some things at the house that I want you to have. They belonged to my mother. Some of them were given to her by her mother. I've saved them for you, even knowing you probably wouldn't want them."

"What kind of things?"

"Useless for the most part. Linens and glassware. Nothing of any value except for the hands that touched them over the years."

"Why me? Why not Heather or Grace?"

"You know the answer to that already. But if you need to hear the words, I'll say them for you."

"Maybe I do."

"You are the link between the women in this family, the only daughter who remembers her mother, the one who cares even deeper than Heather, the one whose heart will be touched when you open a cupboard and see something that you know once belonged to the women who came before you. I had already given some pieces to your mother, who promised to give them to you."

"The blue bowl," Karla said, excited. "Mom loved that bowl, and Dad never understood why. He said it was the ugliest thing he'd ever seen. I remember it always sat in the middle of the dining room table and Mom would put flowers in it whenever we had company."

"I have the matching candlesticks." There had been plates, too, but one by one they'd been broken over the years."

"Are they ugly, too?"

"Hideous."

"Then, yes, I'll take them. And whatever else you've saved for me. I'll even make you a promise. When the time is right, I'll pass everything on to Anna Marie."

"You're assuming you won't have a daughter of your own."

"I don't think that's in the future for me or Grace." She thought for a minute. "But if it turns out I'm wrong, and I do have a daughter, you can be sure I'll start indoctrinating her about these things early, the way my mother did me."

"Think of yourself as a shaman who passes magical stones on to the next generation."

"Why, Grandma, that's downright poetic. I didn't know you had a bent for that kind of thing."

As they made the final sweeping turn north and climbed to the top of the hill, the fog cleared and Anna could see the ocean. She held her breath for several seconds and then let it out with a soft sigh. "I'm home again."

Karla called Jim the next morning and told him she was staying one more day and that it was all right to close the shop until she got there. She thanked him and promised to take him to dinner at the best restaurant he could find the next time she saw him. He insisted he'd give her another day, and they made arrangements to meet at the shop instead of the house.

She could have used another month. Anna had a story for each piece of crystal and linen, some of them funny, some sad. Karla planned to write them all down as she unpacked them again and told Anna she believed that

240

finally, after seven years, her house would at last feel like a home.

Karla cried when she left, but not until she was past the driveway and Anna couldn't see her. For lunch she'd packed a turkey sandwich, the last of the leftovers from Thanksgiving. Her jeans had moved from tight to uncomfortable and she'd already decided it was back to fifteen hundred calories a day when she returned to work. But while she was on the road the calories didn't count, or so she told herself. She picked up a container of milk when she stopped for gas and over the next two hundred miles ate every one of the persimmon cookies she'd saved in the freezer to take to Jim.

Almost as nervous about seeing Jim again as she had been about marrying him in the first place, Karla stopped by the shop before going to the house to unpack. He'd said he would wait for her there no matter how late she arrived.

The day she'd left, the shop windows were painted with leaves and pumpkins; now there were snow scenes with trees and houses and snowmen. Only the artistry was far better, the talent beyond pedestrian. She took a moment to look at the footprints in the snow, her gaze following them to a couple watching their children sled down a hill. The man and woman were holding a steaming mug cupped between their hands. Clever. Holiday, happiness, and coffee.

She let herself in with her key. The bell over the door sounded her arrival, summoning Jim from the back room.

"Welcome home." He came forward, his arms outstretched.

"Thank you. It's good to be back." It was, but not as good as she'd expected. He gave her a hug and the kind

241

of kiss saved for relatives. "The place looks wonderful. I see you bought some new decorations."

"Amy did. She loves doing that kind of thing. At first she was a little worried you might not like it, but I told her you weren't the kind who let things like that bother her."

"Is she here?" Somehow Karla actually managed to make it sound casual.

"She went back to L.A. a couple of days ago. I told her you wouldn't mind if she stayed, but she thought it would be better if she weren't here."

Smart woman. Or maybe just thoughtful. "Still serious about her?"

He nodded. "As a matter of fact, I asked her to marry me."

How could she have convinced herself she was prepared for this? "I assume she said yes?"

"Can you believe it? We've even set the date. The amazing thing is she knows about us, and what I did to you, and she's still willing to take a chance on me." He ran his hand across his mouth as if trying to contain excessive glee. "You're the first person I've told about the engagement."

The gesture reminded Karla of a little boy standing in front of the class telling about his new puppy. "I'm honored. Congratulations." Her throat dry, the lump in it too big to swallow, she was in desperate need of a drink of water. "To both of you."

"That means a lot to me, Karla. I don't want to lose you as a friend."

A quiet acceptance went through her. Jim was truly out of her life, at least in the way she'd talked herself into believing she wanted him there. In its place came the fledgling hope that as unlikely as it had seemed when she left, the friendship thing might actually be possible.

"I would hate to lose you as a friend, too." When had this transition taken place? "I'm not sure I'm up to attending the wedding, though. At least not if it's anytime soon."

"I understand."

She went behind the counter and poured herself a glass of water. She studied him as she drank, and when she finished, said, "You've changed."

"I know. I'm sorry it didn't happen sooner. I'll never forgive myself for the way I hurt you."

She didn't want to hear this. The time for mea culpas had passed. "I've changed, too."

"So you and Anna made your peace?"

"And then some."

"I'm glad to hear it. It was a long time coming. And as much as I hate to say this, she was right about me, you know. I wasn't good enough for you."

The self—effacement was too far over the top for her to ignore. "Oh, please—let's not go there."

He smiled at her impassioned plea. "I have to get going. I told Amy I'd try to get to her place before ten."

She glanced at the clock on the far wall. It was a quarter past six. If he didn't get tangled in too much traffic on the coast highway, he should make it in plenty of time. "Wait a minute and I'll write you your check now."

"I don't want it."

"Of course you do. You earned it—and then some."

"Consider it rent money for the house."

"That's crazy. You could have rented three houses for what I owe you."

"My time here was a favor for a friend. What I owe

243

you is a lot more than I'm ever going to be able to pay, so let me do this one small thing without making a big deal out of it." He smiled. "Okay?"

She saw how much it meant to him and pushed her own pride out of the way. "Okay."

He held out his arms again, gave her a quick hug and kiss, and headed for the door. At the last second he turned and said, "One more thing. I didn't use your bedroom. We stayed in the guest room."

He was gone before she could think of anything to say in reply.

CHAPTER 22

NOT ONLY HAD JIM AND AMY SLEPT IN THE SPARE bedroom, he'd stripped the bed and left the clean sheets and blankets folded on top of the bedspread. The entire house was as clean as the bedroom. Not one room contained evidence that anyone but Karla had ever lived there.

Why couldn't Jim have changed, why couldn't he have been just half this sensitive to her feelings, before the divorce? She would have settled for an effort, a few steps in the right direction, a promise, anything to hang her hopes on.

But then she was beginning to see that she'd made a remarkable transition herself, she didn't fully understand. She didn't want Jim anymore. At least not the way she had when she'd left for Anna's. As usual, because she couldn't understand the transition, she didn't completely trust it. In the back of her mind she was half—convinced she was going to wake up the next morning, or the morning after that, and give into the old, foolish hope that Jim would come to his senses and realize she was the woman for him.

The next morning, she was through with her shower and dressed for work before it occurred to her she hadn't thought about Jim at all. Normally he was the first thing on her mind when she got up and the last thing before she went to sleep. In between she gained freedom with work.

Anxious to get back to that work, she arrived at the shop a half hour early, convinced she would find a dozen small things left undone. Jim could be counted on for most things, but he wasn't a detail person by nature. He had no problem with the obvious, like remembering to inventory the coffee supply every night, but he could never think to check for little things, like stir sticks and napkins.

Karla had her key in the lock at the back door when she heard someone calling to her.

"Hey, Karla—I was beginning to wonder if you were ever coming back."

Eva Karls owned the Christmas shop next door and was a longtime customer. "Me, too."

"How is your grandmother? I meant to ask Jim but kept forgetting."

"She's doing a lot better than I expected. I'd like to talk her into coming down for Christmas." Where had that come from? Heather would be furious if she knew Karla had even considered asking Anna to go to Solvang for Christmas. Since it was impossible to have the family get—together at Anna's, Heather felt she had priority rights for Anna to be with her.

Eva had her own door unlocked and had bent to pick up a package before going inside. "I told Amy I wasn't expecting to get any more of those miniature nutcrackers she used for the baskets, but some came in yesterday, so if you need them, they're here."

Karla had no idea what she was talking about and didn't want to take the time to ask. "Thanks, I'll let you know."

"She sure is a sweet gal. Jim did okay by himself with her." She held the door with her foot and breezily added, "Since Jim couldn't work things out with you, it's nice that someone like Amy came along for him."

"Yeah—nice." Karla's smile was as wooden as one of Eva's nutcrackers.

The early—morning cold penetrated her thin coat, and after telling Eva she'd tap on the wall when her coffee was ready, she hurried inside to turn on the lights and heater.

Something was different, and it wasn't just that the supply shelves were full and in perfect order. She stood and stared and then looked around trying to figure out what had changed. And then it came to her.

There was a new coat of paint on the walls. She looked closer. Sure enough, the scuff mark by the back door and the scratches the plumber had left when he repaired a leaky pipe were now gone. Had she bothered to go into the back room the night before, she would have noticed and could have questioned Jim about it then.

Agitated that he could still act as if the walls were his to do with as he pleased, she went into the main part of the shop and turned on the lights. She'd been so focused on Jim last night she hadn't paid any but cursory attention to the changes he'd made in there. There was the obvious—the Christmas decorations—but she'd missed the subtleties involved with them. Everything was displayed with the same artistry as the painting on

246

the windows. Not only was there a color scheme, burgundy and gold, there was a theme, the toys of Christmas past.

The antique hutch she normally used to display coffee paraphernalia was decorated with fresh—cut greenery laced with expensive burgundy ribbon. The corners were accented with gold balls and stars and small toys. Elegant in its simplicity, it was the perfect backdrop for the dozen—plus gift baskets that had been wrapped in clear burgundy cellophane and tied with gold ribbon. Each basket held two cups, a package of coffee or tea, a tin of imported biscotti, a miniature nutcracker, and a small, hardbound book of Christmas stories. She looked closer and saw that some of the books were about cats and that the nutcrackers and cups had cat themes. Other baskets focused on dogs. The rest were Christmas in general.

Gift baskets weren't anything new. Karla had made them for her customers on Valentine's and Mother's and Father's Days. Only these were better than anything she'd come up with. Not only was the packaging beautiful, the way they were displayed in the hutch gave them importance. Priced to be affordable for a hostess or business gift, they were also perfect for a friend or gift exchange.

Brilliant, beautiful, creative, savvy—those were just a few of the words that came to mind. Only one emotion surfaced, however. Karla was annoyed. Big time.

It was everything she could do not to dig in and rearrange everything Jim and Amy had done. This was her shop, damn it. She'd decorate and display and sell her products her way. If she'd wanted someone to come in to paint her scratched walls or to show her what she was doing wrong, or at least how she could do things better, she would have asked.

But what really grated, what actually hurt, was that the decorating came together better than anything she could have come up with had she spent an entire year in the planning.

She looked around—at the fresh flowers on the tables, the Christmas napkins on the counter, the tree in the corner decorated with ribbon and bows and coffee scoops and tea strainers that had been painted gold.

The gifts under the tree established the theme toys from decades past. At first Karla didn't understand why Amy had chosen the old toy part—and then she spotted a doll like one she'd had when she was a little girl. Her reaction triggered the answer. The tree and toys were meant to appeal to her customers, not children. Nostalgia. A surefire winner if you could figure how to reach a target customer.

And Amy had.

Karla didn't even consider the possibility that Jim had contributed time or talent to the decorating. He could no more tie a bow than walk a tightrope. He had the people skills, the charm that convinced customers they wanted pastry with their coffee and that they couldn't get along without taking a freshly ground pound or two of that same coffee home with them.

Knowing she wouldn't find anything, Karla still checked under the counters and tables and in the corners for something the cleaning service might have missed. She had two absolute rules for her business—serve the best product she could provide, in the cleanest shop.

The back doorbell sounded. She glanced at the clock. The first of the pastry orders had arrived. Tonya and Margaret, her part—time employees, would be there in another hour and the work day would officially begin.

Karla slipped back into the routine of running the shop as easily as a cloud releases rain. At the beginning of December she extended her hours from three in the afternoon to six in the evening. While the days passed in the usual holiday blur, Karla left the shop each night without her accustomed sense of accomplishment. She had come to live for that feeling and was unsettled without it.

The shop was everything, providing her with a social outlet, a sense of family, and a sense of accomplishment at a job well done. But something had changed there, too. Only the answer wasn't as easily found as fresh paint. She still got up each morning with enthusiasm for the day ahead, but for the first time since taking over the shop herself, she looked forward to the end of each day and to her one day off with longing.

When she arrived home at night, she checked the answering machine before she put down her purse or took off her jacket. In the week she'd been home Mark had called twice, leaving funny, intimate messages that she rewound and listened to again and again. She tried returning the calls, but reached his machine so often she started hanging up on the fourth ring.

She'd left a message on Jim's machine thanking him again for the work he and Amy had done at the shop and checking to see if he'd found his own place yet, but she hadn't heard back and was beginning to wonder if he and Amy had eloped.

She'd talked to Heather twice and called Anna every other night and had even chased Bill down at work to ask him if Heather was doing as well as she said she was.

She still hadn't heard from Grace. Karla had had her

hand on the phone to call a half dozen times in as many days. If she'd known what she wanted to say, she would have completed the calls.

Every morning she told herself that she would contact the bank about Grace's car that day. And every night she reviewed the reasons she'd put it off one more time.

Finally, she stopped trying to come up with excuses and decided to wait for Monday, her day off, when she wouldn't be distracted by work.

Grace called Sunday night.

"Have you talked to anyone at the bank yet?" she asked by way of greeting.

"No." Karla ignored the ice coming through the phone. "I wanted to discuss it with you first."

"I need a couple more weeks, but I'll have the money to make the payment by then. If you don't want me messing up your credit rating with a late charge, you can take care of it yourself this month and I'll send you a check as soon as I get paid."

Instead of relief, Karla felt sick to her stomach. Where was Grace going to get that kind of money this soon? "You got a job?"

"What do you care? You made it pretty clear you weren't interested where the money came from as long as I made the payments."

Nothing Karla could say was going to undo the years she'd spent catering to her sister. Instead of being grateful for what had been done for her, Grace now felt entitled. "Just out of curiosity, how long was I supposed to continue supporting you without ever saying anything about it?"

Grace didn't bother answering and said instead, "You have no idea what it's like to want something so badly you'll sacrifice anything to get it."

"What you don't seem to understand is that it hasn't been your sacrifice, Grace. It's been mine—and Anna's."

"So you gave me some money once in a while. Big deal. I'm the one who has to go to lessons every day and then sit in some fucking restaurant so the right people can see me. I'm the one who has to buy clothes that leave me juggling credit card payments every month. And I'm the one who has to go on auditions where they talk about me as if I'm some product on a shelf that doesn't come up to the standards of the national brand. I'm the one who does this day after day and then you expect me to listen when you give me your self—righteous shit about how you've supported me all these years?"

"My, God—do you have any idea how self—centered you sound?"

"Do you have any idea how old you sound—and, I might add, how old you're looking lately? I didn't tell you this before because I didn't want to hurt your feelings, but the last time you were here, one of my friends asked me if you were my mother."

To Grace there was no bigger insult. "And now that I've cut you off financially, it suddenly doesn't matter if my feelings get hurt?"

Grace didn't say anything for a long time. "I'm mad at you, Karla. I thought you were the one person I could count on, the one person who understood me, and you let me down. What do you expect?"

"Isn't that interesting—I could have said the same thing about you."

"There's no reasoning with you. You hear what you want to hear. Are you going to wait for the payment, or not?"

"I need some time to think about it. Call me in a couple of days."

"Why are you doing this to me? Is it because you're jealous?"

"Oh, Grace, I know you're not going to believe this, but whatever I decide it will be because I love you."

"You're right. With love like that, I could use a few more enemies."

"Okay. I've heard enough. I want you to pay attention to what I'm about to tell you, because—"

"I'm through listening to you, Karla. There's nothing you have to say that I want to hear." She hung up.

The empty line hummed in Karla's ear a long time before she replaced the receiver, stared at the phone, and said, "Thank you, Grace. You've just ended my last bit of uncertainty about what I should do."

CHAPTER 23

"WHAT CAN I BRING?" KARLA ASKED, THE STANDARD question in her circle of friends when asked to a dinner party.

"Just yourself," Monica said cheerfully. "Come at seven and wear that spectacular red number you wore to the art show last year."

Karla gritted her teeth. Monica had lined someone up for her. Again. "Who is he?" she said without enthusiasm.

"A friend of John's. Great prospect. He's been married twice, but John says both of the women were losers and it wasn't this guy's fault the marriages broke up."

"What happened to your promise not to do this

anymore?" Karla hadn't held much hope that Monica had actually listened to her when she said she wasn't interested in John's single friends, so she had no real right to be surprised now.

"You weren't serious, were you? I thought that was just something all single women say so they don't sound desperate."

Tonya opened the supply room door and signaled to Karla. "Hang on, Monica." She put her hand over the receiver. "You need me?" she asked Tonya.

"We could use your help. It's like a tour bus just drove up and announced we were serving free coffee."

Karla signaled that she would be right there. "Gotta go, Monica. I'll see you Wednesday night."

Slipping into her work vest, Karla opened the door and was taken aback at the number of people in the shop. She sincerely hoped one of them wasn't the fire marshal. She smiled and said, "May I help whoever is next?"

At two—thirty, she sold the last of the gift baskets she'd put together to replace the ones Amy had made. In all the years she'd owned the shop, she'd never had a Christmas like this one. She'd sold more high—end coffee appliances in the week she'd been back than she'd sold the entire year. Mugs she'd had since she and Jim opened the shop that she threatened to toss every time she dusted sold for full price. She'd even had one woman ask to buy the toys under the tree.

As soon as the customer flow slowed down enough to turn the shop back to Tonya and Margaret, Karla started calling her suppliers to restock the near—empty shelves.

She didn't get home that night until after midnight. Tired and hungry, she took one look at the boxes of Christmas decorations that had been cluttering the living room floor for almost a week, decided what she didn't put up she didn't have to take down, and shoved everything back in the closet.

Next year.

The house felt cold and as forlorn and lonely as she did. It was too late to turn on the heater, and she was too tired to care that no one was there to ask her about her day. Sorting the mail as she moved to the kitchen, she abruptly stopped and looked closer at one of the envelopes. She smiled when she saw CINDY written in childish printing in the left—hand corner.

Just like that she was warm again.

Karla dumped the rest of the bills and Christmas cards on the counter and opened Cindy's letter. Inside was a drawing. Karla studied the picture for several seconds, looking for clues to help her figure out what or whom the picture represented. Finally, as she made out cups sitting on a table and a woman next to a counter with a box that could pass for a cash register, it came to her. Cindy had drawn Karla in the coffee shop.

What Karla had come to think of as her real world, the one she'd built for herself in Solvang, disappeared and she was back in Rocklin again. The friends she'd had for years became secondary to the ones she'd made that past month and had only known weeks. Somehow they'd become more real to her, closer to her heart.

She knew now what was wrong with her, why she'd felt as if pages were stuck together in the book she'd been living. She was homesick for a place she'd never allowed herself to think of as home.

She opened the envelope again to see if there was a note from Mark. Her disappointment at not finding anything was out of proportion to how she felt about him. Or how she'd told herself she felt.

The disappointment turned to joy when she spotted a note on the back of the picture, and her self—delusion eroded like Los Angeles hills in a rainstorm.

Cindy wanted me to tell you she misses you. It doesn't begin to express how I feel.

Mark

Karla looked up from the note and saw Anna's candlesticks on the dining room table. So much had happened in the past two months she didn't know which feelings were real and which were triggered and magnified by fatigue. She had distance; now what she needed was time. Next month, when she wasn't operating on five hours' sleep a night, when she wasn't spending half the day on the phone tracking missing orders or trying to place new ones, when the customers weren't five deep at the cash register, and when she wasn't making obligatory appearances at parties four nights out of every seven, maybe then she could spend some time figuring out why her body was in Solvang and her heart was in Rocklin. Reasonable, even logical, precisely the way she'd lived her life for the past thirty—two years. But instead of heading for the kitchen to fix dinner, she picked up the phone and dialed Mark's number.

Knowing how needy she would sound if she left a message the way she was feeling, Karla listened for the fourth ring and started to hang up.

"Hello?"

"Mark?"

"Karla—is it really you? Finally."

She sank into the chair next to her and brought the

phone closer to her mouth as if it somehow brought him closer, too. "You sound out of breath."

"I was outside when I heard the phone ring. I had a feeling it might be you, and there was no way I was going to miss the call." He paused to catch his breath. "How are you? God, I've missed you. I think about you all the time."

"Me, too," she admitted.

"You know we're going to have to do something about this sooner or later."

"I do know. I just haven't been able to figure out what yet."

"Have you decided what you're going to do about Christmas?"

"Heather really wants us to come there."

He let out a frustrated groan. "We need to talk. Are you home?"

"Yes."

"Can I call you there later? I was on my way to the clinic. There was an accident on the freeway that involved more animals than humans and we've got everyone we could reach coming in to handle it."

"I'll be here. Call me when you can. I don't care how late it is."

"Are you sure?"

"Positive."

"Karla?"

"Yes?"

"Never mind, I'll tell you later when I've got more time."

After she hung up, feeling better than she had since she came back to Solvang, Karla hung Cindy's picture on the chandelier so that she could see both sides. The future was still a mystery, but she was closer to

256

believing it just might have a happy ending after all.

Drawing herself up from the depths of sleep, Karla rolled over in bed to turn off the alarm. But it wasn't the clock ringing, it was the phone. Mark. She smiled as she picked up the receiver.

"Hello?"

"Karla, it's Bill. I'm sorry to call you so late, but I knew you'd want to know."

Her happiness disappeared and she immediately grew sick with dread. "It's Anna, isn't it?"

"No . . . it's Heather. They had to take the baby."

"Oh, my God." She sat up and ran her hand through her hair. "What happened? Is she all right? What about the baby?"

"The baby's little—three pounds, twelve ounces, but the doctor says that's normal for thirty—one weeks. They have her in the neonatal intensive care unit. She's hooked up to a lot of machines, but not a respirator, but the doctor says that's normal, too. Of course I was told there were a lot of things that could go wrong, but for right now, she'd doing okay. Even though she's tiny, she's beautiful, Karla. There's not much of it, but you can tell her hair is going to be a soft brown. And—"

"What about Heather?" she almost shouted. She was glad the baby was okay, but right now she cared more about her sister, and it terrified her that Bill was trying to avoid the subject.

"She lost a lot of blood before we could get her to the hospital."

"We?"

"I had to call 911. She got up to go to the bathroom . .

and then just started bleeding. . . . Jesus, it was everywhere. I've never seen so much blood."

"*How is she now?*"

"She just came out of surgery a few minutes ago. They're setting her up in intensive care and wanted me out of the room while they worked on her. I decided I'd better call you while I could."

"What can I do? Just tell me. I'll do anything. Who's taking care of Jason and Jamie?" She had to focus on something concrete or go out of her mind.

"My mother has them."

"Then what else needs to be done?"

"I'm sorry to do this to you. I know how hard it is for you to leave the shop again, but Heather needs you here with her, Karla."

"I'll be there in a couple of hours. How do I get to the hospital?"

"Come up Main and turn right on Romie Lane. It's a big building, you can't miss it."

"Do you want me to call Grace?" She didn't even consider telling Anna. There was nothing she could do except sit and make herself sick with worry.

"I'll do it—as soon as I have to leave Heather's room again. It will give me something to do besides just stand around."

"Tell Heather I'm coming."

"The minute she wakes up."

"And that I love her."

"She knows, but I'll tell her again anyway."

She started to hang up when she heard Bill's voice. "I didn't catch that," she said bringing the receiver back to her ear. "Tell me again."

"Be careful. It's not going to help Heather if something happens to you."

"Don't do that, Bill. You have enough to worry about without adding me to the list. I'll be fine."

"I'm scared, Karla," he said softly, a catch in his voice. "I don't know what I would do if I lost her."

"She's not going to leave you, Bill." She needed him to believe that so she could believe it, too. "I don't care what's wrong with her or what any of the doctors tell you, *Heather is not going to die.*" She couldn't. She wouldn't. She knew what it was like for children to be raised without their mother. She would never do that to her little boys . . . or to her fragile new baby girl. *Three pounds?* Boxes of candy were three pounds, not babies.

"I think I need you as much as Heather does," he admitted. "I'm not doing very well."

She got up, went to the dresser and started pulling out clothes that she'd put away less than two weeks ago. "Hang on, Bill. I'll be there as soon as I can."

Forty—five minutes later, she was on the road headed north. She'd called Tonya to tell her the shop would be closed indefinitely and why, and had almost cried when she offered to step in and take care of things for long as Karla was gone. While the offer was generous, it wasn't practical, at least not for more than a few days. Tonya could handle the retail end, but had no idea how to place orders, who to place them with, or when to put them in. If Karla was gone more than a week, they would run out of supplies and have to close anyway.

Unless she could find Jim. But she had mixed feelings about asking him to come back. If she could, she'd rather handle this crisis without him. He was out of her life, and she had to start acting that way.

The sun was up by the time Karla pulled into the hospital parking lot. Her fear had grown with every mile, almost overwhelming her by the time she reached Salinas. She'd considered stopping along the way to

259

call, but had turned cowardly at the last minute and driven straight through. Now she could barely get out of the car, she was so scared what she might find.

For hours she'd been avoiding the thought of what it would be like to lose her sister. At unguarded moments a tentacle of fear would sneak past her defenses and give her a preview of profound loneliness. She began a mantra of mental pleas to Heather, begging her to fight whatever forces threatened to take her away.

Karla told her sister to think of her children, of Bill, of sunshine and hummingbirds and Christmas—of a sister who loved her more than life itself. If there were a bargaining table somewhere, a place where she could go to offer her life for Heather's, she would skip the hospital and go there directly. Heather's life was important; she was needed and loved and would leave a giant hole in the fabric of a dozen lives if she died. Karla could slip away and join their mother to make a place for Anna with only fleeting notice. The bargain would be a good one.

Forcing herself to get out of the car and face her fears, Karla went inside the hospital and asked directions. After verifying she was who she said she was, she was let into the maternity ward. She found Bill in the hallway leaning against the wall, his hands pressed to his face.

"What happened?" she asked him. She'd always taken pride in her ability to dig deep and face whatever life sent her way. At that moment all she wanted to do was turn around and walk out of the hospital and not come back until someone told her it was safe. "Why are you out here?"

He looked up, and when he saw that it was Karla, put his arms around her. He held on as if she were the messenger bringing long—awaited good news. "Nothing's changed."

"Why are you out here?"

"Her doctors and a couple of nurses are in there now and I was in the way." He let her go and leaned against the wall again.

"How's the baby?" She asked because she knew it was expected. Not only didn't she feel the same sense of joy that had come with Jason's and Jamie's births, she was angry at the little girl who had put her mother in the hospital and left her fighting for her life.

"The doctor said she's doing fine so far. I spent a couple of minutes with her after she was born, but I haven't had a chance to go back since."

"Who's with her?"

He frowned. "What do you mean?"

"She's not alone, is she?"

"There's a nurse with her."

"No family?"

"There isn't any family to spare, Karla," he said defensively. "My mom is taking care of the boys and my sister's out of the country."

"I'm sorry. I didn't mean to imply—Never mind. I just hate to think of her in there all alone." She put her hand on his arm. "I wish I could have gotten here sooner. You shouldn't have had to go through this by yourself."

"I never should have let her talk me into having another baby. I knew how dangerous it could be."

"As long as it wasn't a hundred percent certain that she would have the placenta previa again, there was no way you were going to talk Heather out of trying for another baby. I've thought a lot about the DNA thing, and as much as I hate to admit it, I understand what

261

drove Heather to do what she did."

"Well, I don't. Why weren't the three of us good enough for her?"

At last she understood why Bill was out in the hall instead of with his daughter. His fear had made him angry, too. Understanding brought a strange kind of peace. "You and Jason and Jamie are Heather's world, Bill. She wasn't trying to take anything away from you, she wanted to share even more of herself by giving you a daughter."

"I'm sorry, but that doesn't make sense. I was perfectly happy the way we were. Heather knew that. She and the boys are everything to me. I didn't need a daughter to feel complete."

"But Heather did."

"We should have been enough for her. It's not as if she didn't know what it's like for kids to lose their mother."

She stood so that he had to look at her. "You're right. And that should tell you that she never seriously considered the possibility anything would happen to her or the baby." Without conscious thought, the protective circle Karla had built around her family expanded to include its newest member. No longer was Heather's little girl "the baby," she was Anna Marie—someone Karla would love and protect with every breath, with every ounce of her being.

"Anna Marie needs you as much as Heather does." She reached for his hand. "As soon as the doctor comes out and I've seen Heather, I want you to do me the honor of introducing me to my niece."

He squeezed her hand in silent communication.

"It's going to be okay," she said.

"I'm glad you're here."

"Me, too."

The door opened and a small parade of people came out. A tall man in a gray suit stopped to talk to Bill. After a cursory introduction to explain her presence, the man she learned was Heather's doctor basically ignored Karla and focused his attention on Bill.

"She's doing better," he said. "We're not out of the woods yet, but I don't expect anything to happen that will slow her recovery. Does she know she's had a hysterectomy?"

Karla flinched at the news. Heather would be devastated to know that the choice of whether or not to have more children was no longer hers to make.

"She hasn't been awake long enough for me to tell her," Bill said.

"She was just waking up when I left. If you'd prefer, I'll go back in and tell her what happened for you."

"No, I'll do it," Bill said. "If she has any questions I can't answer, I'll have the nurse give you a call."

"You can expect her to be depressed—that's natural. Even if the two of you weren't planning on having any more children, Heather's lost an important part of her body. It's not something she's going to take lightly, nor should she. As far as the depression goes, however, we'll only worry about it if it lasts more than a couple of weeks." He turned to Karla. "What she could use from you is someone to listen. Being able to talk about what's happened to her, and giving her some time to come to grips with it, are better medicine than anything we've been able to come up with. Unless it goes on too long. In that case, we've got some other things we can look into."

"Can we see her now?" Karla asked.

"Just don't let her get overtired or too excited."

"You go ahead." Bill said. "There are a couple of other things I'd like to go over with Dr. Agostini now before I forget what they are."

Karla nodded and left them standing in the middle of the hallway. The entire trip she'd tried to prepare herself for what she would see when she walked into the room, picturing everything from Heather sitting up in bed with Anna Marie in her arms to her lying with a sheet pulled over her face. The first image she nurtured, the second she forced out of her mind.

What she'd neglected to take into consideration was the impact the monitors would have on her. On television and in the movies the machines were secondary to the drama, tucked into a corner or behind the bed. Here they took center stage, an ominous reminder that all was not as it should be with the person attached to the wires.

Karla had to move to the foot of the bed to get an unencumbered view of Heather. She prepared herself with a smile, convinced her attitude was as important as her presence. "Sorry it took so long for me to get here," she said softly.

Heather tried to return the smile, but when she moved her mouth, her lips trembled and her breath caught in a sob. "I really messed things up this time."

Karla moved closer, trying not to took at the bag of blood dripping into Heather's arm or to focus too obviously on how pale and frighteningly ill she looked. She leaned over the railing to give Heather a kiss and to take her hand. "How can you say that? You have your daughter, Heather. She's here and she's doing fine."

"Have you seen her?"

"Not yet. I just arrived a few minutes ago and wanted to check on you first."

"Something's wrong. I don't know what it is, but I can feel it."

The sad conviction in Heather's voice threw Karla. Was there something she hadn't been told either? "I swear to you, no one has said anything about Anna Marie having a problem. I would tell you if they had."

"Then it has to be me. Am I going to die?" A tear escaped one eye and slowly rolled down her cheek. "I can't die, Karla. Jamie and Jason need me. Bill can't be both father and mother to them."

"Anna Marie needs you, too." Karla captured the tear with the back of her finger. "Maybe most of all."

"She's so tiny. I try, but I can't picture what she looks like in my mind. I can see Jason and Jamie when they were babies, but she's just this voice crying out to me in pain. I did that to her, Karla. She's suffering because of me."

She should never have come in without Bill. "What makes you think she's suffering?"

"She needed me and I let her down. The doctor told me it was time for me to go to bed and stay there, but I was so sure that if I was careful, I could wait until after Christmas. If Bill finds out, he'll never forgive me."

"Good grief, Heather. Is there anything you don't feel guilty about?" The question had been automatic and one she was sure the doctor wouldn't approve of.

Heather eyed her. "You're supposed to feel sorry for me."

Karla could tell Heather's answer had been just as automatic. She couldn't help but smile. "Well, it didn't take long for us to start acting like sisters again."

The smile she returned barely touched her lips, but radiated from her eyes. "Thank you for coming."

"You couldn't have kept me away."

The door opened and Bill came inside. Karla studied him to see if she could read anything untoward in his expression. He wasn't even aware of her looking at him; he saw only Heather.

She moved out of his way. He went to the bed and leaned close, kissing Heather and touching her face with gentle strokes of his fingertips. Finally, he took her hand and brought it to his cheek. "You are the air I breathe," he said in a hushed whisper. "And I fall deeper in love with you with every breath."

They were the most intimate, beautiful words Karla had ever heard spoken. What she and Jim had shared was an adolescent crush compared to this.

"Forgive me?" Heather asked.

"Yes... now that I know you aren't going to leave me."

"I'm sorry."

"I don't want to hear that. You were right, Heather. Anna Marie was worth the risk."

Karla wondered if Heather had any idea how much that statement had cost Bill. She had no doubt he really would come to feel that way in time, but for now, the reminders of how close he'd come to losing Heather were too real.

She eased her way out, knowing she wouldn't be missed, comforted by the knowledge that Heather had someone who would see her through whatever was ahead.

CHAPTER 24

KARLA WAS IN LOVE—COMPLETELY, UNABASHEDLY, head-over-heels, wildly in love. The object of her attention and affection was less than eighteen inches long and fit comfortably between her cupped hands, had soft, brown fuzz on a beautifully shaped head, eyes full of questions, and her great—grandmother's delicate ears. With hands the size of a quarter she had reached out and captured Karla's heart.

It had taken thirty hours without sleep and an insistent brother—in—law to get Karla to finally leave the hospital the night before. Collapsing on Jamie's bed before she'd even taken a shower, she slept far longer than she'd intended and was in a hurry to get back to the hospital.

The storm that had been sitting offshore for days had finally made it inland, the deluge coming faster than the drains could clear the roads. She had to slow to a crawl to make it through several intersections, the water inches deep, the traffic lights blinking a red warning.

Karla mentally recorded every detail from the thump of the windshield wipers to the howling wind. She pictured telling Anna Marie the story of her birth one day and wanted to get it right.

A trip that should have taken fifteen minutes took thirty. Karla made it without the radio, singing to herself instead. Most of the songs were old standards, but there was one she couldn't remember ever singing before. It was a lullaby, its words tantalizingly out of reach, the melody strong and strangely familiar.

When she arrived at the hospital, she first went to check on Heather. She was asleep. So was Bill. He'd pulled a chair close to the bed and laid his head next to hers. Their hands were clasped, they breathed each other's air. This, too, she would tell Anna Marie one day. She left as quietly as she'd entered and headed for the neonatal intensive care unit.

Before going inside, Karla stopped to peek in the window. Anna Marie's isolette was empty. Karla's gaze swept the room. Anna Marie wasn't anywhere she could see. Forcefully containing a swell of panic that made the hair on the back of her neck stand on end, she motioned to one of the nurses, indicating the empty unit.

The nurse smiled and pointed to a woman in a rocking chair, her back to the window. Karla had missed seeing the monitor wires and warming light that indicated the woman had a baby in her arms. She frowned in concentration. And then it came to her.

Grace.

Bill had told Karla the night before that he'd left a message on Grace's answering machine but that he hadn't heard from her. And yet here she was. The caring, loving woman Karla had been looking for still existed under Grace's self—centered veneer. Whatever wrong Grace had done or would do would be forever mitigated in Karla's mind by her unquestioning appearance at the hospital. Bill made the call; Grace responded. It was all Karla needed to know.

Karla scrubbed her hands and put on the requisite hospital gown before going inside. Before saying anything, or even acknowledging it was Grace holding Anna Marie, she hunkered down and carefully moved the blanket aside to get a better look at her sleeping niece. Bundled snugly in blankets with a tiny knit hat covering her head, there wasn't much to see. Still, when her mouth made a suckling motion and her eyes moved behind spider—veined lids, Karla was convinced she was the most beautiful child ever born.

Karla moved her arm to keep from blocking the heat coming from the warming lamp. The night nurse, a man her age who looked like Gulliver in the land of Lilliputians, had explained that premature babies were confined in isolettes to control their body temperature and prevent water loss that occurred through their skin and simply through their breathing. He said to expect Anna Marie to stay in the isolette until she could perform those functions for herself. Until then, she would be limited to twenty—five minutes out at a time.

Which meant that with Grace there, the line to hold Anna Marie when she did get to come out had grown another person longer. "How long have you been here?"

Grace answered without looking up. "A couple of hours." She moved her arm to give Karla a better view. "Isn't she something?"

"I've been trying to figure out a way to sneak her into my suitcase when I go home." For now, their argument was put aside. They were sisters imprinting and bonding with the newest member of the family.

"You're too late. I've already made a bed for her in my car. She leaves with me."

"Have you talked to Heather this morning?"

"For a few minutes."

"How is she?"

"Still pretty upset about the hysterectomy thing. But she'll be okay once she finally gets her hands on this girl. As soon as she does, she'll realize that what she lost she got back tenfold in little Anna Marie."

This cut—to—the—basics logic was a side to Grace that Karla had never seen. "That's good."

"So is this." Finally Grace looked up. She put her free arm around Karla's shoulders and leaned closer to give her a hug. "I'm sorry I've been such a bitch lately."

"Apology accepted."

"We need to talk."

Selfishly, Karla didn't want to hear what Grace had to say. She was worn down mentally and physically and wanted to save whatever energy she had for Heather and

Anna Marie. "Yes, we do, but not until this is over."

"It's not what you think," Grace said quickly. "I'm not going to ask for anything. Believe it or not, I actually have good news to share with you—with everyone. At least that's the way it looks right now."

"You got a job?" Karla remembered the last time she'd said those words to Grace and the consequences and added, "Is it the role you had an audition for when you got home?"

Grace smiled. "Not bad, Karla. If I didn't know you as well as I do, you might have convinced me you weren't asking if I'd gotten a 'real' job."

"I'll work on my delivery. Now tell me what you're talking about before I say something else I shouldn't."

"I haven't heard back on that particular audition, which was for a movie, by the way. The job I got is for television. Remember the pilot I did a couple of months ago?"

"About the three women who start their own advertising agency?"

"That was a year ago," she said patiently. "This is the one about the family that moves to an island because the father wants to prove they can survive without modern conveniences. I'm the teenage daughter who's pissed about missing her last year of high school. The producer called my agent to say it's a go for eight shows. They're going to give us a summer tryout, and if we pull decent numbers, they'll give us a slot midseason when they dump the shows that haven't made it."

There were more ifs, ands, and buts in Grace's scenario than in a politician's reasoning for not fulfilling a campaign promise. "That's so exciting. Congratulations."

"Thanks. I know the odds are against us making it past the summer, but it's nice to be actually working instead of just sitting around talking about it."

Karla had come to believe the talking was as important as the doing for Grace. She'd sold her sister short but wasn't up to an apology. At least not yet. Their last few run—ins were still too fresh in her mind. "When do you start?"

"Monday."

That gave her five days to get ready. "Are you shooting in L.A.?"

"We're using Florida for the exterior stuff. The rest we'll do in Vancouver."

Anna Marie's nurse, who was always nearby, interrupted them to check the monitor leads that snaked out of the blanket and to write down the readings from the monitors.

"Have you told Anna?" Karla asked when she was gone. "She could use some good news."

"From me, or in general?"

Had Grace always been able to read her this well, or was it a recently acquired skill? Before now Grace had never responded to the nuances in their conversations, and Karla had assumed they'd gone unnoticed. She realized now that she'd been baiting her sister, hoping for a confrontation, and Grace had been too clever to let it happen.

"From you," Karla said bluntly. "I think she's waited long enough, don't you?"

"I tried calling her before I left and then when I got here, but there wasn't any answer."

"Did you leave a message?"

"The machine wasn't on."

"Are you sure you had the right number?"

Anna Marie stirred in Grace's arms, disturbed by the sudden rise in Karla's voice. "Of course I'm sure I had

271

the right number."

"Did you try Susan?" An immediate, sickening image of Anna lying on the floor with her hand inches from the phone came to Karla's mind. "What about that woman who lives next door?"

"I figured I would give her another hour or so first and then call someone to check on her. There are a hundred explanations for where she could have been, and I didn't want to embarrass her by having someone beating on her door."

"An hour from now could be too late."

"It's not like she's on her deathbed, Karla. You told me that yourself. She's probably shopping or at the doctor's. And didn't you say she spends a lot of time at the day—care center with Susan?"

"But she's never gone more than—" Something at the window caught Karla's eye. She looked up and saw Anna standing in the hallway watching them.

"Oh, my God, what is she doing here?"

"Who?" Grace asked.

"Grandma."

Grace's eyes lit up. She tried to turn to see, but couldn't without disturbing Anna Marie. "Help me," she said, as she started to get up.

"Sit down," Karla snapped. "You're going to unhook the monitors."

Grace did as she was told and waited for Karla to turn the chair. She put her free hand under Anna Marie's bottom and brought her up into a sitting position to show her off to Anna, who now had her nose pressed to the window.

Her expression was more eloquent than the collected works of Wordsworth. A woman who had borne a daughter of her own, who might have been blasé, was

272

awestruck. When Anna Marie squirmed and opened her mouth to yawn, Anna's eyes grew misty.

Karla was furious.

"Are you sure you didn't forget and leave a message on her answering machine?" she said under her breath, her pasted—on smile still in place.

Grace answered in the same falsely cheerful voice. "Give me a little credit, would you? I'm not the complete idiot you think I am."

Then who? Bill had promised he'd wait until Heather was out of intensive care before he called Anna. He understood why Karla had been concerned and wouldn't have changed his mind without talking to her first. "I'm going out there."

"You know, Grandma has gotten along just fine for eighty—five years without you running her life for her. I think she's good for a couple more."

"She's not supposed to get upset."

"Says who?"

"Her doctor."

"He told you that?"

"He didn't tell me, he told her."

"Then don't you think she's the one who should decide what will upset her and what won't?" Anna Marie blinked her eyes open and looked at Grace. "Well, hi there, little one. Ready to wake up and check out your habitually arguing aunts?"

"Oh, that's a nice way to introduce us." Karla leaned in close and smiled at her niece.

"She might as well know the truth. We don't want her getting the idea she has relatives who actually like each other."

"I like you."

Grace laughed. "Since when?"

The question offended Karla. "I've always liked you."

"When I'm the sister you want me to be and pay my bills and don't call you for help. I haven't been that person for a long time."

Karla shook her head and put up her hand. "We have got to find a way to stop sniping at each other. We can't go through life like this."

"We can—but I don't like the idea any more than you do."

"Truce?"

"My goodness. How symbolic. A vow of truce with our brand—new niece as witness. Do you suppose it will last longer this way?"

Karla brushed a kiss on Anna Marie's forehead, and on impulse, one on Grace's, too. "I'm going to see Anna."

"How long were you going to make me wait before you called?" Anna asked as Karla came through the door.

"Until Heather was out of intensive care," Karla answered truthfully. "There was nothing you could do but sit around and worry, and it didn't make sense to put you through that when it wouldn't do any good for either one of you."

"I'm not an invalid, Karla. At least not yet." She took several rapid breaths that seemed to contradict the statement. "From now on I would appreciate it if you would refrain from treating me like one."

"All right." It was easier to agree than argue. "I'll keep my opinions to myself from now on."

"I'm perfectly capable of deciding whether or not something is too stressful for me to handle."

"I'm sorry." Apologizing was getting to be a habit

274

lately, but Anna wasn't going to let her off without more concession. "It was presumptuous, but I was worried about you. And I figured it wouldn't help Heather if you wound up in the hospital, too."

Suddenly conscious that Anna had been standing out in the hallway by herself, Karla looked around. "How did you get here?"

"Susan. She'll be in as soon as she parks the car."

A group of people came toward them from the elevator. Karla used them as an excuse to move Anna to the maternity waiting room where they could sit down.

"How is Heather doing?" Anna asked when Karla handed her a cup of coffee.

"Bill didn't tell you?"

"I haven't talked to Bill." She blew on the dark liquid in the styrofoam cup and took a tentative sip.

"Then how did you find out?"

"I left a message for Heather on her machine, and when she didn't call back I knew something was wrong. I tried to reach you at the coffee shop and the woman who answered told me you were gone for a few days with a family emergency. It wasn't hard to put the rest together."

"We almost lost her," Karla admitted. "It was really scary for a while. But Anna Marie is fine." For this she didn't have to pretend or embellish her enthusiasm. "All she has to do is gain a few pounds and she'll be ready to go home. Maybe even before Heather."

"She's so small," Anna said in wonder. "Back when I had your mother there weren't many babies born that size who lived more than a few days. Everyone told those poor women that it was for the best, that their babies would have had a lifetime of problems, and now you hear about ones that are smaller yet who survive."

"They don't just survive, the majority of them come through without any more problems than a full—term baby." Karla had only the night nurse's word on that, but it was something positive to hang onto. She'd been gathering those positives for a day and a half now, like flowers for a bouquet she was saving to give Heather whenever she was frightened or depressed.

"Thank you for telling me that. It's hard to forget all those babies who died and realize it's not that way anymore." Anna put her hands on the chair. "Now I would like to see Heather."

"Shouldn't we wait for Susan?"

She pushed herself up. "Making me wait another five minutes isn't going to give Heather enough time for a miraculous recovery."

Karla hated it when someone automatically assumed a person who was hard of hearing was stupid or that old age made someone childlike or feebleminded. And yet she'd tried to maneuver Anna by distracting her, precisely the way she would Cindy. She took Anna's hand and put it through her arm. "At least let me try to prepare you for what Heather looks like."

"I would imagine she looks like hell. You don't have a baby, lose half your blood, and have a major part of your body removed without consequence."

"How did you know about the blood? And the hysterectomy, for that matter."

"I called Pat." She held onto Karla for support as much as balance, no longer trying to convince her she needed neither.

"Bill's mother?"

"I couldn't reach any of you and the hospital wouldn't tell me anything, so I didn't have any choice. Pat said she'd been too busy with the boys to get to the

276

hospital so she hadn't seen Heather or the baby herself yet, but that Bill kept her filled in on everything that was happening."

Karla could only imagine how the story had been embellished in the telling. Pat loved the dramatic moment as much as Grace but wasn't as good at pulling it off. "So you called Susan."

"Just to take me to the bus station."

"Knowing all along there was no way she'd let you take the bus to Salinas."

Anna had the decency to look embarrassed. "All right, I admit there are times being a little old lady comes in handy and that I'm not above taking advantage of it once in a while. But do you have any idea how long it would have taken me to get here by bus!"

"I suppose I should be grateful Susan's an easy touch. I still wish you'd stayed home, even if you are the best medicine Heather will get today."

"She made me promise I'd be here for the birth of this baby and there was no way I was going back on that promise."

Karla knew as well as Anna what Heather had really meant. She wanted Anna to live forever but was willing to settle for marked special occasions. "After you see Heather I'll take you in to see Anna Marie." Karla softened. Anna was already there. What good would it do to keep telling her she shouldn't be?

"Your great—granddaughter has your ears."

Anna looked puzzled for a second and then smiled as she reached up to touch her ear. "I guess that's not the worst thing she could have gotten from me."

"If I could give her something of yours, it would be your spirit."

"That's a lovely thing to say."

"It's not a bad way to feel, either." Words of affection came hard to Karla. Even with Jim, when the occasion made it necessary to say something, she'd let fancy, expensive cards tell him how she felt. Cards could be ignored or thrown away without permanent damage. Words treated the same way had the power to destroy.

Karla stopped in front of the elevator. "I used to try to tell myself that it was Mom who guided me and Heather and Grace into becoming the women we are, that her love and caring was so strong when she was with us it lasted beyond her death. I think that's true for me, at least partially. But Heather is the mother and wife she is because she found that woman—she found herself—in you. She's worried that you won't be around to give that same gift to Anna Marie. What she hasn't realized yet is that her daughter will find you whenever she looks at her mother."

Anna didn't say anything for a long time. Finally, her voice a rough whisper, she said, "Thank you, Karla. I know how hard that was for you to tell me."

The elevator doors opened and they stepped inside. "After I finally stopped feeling sorry for myself for all I would miss, the worst pain of your mother's death came with knowing you girls would grow up without her and that for Grace at least, she would become nothing more than an image in a photograph. Of all the tears I shed, those were the ones that never stopped."

"When you and Mom finally do see each other again, it's going to take years to catch her up on everything that's happened." Was this one of the stages of grief she'd read about, the acceptance that Anna really was going to die? "I feel strange telling you this, but on the way back to Solvang I found myself making a mental list of things I wanted you to tell her for me."

"Better write them down or I'll forget for sure."

"I'm impressed. You've figured out a way to take things with you when you go."

Anna chuckled. "Wouldn't that be a kick."

"If you were allowed one thing, what would it be?"

Anna considered her question. "A jar of peanut butter." She looked up at Karla and winked. "Just in case it's in short supply up there."

CHAPTER 25

ANNA WAS MORE FRIGHTENED THAN SHE'D LET KARLA see. From the minute she'd found out about Heather she'd tried to strike a personal bargain with God, telling him she realized he wasn't getting much in exchange, but that she would willingly give up whatever time was left to her if he would spare her granddaughter's life.

She rarely questioned his reasoning and had never asked for personal favors—until now. It just wasn't fair for two sets of children in the same family to grow up without their mothers. Surely he could see that.

"I'm going to peek inside and see if Heather is awake before we go in," Karla said.

Anna nodded. *Okay, God, if you want me, you can have me. I'm ready. Right now. No questions asked. I would like just a minute to tell Karla and Heather and Grace how much I love them, though. Heather and Grace know already, but I think Karla needs to hear me say the words again . . . maybe even a couple of times.*

"She's awake." Karla opened the door and stood to the side to let Anna come in.

She hesitated, waiting to see if her heart would stop, not wanting it to happen in front of Heather but in the hallway. Nothing happened. Either God wasn't in a bargaining mood or he was willing to give her Heather and still let her have her allotted time on earth.

"Are you all right?" Karla whispered.

"Just a little slow today." Another lie easily told and accepted because of her age. She and Heather saw each other at the same time. The joy that came to Heather's eyes was a gift Anna would tuck away and savor on the cold nights ahead when she was alone in her room and unable to sleep.

"Grandma—" The rest was lost as Heather started crying.

She'd been right to come. Heather needed her. Knowing so brought a warm feeling to her tired heart. It was good to be needed.

Bill moved to give her his chair. She smiled her thanks. He was another gift she never overlooked when counting her blessings. If she'd been allowed to choose the perfect man for Heather, she couldn't have found anyone to match the one she'd chosen for herself.

She kissed Heather the way she had when she was a young girl, on the forehead, checking her temperature along with dispensing love. "You look like you've had a pretty rough couple of days. Want to tell me about it?"

Fresh tears spilled from the corners of Heather's eyes. Anna reached for a tissue and gently wiped them away.

"I didn't want you to come," she said. "But I'm so glad you're here."

"I'll stay as long as you want me to." Anna settled into the chair.

"I was so scared. . . . It just happened, Grandma. . . . I didn't do anything. . . . I swear I didn't. I was in bed the way I was supposed to be and I just started bleeding."

"Of course you didn't do anything. No one is blaming

you for what happened."

"I should have stayed home Thanksgiving. Maybe the trip was too much. The doctor—"

"Stop that right now," Anna said sternly. "If you can show me that it will help you get better faster and back to your family sooner, I'll sit here and listen to that nonsense. If not, you either talk about something constructive or I'm going back to the nursery to be with my great—granddaughter."

Heather moved her head closer and whispered, "Is she all right? Bill and Karla and Grace have been so worried about how I'll react if they tell me something's wrong that I can't trust them to tell me the truth."

Now was not the time for evasiveness. Anna chose her words carefully. As she spoke, she put her hand on her chest and gently rubbed the tightness in her muscles. She'd either slept wrong last night or pulled something getting in and out of Susan's car. "I haven't seen her up close yet, but from the way the nurses were acting around her, and the way your sisters are fighting over who gets to hold her, I would say Anna Marie is doing better than her mother."

"What does she look like?"

Anna wondered how many times Heather had asked the same question and why no one had thought to take a picture to give to her. "Now remember, I haven't been inside the nursery yet, so my observations are from a distance."

"That's okay."

"She was all wrapped up in a pink blanket and had a knit cap on her head. When Grace held her up for me to see, she had her mouth open in a big yawn. Afterward she blinked and looked around and made one of those faces that means someone was going to be changing the diaper soon."

"Did she cry?"

"Not that I saw."

"You said Grace was holding her?"

"As if it was something she did every day."

"She wasn't afraid of her?"

"I didn't pick up anything like that, from either of your sisters." Finally Anna understood. It was Heather who was afraid of her baby. Somehow they had to find a way to get her to the nursery so she could see for herself that Anna Marie was safe to love.

Heather started to cry again. She reached for Anna's hand. "I'm so glad you're here."

Feeling like an intruder, Karla decided to find Susan and thank her for giving Anna a ride. She'd been right to be worried about Anna, but wrong to try to keep her away. She looked at Bill and motioned that she was leaving. He followed her out into the hall.

"Thank you," he said and gave her a hug. "This was the best medicine Heather could get. She needed Anna." He smiled wearily. "I guess there are times when only a mother will do."

The statement sent a sharp pain through her chest and tears to her eyes. She blinked them away before Bill could see. "I didn't have anything to do with her coming." There was more. "But I'm glad she's here, too." The admission was like arriving at the far side of a swollen river, giving her both freedom and comfort.

"I think we're going to be okay."

"I think you already are okay," Karla said. "Now why don't we take a little stroll down to the nursery. After two days of me and Grace, that daughter of yours needs some male company."

When they arrived at the nursery they found Susan at the window, her attention so focused on Anna Marie she didn't hear them come up. Finally she turned, saw them, and put her arms around Bill. "She's definitely a keeper. I'm so jealous I'm thinking about going home and talking to Allen about getting one of these for ourselves."

Bill looked in at his daughter unwrapped and asleep in her isolette. "It's hard to picture her ever holding her own with her brothers."

"Wait until you get a good look at that twinkle in her eyes and then tell me that," Karla said. She understood Susan's surge of maternal feelings. For the first time in her life, Karla had felt them, too, and it had left her reeling. She thought she'd accepted the running down of her biological clock when it became clear she and Jim were never going to get back together. And now this.

As much as Karla loved Jamie and Jason, she hadn't experienced this lioness emotion when they were born. But then they'd been big, ready—to—take—on—the—world, full—term babies. This bundle of perfection in miniature struck a protective chord in Karla, one she had believed so deeply buried it would never surface again. This was exactly the way she'd felt about Heather and Grace when their parents died. Her determination to protect her sisters had left her at odds with her father's family, making her the outsider, and in the end, bringing them to Anna.

Obviously it was a feeling one didn't want to ignore.

"I'm going in," Bill said. "Would either of you care to join me?"

Karla and Susan looked at each other in silent agreement to give Bill this time alone with his daughter. "I'm in desperate need of a cup of coffee," Karla said.

"We'll be in the cafeteria if you need us."

They stood at the window until he was inside. A nurse brought a chair and opened the round window for Bill to reach through and touch Anna Marie. The moment was so intimate, so personal, so wrenching, Karla could hardly stand to watch.

Susan nudged her. "Let's get out of here."

The cafeteria was nearly deserted, the coffee hot, the doughnuts surprisingly fresh. A live tree sat in the corner wrapped in silver garland and twinkling Christmas lights. Paper elves and reindeer cavorted on the walls and small potted poinsettias sat in the middle of the round tables.

Karla led the way to a table by a window. "If you tell me you're ready for Christmas I'll gleefully wring your neck."

"I've got everything for school taken care of, but I'm not even close to being finished with my shopping for the family. But what's the hurry? What do we have . . . about two weeks left? Plenty of time."

"Even taking unexpected trips into consideration?"

She shrugged. "In the end, it all seems to get done one way or another."

Karla looked at her maple bar. "I really shouldn't."

Susan grinned and took a bite of her jelly doughnut. "But you're going to anyway."

"Damn straight." Luckily, it didn't taste as good as it looked and the second bite was easier to resist. "I haven't thanked you for bringing Anna."

"I know why you didn't want her to come, but once she found out Heather was in the hospital, there was no way she was going to stay home."

"Heather needed her here. I had no idea how much until I saw the two of them together."

"I loved having my mother with me when Bobby was born. We understand what the other one is thinking without having to say a word. And we laugh at the same things. There was this woman in the room next to mine when I was in labor. We couldn't figure out why she'd be screaming her head off one minute and quiet the next. Turns out she stopped when her husband went outside for a cigarette. After that Mom and I just roared every time the room got quiet. The doctor and nurses thought we were nuts."

Karla managed a smile. "My mother and I were like that, too. We'd go to a movie and be the only ones laughing and then not get the joke when everyone else was rolling on the floor."

"If she was anything like Anna, she must have been a wonderful woman."

"Heather is more like our mother than I am." There it was, admitted aloud for the first time, and it hadn't hurt at all.

Susan took a sip of coffee. "I've been instructed to ask if you're coming home for Christmas."

"By whom?"

"Mark."

"Mark . . . or Cindy?" She refused to let herself get excited over a casual question.

"You're kidding, right? You have to know how Mark feels about you."

"I know he likes me—as a friend," she quickly added.

Susan stared at her for a long time without saying anything.

"What?" Karla prompted.

"I'm trying to figure out which one of you is putting me on. I can't believe you don't know how much Mark likes you. He hasn't had any problem telling me."

"Thanks. I needed that. My ego has been scraping bottom lately."

"You can't think I would make up something like this. To what point?'"

Not make up—just exaggerate a little. Maybe a different time and place and we could have worked things out. Right now his life is in Rocklin and mine is in Solvang."

She shook her head and crumpled her napkin. "That's too bad. In my humble opinion, I think the two of you were made for each other."

"Humble opinion? I think that's an oxymoron where you're concerned."

Susan laughed. "I'm going to take that as a compliment."

Karla finished her coffee and took another bite of the maple bar. She'd finally figured out that she ate when she felt stressed. And bored. And happy. Hell, she ate because she liked to eat. But she was not going to eat the rest of the maple bar.

Before she could change her mind, she got up and tossed everything in the garbage. "When are you heading back?"

"I told Anna I'd stay the night and we could leave after lunch tomorrow."

"If you have to get back, I can take her home."

"There's more than a good—neighbor policy working here. When I told Allen I was going to be gone a couple of days with Anna, he volunteered to put up the tree by himself. If I get back early, I'll have to help."

It was a typical Susan story. True, but embellished to make Karla feel she was doing a favor rather than imposing. "To answer your question, I wasn't going to come up for Christmas, but I've changed my mind. I don't want to be alone any more than I want Anna to be alone."

"Since it will just be the two of you, why don't you have dinner with us. We eat around six, but you can come anytime." She warmed to the idea. "This is perfect. My folks can't come this year, so we won't even have to borrow extra chairs. And did I mention Mark and Cindy are coming?"

"And Linda?"

"Good God, no. She hasn't made it home for Christmas since she and Mark divorced. Besides, if she did, she'd spend it with her mother."

A minute ago Karla had had no plans for Christmas, and now everything was in place, tucked in a gold box and tied up with a bright shiny red ribbon. "I'll talk to Anna."

"Oh, she'll come. She's never turned me down about anything. You're the only one I have to convince."

Karla laughed. "Oh, you've convinced me." She'd been on board with the mention of Mark's name. "I'll be there." For once Christmas was turning into something other than a good retail month. "I'll even make the pies."

CHAPTER 26

ANOTHER STORM MOVED IN, THIS ONE FROM THE GULF of Alaska, colder than the last and packing a bigger punch. Karla was exhausted from fighting the wind and rain on Highway 101 as she drove home and felt a little like the horse with the barn in sight when she hit Santa Maria.

She would have liked to stay another day with

Heather. Not because she was needed, but to stagger the leave—taking with Grace and Anna and Susan. As it was, there had seemed enough goodbyes that afternoon to see a ship set sail. While the quiet was undoubtedly welcome, all of them taking off at once must have created a small vacuum for Heather.

She'd started getting better from the minute Anna arrived. The progress wasn't slow and steady but in great leaps.

The highlight for all of them came as they stood with their noses pressed to the neonatal intensive care window and watched Heather hold Anna Marie for the first time. Even Grace was swept away, her control so far gone she ended up with swollen eyes and a face wiped clean of makeup.

The night before they'd gathered around Heather's bedside and toasted Anna Marie's birth and Grace's new job with sparkling cider.

Finally the world held such promise for them all.

And then, just as Karla was leaving Santa Maria, a scant twenty—five miles from home, her cell phone rang.

Between waiting for a break in traffic and following the cord from the lighter to where she'd tucked the phone under the seat, it took five rings before she answered.

"Hello?" There was no way this was good news. She was tempted to end the call and blame it on the weather and give herself a few more minutes to prepare.

"Karla, it's Susan. I'm sorry about chasing you down like this, but I've tried you at home several times and at the shop and—"

"What's wrong?" Karla's stomach convulsed in fear. Her skin turned cold and sweaty at the same time.

"It's Anna. She's in the hospital."

She didn't want to hear the answer but had to ask. "What happened?"

"She had a heart attack."

"When?"

"I'm not sure, but I think it started a couple of days ago. At least that's when she started swelling. By the time we got home, she could hardly breathe. I took her to Sutter Roseville to have her checked out and they admitted her right away."

"What did they tell you?"

"That the attack itself was minor. But she has acute pulmonary edema—at least I think that's what they called it. It's part of the congestive heart failure. They're giving her digitalis and a ton of Lasix. I'm not sure I'm getting all of this right, but what's important for you to know right now is that everything that needs to be done for her is being done."

"Did they have to put her on a respirator?" On her second visit to Dr. Michaels's office Karla had quizzed him on what to expect if Anna had to be hospitalized. But hearing the clinical details in his office was a long way from hearing them from Susan.

"Yes," Susan reluctantly admitted.

Karla recoiled at the thought of Anna lying in a bed without the ability to breathe for herself, her ability to communicate gone. "Is she awake?"

"She fights the respirator, so they're keeping her sedated."

"I'm coming up." Karla glanced at the dashboard clock. "Look for me around midnight. Can you stay at the hospital with her until then?" She couldn't bear the thought of Anna being alone.

"Where are you now?"

"About a half hour from home."

"It's crazy for you to turn around now, Karla. Go home and get some sleep. Allen and I will stay with Anna until you get here tomorrow."

"What about Bobby?" She felt guilty for asking, but needed to know that Susan was free to fulfill her promise.

"Mark said he could spend the night with him and Cindy."

She was relieved Susan hadn't taken offense. "Did you call Heather?"

"No. I wanted to talk to you first. She'll be furious if we don't tell her, but I just couldn't do that to her and Bill. Not after everything they've been through. Unless you think I'm wrong?"

"This is the last thing they need to hear right now." The sky opened and it no longer rained, but poured. She slowed the car and turned the wipers on high and still had trouble seeing the reflectors on the road. "What about Grace?"

"I tried, but I couldn't reach her. I didn't want to leave a message on her answering machine, so I thought I'd just keep trying until I found her home."

Grace had taken off a couple of hours before Karla. With a straight shot down I—5 and the speed Grace drove, it was possible she'd been home and had left again already. Karla wished she'd paid more attention to Grace's chattering about where and when and how long she was going to be gone on location in Florida. If she'd already gone, Karla had no idea how to find her without launching a minor investigation.

"I have to stop by the shop before I do anything," she told Susan. She'd talked to Tonya the night before and everything but the number of customers coming into the shop was in chaos. None of the orders had come in correctly. They were ass—deep in cups and out of their two best selling coffees. "I'll call you from there as soon as I decide what I'm going to do. Is there a number at the hospital where I can reach you?"

"I left it on your answering machine."

A dozen parting thoughts crowded her mind. She wanted to tell Susan to hold Anna's hand, to tell Anna to stop fighting the respirator and let it do its work, to say that Karla was coming and that she loved her . . . and most important, that she wasn't to die. Not now. Not yet. Not for a long, long time.

After she hung up, she became passive to familiar landmarks that only minutes before had brought comfort that she was nearly home. Finally, without conscious thought, she did what her heart demanded and ignored her mind, giving into emotion rather than logic. At the next off—ramp she turned the car around and headed north.

As soon as she was sure she could talk without breaking down, she picked up the phone again and called Tonya to tell her to fill all the promised special orders that she could and then close down the shop for the holidays.

The rain slowed after Karla left Paso Robles and took the cutoff to I—5. With little traffic to occupy her mind, she began counting the swipes of the windshield wipers to keep from thinking about the miles that separated her from Anna and what could happen in the time it took to travel those miles. When counting didn't work, she went through the alphabet, listing all the states in order. Next came the names of every teacher she'd had since kindergarten.

The teachers provided more of a challenge. She had to remember the year, where she had lived, and which school she'd attended. Between third and fifth grades, three moves had equaled five schools and as many teachers.

She stopped for fast food in Kettleman City and bought a book on tape at the service station. Her mind was back on Anna before the deep—voiced narrator had made it through the introduction.

Somehow, even after everything that had happened, the doctor's appointments, the estate planning, the signs that indicated Anna wasn't moving as quickly or breathing as deeply or staying up as long as she had the week before, Karla had still managed to convince herself they had time.

A part of her mind had refused to believe Anna was really dying. She'd compartmentalized the information for later. Even with intimate knowledge of how abruptly life could end, she'd allowed herself to become one of the people she'd always wondered about—the ones who attend funerals and grieve for words left unsaid, for love unexpressed, for questions unasked when the person who died did so slowly and painfully and alone.

Finally Karla stopped trying to distract herself and made a mental list of the things she would say to Anna if they were granted the time. She hadn't fulfilled her end of their bargain. There was so much more she could say about her mother—how she'd helped Heather catch fireflies on summer nights, how she'd taught Grace to swim before she was two, how she and Karla had wandered through the woods to pick blueberries and come home with poison ivy all over their arms.

And then there were the questions she wanted to ask. How did her mother come to love the mountains and

292

Anna the ocean? She'd never asked Anna about her wedding day. Or if she'd gone on a honeymoon. The Depression was something Karla had read about in books, never thinking to ask Anna how she had made it through those years. Had she lost friends in World War II?

In the end, it was the memories, not the wealth or belongings, that marked the sum of a person. If Karla allowed those memories to die for lack of the right questions, she would be witness to two deaths.

When she saw the exit for Santa Nella she reached for the phone to call the hospital but flipped it closed before she had completed the call. No matter what anyone told her, the only thing she could do was what she was doing right then.

Anna had waited for nineteen years; Karla refused to believe she wouldn't wait just a little longer.

At two o'clock in the morning even businesses had turned out their Christmas lights. Karla spotted an occasional house still lit up from the freeway and assumed the owner had gone to bed and forgot to turn them off, but for the most part, the holiday was on hold for another six hours.

Not at the hospital, however. Here the trees and decorations were lit, the employees in the wide—awake time warp dictated by shift work. Exhausted to the point of numbness when she'd arrived, her pulse quickened and her mind focused sharply as she crossed the entrance to the reception desk. By the time she had received directions and was halfway down the long hallway to the Grove Region wing of the hospital, her hands were shaking.

She experienced a chill of apprehension when she

saw a sign that instructed her to turn off her cell phone. Reality became a battering rain against the wall she'd built to protect herself. Anna wasn't just in the hospital, she was in the part of the hospital where death, not life, was the accepted outcome.

She picked up the receiver to the visitor's phone outside the locked door to the cardiac intensive care unit, identified herself, and waited for the buzzer. The nurses' station was to her right; to her left was an arc of private rooms with glass walls between the patients and their caregivers. The lights had been dimmed in the rooms but were bright in the hallway and at the station.

A woman in a multicolored nurse's uniform saw Karla peering into a room and asked, "Can I help you?"

"I'm looking for Anna Olsen."

"She's in number five."

"Thank you, Karla said automatically.

When she found the room, she stood at the door, her gaze intently focused on the waiflike figure under the unnaturally smooth bedspread. An obscene tube protruded from Anna's mouth, connected to a machine that quietly hissed and thumped in rhythm to the movements of her chest. A bag of clear liquid hung suspended from a pole attached to the bed, its fluid dripping into a tube connected to the back of Anna's frail—looking hand.

Monitors filled the small space. Some she recognized from Heather's hospital room; others she'd seen on television. One flashed numbers, another heartbeats. Even those that were familiar scared the hell out of her because she didn't know if their readings were good or bad.

Karla slowly moved closer, a terrified gazelle ready to bolt. Anna looked insignificant and utterly defenseless in the generic mechanical bed. With her skin a translucent blue—white, her eyes closed, her face swollen and unanimated, it was almost as if her life weren't hers anymore but had been given over to the machines.

Karla stood perfectly still, her body rigid with shock. This was not the same woman she'd hugged good—bye less than twenty—four hours ago.

A figure rose from a chair in the corner of the room and came forward. Assuming it was Allen, she didn't look at him when she said, "She's going to die, isn't she?"

"Someday. . ." It wasn't Allen's voice. "But not now."

Startled, Karla lifted her gaze from the bed to look at Mark. She didn't question his being there. She realized as soon as she saw him that somehow she'd known.

He opened his arms. She leaned into him, burying her face in his neck. When he pulled her closer, she felt a powerful, consoling release. She wasn't alone anymore. She didn't have to be strong, or pretend she wasn't afraid, or explain why she'd come that night instead of waiting for morning.

Mark understood.

She had no idea how she knew this either, only that she did.

CHAPTER 27

SUSAN TOOK OVER FOR MARK IN THE MORNING. KARLA tried to talk her out of staying, but to her relief, she was ignored. The cardiologist came in at eight, a woman Karla had never met. She introduced herself as

295

Elizabeth Faith and explained that she was covering for Dr. Michaels, who was on vacation.

Karla didn't believe in omens, but liked that Anna's new doctor was named Faith. When she was through reading the chart and examining Anna, she looked from Susan to Karla. "Which one of you is Mrs. Olsen's granddaughter?"

Karla held up her hand. "I arrived this morning."

"So you weren't here when she was admitted." She shoved her hands in the pockets of her blazer. "I don't know how much you've been told, but I'm sure the situation seems pretty frightening to you right now. Actually, I'm very optimistic about your grandmother's recovery. She's responding well to the medication and I hope to have her off the respirator by this afternoon."

"Why was it necessary to put her on one in the first place?"

"There was an acute buildup of fluid in the lungs. We had to be sure she was getting the oxygen she needed while the Lasix did its work."

"When will she be able to go home?"

She considered the question for several seconds. "A week, maybe a few days longer. I'm sure Dr. Michaels explained that she's not going to be as strong as she was before an episode like this. From now on, your grandmother will need to rest more than she did before and will tire more easily, but other than that, I think she'll do just fine."

Karla had sworn she wouldn't ask what logically came next, but her need to know was stronger than her will to resist. "How long do you think she has?"

"Congestive heart failure isn't the automatic death sentence it used to be. I have several patients who are in a lot worse shape than Mrs. Olsen who've been through several episodes like the one she just had. There isn't any reason to think she won't do just as well and be around for several more years."

"What about the heart attack?"

"That's a consequence of the disease. Luckily, there wasn't any major damage."

The next was harder. "What about her quality of life?" When Anna signed her living will, she'd made it clear she did not want her life prolonged just because it could be. She'd given Karla the right to decide should she become incapacitated, but Karla was no longer sure she could handle the responsibility.

"She's not going to be running any marathons, but with medication, she can lead a comfortable and productive life for several more years."

Karla had heard the words she needed to hear, the same ones she'd spoken to Heather and Grace and believed herself before Anna wound up in the hospital. "Thank you."

She smiled and handed Karla her card. "You're going to have a hundred more questions for me in a couple of days. If I don't see you here, give me a call and I'll get back to you as soon as I can."

Karla held up okay until after the doctor was gone. Feeling as if her legs could no longer hold her, she lowered herself into a chair. Her hands were shaking, and the tears she'd managed to keep at bay for hours abruptly filled her eyes.

Susan came over and knelt down beside her. "Can I get you something?"

"I was so scared," she said, her voice little more than a whisper. "I've been so stupid. I already let years go by as if we had an endless supply. And then I blithely went home two weeks ago ready to let it happen all over again. Somehow I've got to figure out a way for us to be together even if it means I hire more help and start commuting here for long weekends."

"Now you know that you still have time. All of you do." She took Karla's hand and smiled. "This will make a wonderful Christmas present for Heather—once we tell her that it happened at all, that is."

Susan left at ten—thirty to take care of some work at school that needed to be done and came back at a quarter to twelve with coffee and a chicken sandwich from La Bou restaurant. The nurse was busy with Anna, so they got out of his way and went out to the lobby to eat, sitting on overstuffed chairs in front of floor—to—ceiling windows that faced the main parking lot.

"I know it's not as good as yours," Susan said about the coffee. "But it's the best we have around here."

Karla took a sip. "It's wonderful. Reminds me of the Thanksgiving blend I made for the shop last year."

"Is everything okay there?"

"No . . . not really." She started to take a bite of the sandwich, but wasn't yet ready to put something solid in her stomach. "I had to have Tonya close down. She was out of too many things to stay open."

"What about Jim? Have you thought about asking him to pinch—hit for you again?"

"I don't want to put him on the spot like that. If it were any other time I would, but not Christmas."

"What's the harm in asking? He can always say no."

She thought about it before answering. "It sure would take a big worry off my mind. Once people get it in their heads that they want special coffees for the holidays, they hate it when they can't have them. That Closed sign I told Tonya to put up is going to cause a lot of ill will." She gave Susan a tired smile. "I've spent

298

years convincing people they shouldn't have a party without my coffee, so I guess I have no right to complain when my words turn around and bite me in the rear."

"Why don't you get out of here for a while? You could go to Anna's and take a nap or a shower or just splash some cold water on your face. I'll call the school and tell them not to expect me for a couple of hours."

"The doctor said she might take Anna off the respirator this afternoon and I want to be here when that happens."

"I tried Grace again while I was at school. Still no answer."

"I tried her, too." Karla watched a woman with a little boy cross the street from the parking lot. She was trying to keep them both dry under the same umbrella and was hunched so low she looked like a duck waddling from puddle to puddle. "If I haven't reached her by tonight, I'm going to ask her roommates if they know how to reach her."

"What about Heather?"

"I reached Bill at the hospital and told him what happened and he agreed we should wait a couple of days before we tell Heather. He did have some good news. Heather's doctor says she can go home day after tomorrow."

"Wow, that's great. What about the baby?"

"They're saying a month, but hoping it will be sooner."

Karla glanced at her watch. A hundred doctors could tell her Anna was going to be all right and she would still have the tiny seed of doubt that had been planted when her parents died. She accepted miracles, but she didn't believe in them.

"I'm going to go back in," she told Susan.

"You haven't eaten your sandwich."

"I'll take it with me and eat it later."

"If you don't take care of yourself, you're going to wind up in the hospital, too."

Karla smiled. "Spoken like a true mother."

"That doesn't mean I'm not right."

"I'll eat something. I promise. Just as soon as I'm sure it will stay down."

Susan swept the crumbs from her lap into the sandwich wrapper, crumpled it up, and put it back in the bag. "I'll be back this afternoon."

"You don't have to do that. I know you must have a ton of things to do to get ready for Christmas. I appreciate the thought, but I'll be fine."

"Speaking of Christmas . . . I almost forgot." She reached inside the oversized bag she carried with her everywhere. "Cindy wanted me to give this to you."

"Another drawing?" She was falling for that little girl in a big way.

"What else?" Susan smiled when she handed the folded paper to Karla.

Karla studied the picture, looking for clues. There were the obvious stick figures, but nothing else connected. "You're going to have to help me out here."

"This is her new kitten. . ."

"She has a new kitten?"

"The mother was run over by a car."

It was all that needed to be said. "And what's this?" Karla pointed to what looked like a red snowman.

"Santa Claus. And those are his reindeer."

Once everything was pointed out to Karla, it all came together. Cindy was in her holiday picture—making mode, determined to single—handedly decorate the worlds of the people she liked.

"And this goes with it." Susan handed her another piece of paper. On it was written, I LOVE YOU ANNA. LOVE CINDY.

"She'll be so pleased. Tell Cindy I'll give it to her first thing when she wakes up." Karla rewrapped her sandwich and slipped it into her purse. She stood to walk Susan to the door, looked up and saw Mark headed toward them.

Before he even said hello, he took Karla in his arms and gave her a hug and then a kiss—not the sympathetic, generic kind, but on the lips and lingering. She could see by the look Susan gave them that the hug didn't surprise her, maybe not even the kiss. What had undoubtedly put the self—satisfied grin on her face was Karla's ready acceptance and return of the affection.

Mark let Karla go but kept his arm around her shoulders. "How is Anna doing?" he asked them both.

"The same," Karla said. She reached up to wipe rainwater from his forehead. "What are you doing here? I thought you weren't coming back until tonight."

"I switched a couple of appointments." He gave Susan a quick kiss and pointed to the bag in her hand. "Thanks for bringing her lunch. I was afraid I was going to have to hand—feed her to get her to eat."

"You may still have to. All she's had is coffee."

Karla looked from Susan to Mark. She was being taken care of—gently by Susan, proprietarily by Mark. The strange part was that she didn't mind. She almost thought she liked it. No one had taken care of her in a long time. No one had even tried. She felt like the wallflower who'd finally been asked to dance.

Mark said to Karla, "My mother and stepfather will be here on Friday to take care of Cindy over the

301

weekend so I can spot you shifts with Anna."

"They didn't have to come up," Susan said. "Cindy could have stayed with us."

"I know, but they liked the idea of having some time alone with her before Christmas, and my mom's been looking for an excuse to meet Karla."

"You told your mother about me?" The simple fact held a world of meaning. "When?"

He grinned. "After our first date—well, actually our only real date. She told me any woman who would let me sing to her had to be tone—deaf or enamored and was someone she wanted to meet. She knows you won't have time this trip and asked me to be sure to give you and Anna her best wishes."

"Are you staying now?" Susan asked.

Mark looked at his watch. "For another forty, five minutes. It's been a madhouse today. I've had two dogs that ate an entire three—pound box of chocolates, a cat that swallowed curling ribbon, and a bird that flew into a sliding glass door. This on top of a schedule full of regular appointments, and the day is only half over."

"As much as I appreciate both of you being here with me, I think I can manage the afternoon alone. Especially now that I know Anna is going to be all right."

Mark and Susan exchanged glances. Susan was the first to answer. "I'll make you a deal. I'll leave you alone if you promise you'll let me take over this evening. You need to get out of here, even if it's only for an hour or two."

"Sounds good to me," Mark said. "I'll be here to pick you up as soon as I can get away from the clinic."

Again, they were taking care of her and she still didn't mind. "What about Cindy?"

"She and Bobby are going to a friend's house."

"I really would like to take a shower," Karla said. "I guess it wouldn't hurt if I left for a little while—as long as I'm here when Anna wakes up and she's still improving when I leave."

Susan nodded. She hooked her purse over her shoulder. "Do you want me to bring you anything when I come back?"

She thought a minute. Whatever practical things she needed she could pick up for herself when she went to Anna's later. "Another picture from Cindy. Tell her I'm going to put this one up where Anna can see it when she wakes up."

"Will do." Susan gave her a quick hug, said good—bye to Mark, and left.

"I'm sorry I can't stay very long," Mark said when they were alone.

"You'd be here if I really needed you."

"I'm glad you know that." He sat down and brought her with him. "I went by the house and picked up the messages. There was a breezy one from Grace saying she'd gotten home and was on her way to the airport and that she'd call again in a week or so."

Karla had been worried Heather would call and get upset when she couldn't reach Anna, so she'd given Mark Anna's key so he could check the answering machine for her. "Did she leave a number?"

"As a matter of fact, she did. I have it right here." He reached into his pocket and handed her a piece of paper from the tablet Anna kept by the phone.

"Nothing from Heather?"

He shook his head. "She may be waiting for Anna to call her."

"Or Bill could have headed her off somehow." Normally it was hard for her to sit as close as she and

Mark were sitting for very long. Jim had accused her of being territorial and unaffectionate. She'd tried to make him understand that she was simply one of those people who needed a cushion of empty space around them to feel comfortable and that it had nothing to do with how she felt about him personally. But somehow, with Mark, it didn't bother her that the length of her thigh continued to rest against his or that he still held onto her hand. Had they not been in a public place, she probably would have moved even closer. Being in his arms brought her a comfort she felt with no one else.

"Did you ask the doctor how long she thought Anna would be here?"

"A week to ten days."

"I know that it's still a little early to be thinking about this, but I wanted you to know that Susan and Allen and I will take care of Anna if and when you feel you have to get back to take care of things at the coffee shop—"

"I've decided I'm going to call Jim and ask him if he'll pinch—hit for me again." She hadn't realized she'd made up her mind to do so until the words were out. "If I can't reach him, or if he's tied up and can't take over for me, I may have to take you up on your offer."

"I hate to think of all the business you're losing. If you can't arrange something, it's going to be hard to win those customers back."

Finally, someone who understood. "I've worked so hard to get the shop where it is. It's like being hit in the stomach with a baseball bat to think all that work could be for nothing." She didn't like the way that made her sound. It was important that Mark understand what she was trying to say. "I know what you're thinking. How can I be worried about the possibility I might lose business when Anna is—"

"Stop right there, Karla. One of the things I love about you is the passion you have for your work."

He'd taken her off guard with the simple, potentially life—altering statement, and she was too surprised to say anything.

"Bad timing, I know. With everything else you've got going on in your life right now, I wanted to wait—at least until I could plead my case with champagne and caviar. But there it is. I love you, Karla."

"You're out of your mind. You can't possibly love me. You hardly know me."

"Tell me how long you think it should take and I'll wait that long before I tell you again."

She stared at him looking for something that would tell her Mark was only trying to make her feel better, that in a fit of misguided kindness he'd decided this outrageous fabrication was the answer. What she saw was a love so pure and direct that it held no room for anything but his feelings for her.

Somewhere in the back of her mind she heard her father's voice telling her about the love that would come to her one day, how it would arrive so gently she wouldn't recognize it at first. Mark was everything she admired in a man. He carried the traits so integrally and effortlessly they were as much a part of him as his dark hair and blue eyes.

His kindness wasn't something he saved to bestow on those he felt worthy at special moments, it was in the things he did every day, the animals he rescued, the lunch that included Anna, the friendships he nurtured, the child he loved. He was sensitive and intuitive and had figured out before she had how desperately she needed someone to simply listen to her the night he canceled their dinner reservations and gave her a quiet evening in his home. He could have used her, easily, and with her permission that night. She was willing, even eager, to make love to him. But he had a sense of honor, a quality so old—fashioned and rare it was nearly unrecognizable anymore.

Mark was the quiet hero her father had told her about, the man she would be slow to recognize, the man who would bring her the love poets would be unable to find words to describe.

"Karla? Are you all right?" He put his hand on the back of her neck and brought her forward until their foreheads were touching. Softly, he added, "Too soon?"

She brought up her chin to kiss him, not caring that they were in the lobby of a hospital sitting in front of a window for all the world to see. "The beginning of forever."

CHAPTER 28

"YOU TOLD ME SHE WAS GOING TO BE ALL RIGHT," Grace said accusingly, the words coming between hiccuped sobs.

Karla was dumbfounded at Grace's impassioned reaction to the news about Anna. After what had happened at Thanksgiving, she'd expected concern, not trauma. "She *is* going to be all right," Karla repeated.

"I'm coming home."

"That's crazy. There isn't anything you can do here. Besides, won't you lose your job if you leave? That's the last thing Anna would want."

"Let me talk to her. I want to hear for myself that she's okay."

"You can't talk to her yet."

"Why not?"

Karla considered coming up with something to pacify Grace, but chose the truth instead. She needed her credibility. "She's still on the respirator."

"She's on a respirator? My, God, she can't even breathe for herself and you're trying to tell me she's going to—"

"Calm down and listen to me. The respirator isn't because she can't breathe for herself, it's to make sure she gets plenty of oxygen while they reduce the fluid in her lungs."

"She has fluid in her lungs?"

Karla leaned her head against the wall and closed her eyes. She wasn't handling this very well. She should have waited to call Grace when she'd had some sleep and her mind was sharper. She heard someone coming and looked up expectantly, thinking it might be Mark, even though she knew he wouldn't be there for hours yet. Her pleasure at having him with her had become a need, and her disappointment was acute when she saw that it was only another group of visitors headed for the maternity wing. "How long are you going to be in Florida?"

"Until it stops raining and we can get the shots we came for."

"I need a time frame. Days? Weeks? Months?"

"Mid—January. Why?"

"I'm going to get some material on congestive heart failure and send it to you."

"You don't have to do that. Just tell me about it. I'm sure you've already read everything there is."

At last, something Karla could smile about, even through the smile was more dry than happy. Grace had never been a reader, acting as if it there were only so many words her mind could absorb and she wanted to save them for important things, like scripts. "Then you're going to have to trust me when I tell you I know what I'm talking about."

"Does that mean I'm not allowed to ask questions?"

"Of course not. Just don't question everything I tell you." She ran her hand through hair desperately in need of a good shampooing, knowing she was only making it look worse but was too tired to care. "I'm going to let you go now. If you want an update tonight, I'll be at Grandma's. You can catch me there or leave a message where you'll be and I'll get back to you."

"Give her a hug for me and tell her I love her. Oh, and I want to send flowers. What's the name of the hospital?"

"She's in Sutter Roseville, but why don't you hold off on flowers for a couple of days? I'm not even sure they allow them in intensive care."

"She's in intensive care? You didn't tell me that."

Frustrated beyond patience, Karla was tempted to bang her head against the wall. "Don't panic," she said calmly. "It's just the way they do things here."

"You have no idea how hard it is to be this far away. You're lucky because you're there and can see everything for yourself. I don't have a doctor or nurse to explain things to me. All I have is you."

"I'm sorry. I'll try to do better from now on."

"I love you, Karla."

The words startled her. She couldn't remember the last time Grace had told her she loved her. Or, for that matter, the last time she'd told Grace. "I love you, too." She started to tell her good—bye, but thought of one more thing she wanted to say. "I'm really proud of you, too. Now go break a leg and let me take care of Grandma."

Karla got her wish. She was the first person Anna saw when she woke up. Karla took her hand and gave her a smile that put her heart on her sleeve. "Welcome back."

Anna opened her mouth to say something, but no words came out.

"She's just hoarse from the tube that was in her throat," the nurse said.

"Do you know what happened and where you are?" Karla asked. "Just nod or shake your head," she added quickly.

Anna closed her eyes and nodded as if she were a child being chastised for bad behavior.

"I'm not going to wear you out with details; all you need to know right now is that everything is being taken care of—including me. Susan and Allen have been wonderful."

Anna smiled.

"And Mark—well, I guess the best way to tell you about Mark is that he's everything my father said he would be."

"You found . . . your gentle hero," Anna whispered.

"But you already knew that, didn't you?"

"I . . . hoped he was . . . the one."

"Now all I have to do is figure out what I'm going to do about it."

Anna squeezed her hand. "It will . . . come to you."

Karla settled back in her chair. She was suddenly ravenously hungry and wished the chicken sandwich weren't five hours old. "Bill knows you're in the hospital, but we both agreed it was better not to tell Heather for a couple of days. I did talk to Grace, however, and she—"

Anna had no doubt Karla had taken care of whatever she felt needed to be taken care of and that it was safe just to lie there and half listen. She'd already heard the important part—the part about Karla and Mark. She'd worried she might not live to see Karla find the happiness long overdue her. It seemed she wasn't as ready to let go of this life and move on to the next as she'd tried to convince herself she was.

She'd been on her second nitroglycerin tablet on the trip home from Salinas with Susan when she finally had to admit that she was in deep trouble. When she was being rushed to the hospital, a dozen memories surfaced and fought for recognition. She still had so much to share with Karla, so many stories to tell. The world would go on if Karla never knew why Frank hadn't fought in the war or how many years Anna's parents and her six brothers and sisters had lived in the basement of their uncompleted house in North Dakota before they could afford to finish building. Karla didn't need to know these things, but Anna needed to tell her.

Now that she knew she had more time, she wouldn't waste a minute. If necessary, she would go to Solvang to be with Karla to tell her the stories, to share the memories.

Mark listened for the shower to stop before he tossed the mushrooms and green onions into the pan with the turkey sausage, calculating it would take Karla another ten minutes to get dressed and be ready to eat. He'd offered to take her out to dinner, but she'd said she preferred to eat at home where they could be alone and talk without being interrupted. The mushrooms were still a milky white when he heard her come into the

310

kitchen and felt her arms slip around his waist.

He was a simple man, easy to please, undemanding in everything and everyone—with the exception of the woman he loved. In this he was intractable. He'd been ready, even willing, to live the rest of his life alone if he couldn't find the woman whose smile brought a quickness to his heart and whose tears touched his soul. He'd had no idea what she would look like, how she would sound, or whether she would laugh at his jokes. All he knew for sure was that when he looked into her eyes he would see tolerance and love and caring. She would glory in a child's hug, that a cloud looked like an umbrella, that on August nights there were meteor showers. And she would respond when an old woman needed her no matter how inconvenient the time or place.

He turned and saw that Karla had come to him fresh from the shower, her hair wet and combed straight back, her feet bare, her body covered by a terry cloth robe. He kissed a drop of water from her nose and brought her into his arms. She snuggled against him, her head on his shoulder. "You smell good," he told her.

"It's the shampoo."

"Whatever it is, I like it."

She put her head back and smiled. "You can borrow it. Anytime."

"It wouldn't be the same." He lowered his mouth to hers and kissed her before running his tongue across her lower lip. "You taste good, too."

"It's the toothpaste."

"Can I borrow that, too?"

"Of course." She put her arms around his neck and stood on tiptoe to kiss him again. "Anytime."

He deepened the kiss and she responded with an

energy that filled him with a burst of longing. "I thought you were hungry."

"Me, too. But something happened when I saw you that made me forget all about food."

He reached behind him and turned off the stove. "Maybe you picked up on the thoughts I've been having."

She smiled. "About me?"

He gave the sash she'd looped around her waist a tug and opened her robe, exposing a long, narrow path of pink skin. He followed the path with the tips of his fingers, confirming the softness he'd imagined, the way she would catch her breath, the desire that would pound through him like waves in a storm.

"Would you like me to tell you what water looks like as it flows over your body?" he asked. "Perhaps you'd like to have me describe how it runs over your breasts or down your back?" He touched the hollow at the base of her throat with his tongue. "While you were in the shower I imagined myself licking the water that gathered here. . . ." He moved to her shoulder as the robe opened farther and touched his tongue there, too. "And here. . ." This time he showed her with his hands as he moved the robe aside, circled her waist, and touched the small of her back. "And here. . ." His voice grew husky with wanting her.

"You could have joined me," she said.

"And now?"

"Now is good, too."

"Do you want to eat first?"

"Are you kidding?"

He smiled. "Yes, I am."

He followed her up the stairs, to the room she told him had been her mother's. He took the protection he'd brought with him out of his pocket before he laid his jeans over a chair. When he joined her under the covers, the bed softly protested his added weight. "Are you cold?" he asked when he took her into his arms again.

"Not now." She looked into his eyes. "With you in my life, I don't think I will ever be cold again."

"You're giving me a lot of power, Karla. I'm just a man—one who loves you more than you've ever been loved, or ever will be loved—but still just a man." He brushed the damp hair from her forehead with his fingers. "If I were more I would move the mountain you didn't want to climb and arrange for sunshine when you grew tired of rain . . . and I would make Anna well again."

As much as he ached for his own pleasure, he wanted to please her more. He wanted them to be old lovers so that he already knew where to touch her, to be at that level where he'd discovered the secret parts of her sexuality she hadn't known existed herself, where her excitement reached a place not even imagined until they'd discovered it together. He wanted that now because he wanted to give her a night that would make her forget, if only for the moment, all the pain that had gone before.

"That we found each other, that you love me, is miracle enough," she said.

"Miracles are for things that are difficult, maybe even impossible, they have nothing to do with how I feel about you. Loving you is the easiest thing I've ever done, it's as natural for me as breathing. You've become a part of me, Karla, as integral as my hand, as impossible to do without as my heart."

He pressed a whispered kiss to the tip of her nose, to her cheeks, and then to her lips. Nearly overwhelmed with her thoughts and feelings, Karla closed her eyes to hold in her tears of joy. Her father may have been right about the poets not finding words to describe how she felt about Mark, but Mark had found the words that she needed to hear, the ones to touch her soul and make it sing with happiness.

"I love you," she said against his lips as he kissed her again.

"Tell me again."

"I love you."

"Again."

"And again, and again," she said. "For the rest of my life."

"I'm going to hold you to that, you know."

She knew as powerfully, as clearly, as she knew the North Star was in the sky outside her bedroom window that Mark would be at her side through all the good and bad that was ahead for them, that he would love her knowing her strengths and weaknesses, and would bring her the happiness she'd believed only existed in her mind.

"Thank you for loving me," she said.

He kissed the corners of her mouth. "You can't give me what you've given me and thank me, too. It's not the way things are done. I suppose I could reciprocate by thanking you for coming into my life. But then maybe Anna is the one I should thank. I have a feeling she had more to do with us finding each other than we'll ever know."

"She would never admit it, but I think you may be right." It also wouldn't surprise her to learn one day that Anna had had a little help. She didn't know about Heather's DNA thing, but she'd come to understand there was a definite, powerful connection between the women in her family, both past and present. An unseen hand had guided her home back to Anna, forward to Mark.

"Karla?"

"Yes?"

"I'm through talking."

She smiled. "I was beginning to wonder."

"Well, wonder no more." He covered her mouth in a kiss that burned a path to her toes. Unerringly he followed that same path with his hand and then his lips. By the time he'd found her mouth again and was moving inside her in a hard, demanding rhythm, her mind was lost to everything but her own building need. She cried out when she climaxed, then caught her breath as wave after wave of pleasure washed over her.

Afterward Mark cradled her in his arms and gently plied her with questions. He wanted to know her favorite color, and time of day, and meal. He asked dumb things, like if she were a flower which one she would be, and hard ones, like where she'd been when she heard about her parents' accident.

Hearing her stomach growl, he made her stay in bed while he fixed them a snack and brought it upstairs. They ate and made love again, only stopping when Mark had to leave to pick up Cindy.

Karla was smiling when she went to bed that night. As she felt herself being pulled into the depths of sleep, the last thing she heard was her mother softly saying, "Have a good life, sweetheart."

CHAPTER 29

KARLA WAS HALFWAY OUT THE DOOR WHEN THE phone rang the next morning. It was Jim.

"Is she gone?" he asked.

"Is who gone?" Karla was so surprised to hear his voice she didn't immediately connect to the question.

315

"Anna."

"What makes you think—"

"I went by the shop to find you, and when I saw that it was closed I thought you were up there because . . . Never mind, it's not important what I thought."

"Anna had a heart attack." She was pleased that he'd cared enough to call to check on her. "She's going to be all right, but it was pretty awful there for a while."

"You should have called me. I would have come up to take care of things for you again."

"I tried, several times, but you were never at home and it wasn't something I wanted to leave on the machine."

"Well, I'm here now. What do you want me to do?"

"I don't know if there's anything you can do. Everything is in such a mess there." She quickly explained how she'd let everything slide while she was at Heather's and that she had no real idea what it would take to get the shop up and running again.

"Why don't I check things out and get back to you. You said Tonya has the keys?"

"Are you sure you want to do this? I don't know how much longer I'm going to be gone—through Christmas at least. You and Amy must have plans."

"I'll talk to her, and if it's a problem, we'll work around it."

"Why are you doing this for me?"

"That's my Karla, never accept anything at face value."

"I'm not like that," she told him, knowing in her heart he was right.

"You didn't used to be, at least not when we first met. I'm afraid you've got me to thank for the change. I'm sorry I did that to you."

316

She thought about what she would say next, wanting to understand her reasons before she told him about Mark. "I've met someone, Jim."

There was a long pause. "I'm happy for you. Really, happy, Karla, not the lip service kind. I only hope he deserves you."

"I'll tell you more later. Right now I'm on my way to the hospital."

"When can I reach you about the shop?"

"Tonight. Try me around seven. And thank you— your doing this takes a big worry off my shoulders."

"You're welcome. I only wish I could do more."

Karla was at the hospital before she realized she hadn't asked Jim if he'd found his own shop yet.

Karla arrived at Anna's from the hospital that night to find Mark and Cindy on the porch waiting for her, a Christmas tree leaning against the railing. Cindy came bounding down the stairs and into Karla's arms as soon as she got out of the car.

"We brung a surprise," she said. "And Daddy said we could have pizza for dinner. And I made a new picture for Anna. Daddy said maybe I could go to the hospital to see her and give it to her myself as soon as she's not in the really sick place anymore."

"I think maybe you could. How about after school tomorrow?"

"My grandma and grandpa are coming to my house. Could they see Anna, too?"

She hesitated. "Why don't we wait until they get here before we decide that?" It was the only way she knew to answer. Thankfully, Cindy seemed satisfied. She was open and adventuresome and easy to love and Karla had to hold back to keep from overwhelming her with all the

317

affection she had stored up to give a child.

Mark met them at the top of the stairs. He took Cindy, held her with one arm, and put the other around Karla. His kiss was warm and welcoming and made her feel as if she belonged exactly where she was.

"I missed you today," he said.

She touched his face. "Me, too."

"How is Anna?"

"Bouncing back. She's unbelievable. She was telling the nurses jokes when I walked in this morning, and she actually ate all of her lunch." Karla gave Cindy a playful tickle. "What's this surprise you have for me?"

"Look." She pointed to the Christmas tree. "Daddy said we could help you decorate it and that it could be a surprise for Anna, too."

Until that moment, Christmas had been something to get through, not celebrate. But the sparkle in Cindy's eyes, her obvious excitement and pleasure at her and Mark's surprise, made Karla want to be a part of the holiday as much as she wanted to be a part of their lives. She went to the tree and held it upright. "It's beautiful." Putting her nose against one of the branches, she took a deep breath. "And it smells wonderful." She gave Mark and Cindy a big smile. "This is a great idea. We can string popcorn and cranberries and make it look like a real old—fashioned tree, just like the kind Anna had when she was a little girl."

Karla let go of the tree and took her key out of her pocket to open the door. The more she thought about decorating the house for Anna's homecoming, the better she liked the idea. If Anna continued to improve the way she had been, she would be home for Christmas for sure.

"Do you know where Anna keeps her decorations?"

Mark asked when they were inside.

"In the hall closet under the stairwell."

Mark started for the kitchen to call for the pizza, then came back and took Karla in his arms again. "It's a good thing Cindy's here to chaperone."

She put her arms around his neck. "I was just thinking the same thing."

"I'm thirsty," Cindy said, as if on cue. "Can I have some water?"

Karla ran her hand through Mark's hair and gave him a very private smile. "I'll get it for you, Cindy."

Karla and Cindy moved coats and sweaters out of the way to get to the back of the closet while Mark put the tree in its stand. They had boxes scattered everywhere when the pizza arrived and ate while they explored their contents.

Karla had paid little attention to the ornaments on Anna's tree when she lived there, never noticing how many were handmade and how many appeared old enough to have come from Anna's tree when she was a little girl. What had started out a fun chore became a journey of discovery as she unwrapped each new treasure.

Mark saw what she was doing and came to sit beside her. "They look like family heirlooms."

"I wish I could tell you about them."

"You'll have to ask Anna when you take down the tree. I'll bet she has a story to go with every one."

Karla picked up a hand—painted papier—mâché ball. "It weighs a ton. I wonder what's inside."

"Is it your mother's?"

Karla stared at the ball for a long time. "I hope so. I like the idea of having something she made be a part of this Christmas."

"Why don't you put it aside and ask Anna."

"Why put it aside?"

"I was just thinking it would make a good present for your new niece. Didn't you say she was named after your mother and Anna?"

"That's a wonderful idea." The more she thought about it, the more wonderful it became. She would have to find a special box, a silver one lined in velvet. "Once Heather sees this she might even forgive me for not telling her about Anna being in the hospital." She leaned over to give him a kiss. "You're really good at this sentimental stuff."

"And I'm really good at putting on lights—when they work. Which Anna's don't. So, I have to go to the store before I can go any farther. Is there anything you need?"

"Popcorn and cranberries."

He put his hand on Cindy's head and turned it until she was looking at him. "You want to go with me or stay here with Karla?"

"Stay," Cindy said.

It was a small thing, certainly nothing anyone else would get excited about, but it pleased Karla that Cindy had chosen to stay with her. "We'll have everything unwrapped and ready to go by the time you get back."

Three hours later, after two more trips to the store for an extension cord and then a replacement bulb for the star in the nativity set, they had the tree decorated. They'd saved the final honor of placing the angel on top of the tree for Cindy.

"I think it could use a couple more strands of popcorn," Mark said diplomatically.

Karla adjusted the four—foot—long string that had taken her an hour to put together. "Give me another month and I'll have it looking the way it should."

Standing between Mark and Karla as they admired their work, Cindy said, "You need presents."

"Next time you come over there will be lots and lots of presents." She'd thought of a dozen things she wanted to buy for Anna, including a new bird feeder. She already had something for Cindy, but it was still in Solvang sitting on her dining room table ready to be mailed. She still had to think about what she would give Mark. She wanted it to be something special, something that would always remind him of their first Christmas together.

Cindy's absent presents made her think about the shop and Jim. He should have called by now. "What time is it?" she asked Mark.

"Almost ten." He looked at Cindy. "Long past your bedtime."

"I could sleep here with Karla. She would let me."

Mark chuckled. "Yes, she probably would. But you're coming home with me tonight. You have school tomorrow."

Karla felt a swell of pleasure that Cindy had even come up with the idea. She knew she would have to move slowly in their relationship, but it was going to be hard. Cindy had a mother and yet was in desperate need of a woman who was a constant in her life, someone she could count on to always be there for her. Karla had to find a way to be that woman for Cindy without taking anything from Linda. it wouldn't work any other way.

Mark held Cindy's jacket while she put it on. "If you don't want Anna getting suspicious, I'd suggest you hide your hands when you see her tomorrow."

Karla looked at her fingertips, dyed dark red with cranberry juice. "I'll have to—"

"If you and my daddy got married I bet he would let

me sleep here," Cindy said.

Karla looked at Mark to see how he had reacted to Cindy's innocently self—serving statement.

He smiled and shrugged. "Out of the mouths of babes."

"I think that's a pretty good idea myself," Karla said, surprising herself. "How about if your daddy and I talk about it someday soon?"

"Okay."

"I'm holding you to that," Mark said. "Remember, I have a witness." He finished buttoning Cindy's coat and started toward the door.

If happiness could be measured, there wouldn't be a number high enough to calculate the way she felt at that moment. "Drive carefully," she told him.

He stopped to look into her eyes and then cup her face with his hands. "I love you, Karla. Get used to hearing it because I'm going to tell you every day for the rest of our lives." The kiss he gave her then was long and achingly tender, with promise and restrained passion.

"And I love you," she said as he let her go.

Cindy wrapped an arm around Mark's leg. "How 'bout if Karla comes home with us?"

Mark looked at her and smiled. "Someday. Soon, I hope."

Karla followed them out and stood on the porch until they were gone. She knew it was cold because she could see her breath, but the chill never penetrated her thin turtleneck and light wool slacks. She started to go inside when she remembered that the feeders hadn't been filled in days and headed for the garage. Finally, satisfied her corner of the world was in order, she went in the house and called Jim.

She reached him at the shop.

"I had no idea it was so late," he said. "I lost track of time. But everything's taken care of. I got the suppliers to overnight what we needed to stay open tomorrow, and second—day the rest, so we're back in business. And from what I saw today, not a moment too soon. Even though you've been closed a couple of days, there were customers lined up outside when I opened this morning. Tonya and Margaret worked the machines all day and Amy I handled the register while I was on the phone pleading with the suppliers for coffee and cups."

He sounded excited when he should have sounded exhausted. "Where are you staying tonight?"

I don't know yet. Probably at the Hansen Lodge."

"Why don't you stay at the house instead? There's an extra key under the brick in the walkway. The same place we always kept it."

"Are you sure?"

"You'd be doing me a favor. I'd feel better if the house didn't sit empty, and there's a whole refrigerator full of food that's going to go bad if someone isn't there to eat it."

"I've been thinking about what you told me this morning."

"Remind me."

"About you meeting someone. It took me a while, but I finally figured out I was jealous. Crazy, huh? I'm worried about losing you even though you're not mine to lose anymore."

"No, not crazy at all. I felt the same way about Amy. And stop worrying, you're not going to lose me. We'll always be friends."

"That's easy to say, Karla. A hell of a lot harder to do."

"You'll like him, Jim." She knew this as surely as she knew Mark wouldn't feel threatened by Jim or by their friendship. "He's a remarkable man. Not someone I would have ever picked for myself ten years ago—I had to grow up first."

"You'll understand if I tell you I need a while to get used to the idea before I start thinking of him as a good guy."

She laughed. "That's fair."

"I'm going to take you up on the house. You know how I hate staying in hotels."

"I remember." They would always be tied together by their memories. And she knew now that she really didn't want their friendship to end.

"I'll call in a couple of days and let you know how it's going."

"Thanks—oh, one more favor?"

"Name it."

"There's a package on the dining room table. Would you send it to me at Anna's address?"

"Tomorrow. As soon as Tonya comes in."

She thought about what she would say next, hesitated, and then plunged ahead. "Tell Amy hi for me, would you? And thank her for all the work she did at the shop at Thanksgiving. It took me a couple of days, but I finally came around to appreciating what she'd done."

Jim laughed, not the polite kind, but a belly laugh. "I'll tell her—all of it. She was worried she might have gone a little overboard."

They talked for a few minutes more and then said good night. Karla made herself a cup of tea and took it into the living room. Her feet propped up, her hands wrapped around the mug, she stared at the tree and thought about Christmases past and those yet to come.

Her tea finished, she picked up the bowls of popcorn and cranberries and went back to work.

CHAPTER 30

"IF YOU DON'T LET ME DO THE THINGS I'M STILL capable of doing, what little muscle I have left is going to atrophy." Anna followed the gentle rebuke with a smile as she struggled to get out of Karla's car.

"It's Christmas," Karla said. "Chapter five of my good girl handbook says that during the month of December I have to be kind to surly shoppers and help little old ladies out of cars."

"Well, since I've got years ahead of me before I'm a little old lady, you're off the hook."

The humor helped ease the tension over having Anna released from the hospital days after either of them had expected. After a straight shot at recovery, she'd come down with a virus that settled in her lungs and had needed to be given oxygen again. Now Karla was caught between happiness at having Anna home and fear it might be too soon.

"Is that a tree I see in the window?" Anna asked as she leaned against the car door and waited to gather her strength.

Karla had purposely left the lights on when she went to pick up Anna, knowing it would be dark by the time they got home. "Mark and Cindy and I put it up to surprise you."

She started toward the house, making the concession of holding on to Karla's arm. Before she started up the stairs, she paused to look at the other decorations—the wreath on the door and the pine swags attached to the porch railing with red ribbon. "How did you find time for all of this?"

"I don't know," she admitted. "I guess when it's something you enjoy you don't notice the effort or how much time it takes."

They slowly made their way inside. Karla took Anna's coat and purse and hung them in the closet before she led her into the living room. After uncounted hours of stringing popcorn and cranberries, she finally had the tree completed to her satisfaction and was anxious for Anna to see it.

"Oh, my . . . I don't think I've ever seen anything as beautiful," Anna said in awe. "You must have spent days on this. And look at all those presents. Where did they come from?"

"Santa dropped by early."

Anna gave her a scolding look before she moved closer. "Goodness, the popcorn and cranberries are real."

"And I have the stained fingers to prove it." She didn't even try to keep the note of pride from her voice.

"I used to talk about doing a tree like this, but never did."

"Wait a minute. I only did this because I wanted to give you a Christmas like the ones you used to have when you were growing up."

"I can see we have a way to go on the family history. Your great—grandmother wasn't the old—fashioned type. She was always the first in line to buy whatever was new. If those aluminum trees that revolved had been around when she was, she would have had one for sure."

Karla laughed. "So much for tradition."

Anna looked at her, her eyes grown misty. "But don't

326

you see? You've started your own. You and Cindy and Mark. And you've made me a part of it by having your first tree in my house. Nothing could have pleased me more."

Karla put her arms around Anna and gave her a long hug. "Welcome home, Grandma."

"Thank you, sweetheart. You've made it a real home for me again."

Two days later, on Christmas Eve, Karla was about to give up on the book she'd been reading and turn out the lamp on the nightstand when she heard a car pull into the driveway. She listened to see if it was just someone turning around, but instead heard a car door slam.

Puzzed at who would be there at ten—thirty at night, she put on her robe and went downstairs. She looked through the window and saw Grace struggling toward the house, her arms overloaded with packages. Hit with conflicting emotions, Karla simply stood and stared rather than immediately going out to help. She was as happy to see Grace as she was concerned about how and why she was there. The packages were in keeping with her excessive personality, which was fine in itself—but how had she paid for them?

In the end, nothing mattered more than the fact her little sister had come home for the holiday. Karla opened the door and was greeted by a rush of cold air. She pulled her robe closer, huddling into the collar and said, "To say I'm surprised to see you would be the understatement of the year."

"Then don't bother," Grace said. "Just tell me you're glad to see me."

"Of course I am." She took the most precariously balanced presents and followed Grace inside. "Grandma will be beside herself when she gets up tomorrow and finds you here."

"I know I should have called, but I was on standby and wasn't sure I would get here at all. As it was, I had a seven—hour layover in Denver." She put the presents under the tree, shrugged out of her coat, and gave Karla a hug. "But as you can see, I didn't let the time go to waste."

It took a second for what she was saying to sink in. As Karla plugged in the tree lights, she took inventory of all the presents and said, "You mean you bought all this stuff at the airport?"

"I didn't want to come empty—handed, and there wasn't any time to shop before I left. We've been filming all day every day." She stood back to admire the tree. "It's beautiful." She came forward again and ducked, and bent, and stood on tiptoe to look at individual ornaments. "There's my angel . . . and my teddy bear. Oh, and there's Heather's cowboy boots. Remember the year she ran for Miss something or other and was supposed to sing the thing about riding the range but then started choking when she tried to yodel and had to be taken off the stage? Grandma was furious with the organizers and bought those boots for Heather as a consolation prize. I'm not sure whose idea it was to put them on the tree, but it wouldn't be Christmas around here without them."

Karla did remember, but only from Heather's letters. She'd been a sophomore at college at the time and indignant that Anna had let Heather enter a beauty contest, let alone that she'd thrown a fit when Heather didn't win.

"I'm not staying long," Grace said. "I have to leave again in the morning. It was the only flight out of here

328

that was guaranteed to get me back to work in time. It seems hardly anyone flies on Christmas day itself, but every other day between now and New Year's is booked."

"What time in the morning?"

"Eleven—thirty. But don't worry, I can take care of everything myself, you can stay here and have Christmas dinner with Anna just like you planned."

"You came all this way for one night?"

"Yeah. Kinda dumb, huh?"

"Damn it, Grace. Just when I think I've got you figured out, you do something like this."

She laughed. "Don't worry. I'll be back to being my old self—centered pain—in—the—ass self by the next time you see me."

"If you're leaving tomorrow, I guess we're just going to have to get our visiting out of the way tonight. I'll fix us some cocoa and we can—"

"Cocoa?" She made a face. "Don't you have anything stronger?"

Karla thought a minute. "I saw some sherry in the back of the cereal cupboard, but there's no telling how old, or how good, it is."

"As long as it hasn't turned, I don't care. Anything's better than hot chocolate."

Karla found the sherry and poured them each a glass. They both agreed it was pretty bad, but drank it anyway. When they were curled up in opposite corners of the sofa, Grace held her glass out to Karla. "Here's to the old, and the new, and the good things yet to come."

"I have a feeling there are going to be a lot of good things to come for the Becker sisters next year."

"Like?"

"Your show is going to be a big hit."

329

"Oh, no. If you're going to be passing good thoughts my way, don't make it those. What you have to do is hope the show fails but that I get outstanding reviews that will lead to bigger and better roles in films."

"But wouldn't that be easier if the show was a hit?"

"The show sucks, Karla—stupid premise, terrible writing, bad acting. The last thing I want is for it to be a success and be tied down for seven years. I'd be typecast in a role that has nowhere to go." She took a drink. "I have to admit it's nice for once to have more money coming in than going out. Which reminds me—" She reached for her purse. "There's something I want to show you." She handed Karla a slip of paper.

Karla looked at it for several seconds but didn't see what Grace plainly wanted her to see. "What is it?"

"I'm paid up on the car for a year. I'll take care of the next year as soon as I get my next check. Three more after that and the car is mine."

Planning ahead was a major step for Grace. "That's fantastic. You must feet as if you've really accomplished something."

"Oh, please. I didn't do this for me, I did it for you. If it had been up to me, I would have stretched the payments as far and as long as they would go."

"Well, you're right about one thing. It does make a great Christmas present, for me at least. Thank you."

"You're welcome." She poured herself another splash of sherry. "Now tell me about you and Mark. I assume if he's half as smart as he looks, he's still hot on your trail."

"He is."

"And?"

"It's getting serious."

"Serious like he's talking about setting up practice in

Solvang, or like he's arranging to take a couple of weekends off to come down to visit?"

"I love him. And he loves me." Grace's delighted reaction was everything Karla could have hoped for. "Pretty cool, huh? Here I had my whole life planned out as a single woman and he walks in and changes everything."

"With a little girl in tow." Grace pulled her legs up, wrapped her arms around them, and put her chin on her knees. She looked young, and vulnerable, and ethereally beautiful. "A very lucky little girl, I might add. She's going to be getting a great second mom."

"I hope so. I think about what's ahead on that front and can't imagine how Grandma coped with the three of us. Especially with me."

"Ha—you were a walk in the park compared to me. You were long gone by the time I started rebelling and didn't have to witness the hell I put her through. I remember being so embarrassed when she would show up at school that I never brought home any of the notices about parent—teacher conferences or open houses. She was ancient compared to my friends' mothers, and I didn't want her anywhere around them or me. God, I'd give anything to take back all the pain I must have caused her."

Grace was finally growing up. Karla liked the woman she was becoming. "Being here when she wakes up tomorrow is a good start. Of course she's going to tell you that you shouldn't have come all this way for only a few hours, but she's going to be very happy that you did."

"And what about you?"

"It makes me happy, too," Karla told her.

"I wish Heather were here."

Karla had been thinking the same thing. She'd told herself not to dwell on the future, to stick to one day at a time where Anna was concerned, but there was no way around the fact that Anna was not going to be with them forever. "If I make the arrangements for the rest of us to be together for Easter, will you promise to do what you can to be here, too?"

"I promise," she said without hesitation. "Whatever it takes, I'll be here." She leaned forward to put her glass on the coffee table. "You know . . . you could save me a second trip if you and Mark arranged to get married at the same time."

Karla laughed. "We've got a lot of things to work out before that happens."

"You don't want to wait too long. You're not getting any younger, you know."

"Thanks for pointing that out."

She grinned. "No problem. It's what us younger sisters are for."

Karla stood and stretched. "It's time this old woman went to bed. I've got a long day ahead of me tomorrow."

Grace stretched, too, and yawned. "First tell me if you've told Heather about Anna yet. I don't want to answer the phone in the morning and have it be her and let something out that I shouldn't."

"Bill did it for me last week. She wasn't nearly as upset as we thought she would be. Probably because I agreed to drop Anna off at her house for a visit when I go back to Solvang."

"Is Heather still trying to talk Grandma into moving in with her?"

Karla nodded. "After this last episode, it's become a mission. She's convinced that with the right food and lots of attention, Grandma can live to be a hundred."

"When are you leaving?"

"In a couple of days. I told Jim I'd be back as soon as I felt Anna could take care of herself between visits by Susan and Mark." Karla automatically started to unplug the tree lights, then thought to ask, "Are you coming to bed?"

"Not yet. I'm going to get a blanket and pillow and stay here to look at the tree for a while."

"I'll see you in the morning, then."

"Wait—" She had a twinkle in her eyes. "You didn't leave the cookies and milk for Santa."

"I'm passing that job on to you." She turned to look at Grace when she got to the hall. "And don't forget carrots for the reindeer or they'll leave a mess out of spite."

Grace laughed. "One more thing."

"Yes?"

"My new niece—to—be—tell me her name again."

"Cindy. Why do you ask?"

"I left the name tag blank on her present."

"You bought Cindy a present?" As easily as that, Grace had made Cindy a part of the family. "How did you know?"

"My psychic told me."

Karla made a futile attempt to hide her distaste. "Don't tell me you actually—"

"God, Karla, you're so easy you ruin all the fun. Think about it. Can you picture me spending money on something like that over a new pair of shoes? I don't think so."

"So how did you find out?"

"I talked to Grandma."

"Oh—she didn't tell me you called."

"Why should she?"

"You have a point."

Grace held up her hands and looked at the ceiling. "Did you hear that, God? My sister gave me a point. You said it would happen one day, but it seemed so far—fetched I didn't believe you."

"I'm not that bad," Karla protested.

Grace gave her a steady look. "And I'm not either."

"No . . . you're not." She blew her a kiss. "But you can be a real pain in the ass sometimes."

Grace didn't say anything, letting Karla have the last word.

CHAPTER 31

"ARE YOU SURE YOU HAVE EVERYTHING?" JIM ASKED.

Karla nodded. "I've been through the house half a dozen times." The movers would be there first thing in the morning to pack everything up and put it in storage. What she would need for the next several months she had in the car with her. The amazing part was how much she'd decided she could do without.

"I guess this is it, then?" He held his arms open to give her a hug.

"You'll call me if you run into any trouble?" she said. She stayed in his arms longer than she had since their divorce.

"Of course. Who else?"

"I don't see why you should, but just in case." The decision to sell him the shop and house had been obvious, and they'd managed to pull it off in less than a month. She'd asked a fair price for both and he'd paid it without hesitation, delighted to have the shop he'd wanted all along and the house Amy had fallen in love with the first time she'd stayed there. Oddly enough, Mark had been her only stumbling block. When she told him what she planned to do, he flew down the next weekend to tell her it wasn't necessary for her to give up anything for him. He was willing to come to her. She convinced him it wasn't the solitary sacrifice it seemed, but a decision she'd reached for herself and Anna, too. The weekend she'd spent with Mark had given her a glimpse of what their life would be like. She'd thought she couldn't possibly love him more. She'd been wrong.

Jim let her go. "You're stalling, Karla."

"I'm going to miss this place," she acknowledged. "And you, too."

"No, you're not." He kissed her on the cheek. "And that scares me a little. Remember, you promised to keep in touch."

"All the best to you, Jim." She opened her car door to get inside.

"You, too, Kay Bee."

She drove away. When she reached the corner she was tempted to turn and look back, but only for a second. She wasn't leaving anything that truly mattered; she was going to something she'd been seeking her entire life.

Karla arrived at the clinic at four o'clock that afternoon. She'd planned to go to Anna's and get cleaned up before she saw Mark, but lacked the will power to be in the same town and stay away even that long. He was at the desk giving a patient instructions on medication for her dog when he glanced up and saw her standing in the waiting room. His reaction was a reflection of her own feelings—warm, excited, intimate, beyond words.

He finished what he'd been saying to the woman, excused himself, walked over, and took Karla in his arms. He hugged her so hard he lifted her off her feet. "You weren't supposed to be here until tomorrow."

She picked up a thread of something in his voice. "You had something planned. . . ."

"Cindy and Susan insisted. I let them have their way and postponed my own plans for a little later." He touched her face and looked into her eyes. "I can't believe you're actually here."

She smiled. "I feel as if I should say something really corny about this being the first day of the rest of our lives, but you deserve better."

"Just tell me you love me—there isn't anything better than that."

"I love you, I love you, I love you." Suddenly, acutely aware of the people around them, she added in a whisper, "The rest I'll save for later."

"Now how am I supposed to go back to work after that?"

She laughed. "This is only the beginning. Wait until I get you alone."

He walked her to the door. "I'll pick you up in a couple of hours."

"After sunset," she said. "I want to watch the sun go down with Anna tonight." After a week of storms, the sun had finally broken through, and she'd decided it was a gift to her and Anna that she couldn't ignore or put off until another time.

Karla spotted an early daffodil blooming as she pulled into the driveway. In a couple of weeks the flower beds would be filled with a half dozen varieties of jonquils, with tulips primed and ready to take their place when they began to fade. Anna's simple, basic passions—birds and flowers and sunsets—had become Karla's, too. She'd come to understand about the subtleties of life that added to the whole. She would not trade Mark's Christmas tree for a diamond necklace, or Anna's pumpkin seeds for a trip around the world.

Although they'd talked on the phone every day, Karla hadn't told Anna about selling her house and business because she knew Anna would question her motives. Anna needed to see for herself that Karla wasn't sacrificing anything, she was freeing herself of possessions that had become anchors rather than wind.

Anna must have spotted her from the window, because she came out on the porch as Karla got out of her car. "What a wonderful surprise. Have you come to see Mark?"

"Yes—but I came to move in with you." She stopped in the middle of the walkway and looked at Anna. "I hope that's all right."

"Of course you can stay with me. You're always welcome here. You know that."

"This isn't a visit, Grandma. I'm moving in." She pointed toward the car. "See? I've brought all my stuff."

"But how can you do that? What about the shop?"

"I'll tell you all about it later. Right now we have tea to make and a sunset to watch." She came up on the porch to wrap her arms around Anna and was filled with a sense of homecoming.

"I'll go along with the tea and sunset, but you've got a lot of explaining to do about the other, young lady."

Karla laughed and then kissed her. "I love you, too, Grandma."

As soon as the water was on the stove, Karla ran an extension cord out the window and hooked up the electric blanket she'd given Anna for Christmas. She spread the blanket over the rocking chair and turned the heat on low.

"Very resourceful," Anna acknowledged when Karla had her tucked into the chair. "Now I suppose I have to be careful not to spill my tea and electrocute myself."

"Sounds like a good plan to me." Karla brought a chair from the kitchen and sat down next to Anna. She was going to have to look into getting her own rocking chair for the porch.

"You do realize there's never been a sunset anywhere on this earth that could live up to these preparations."

"I'm not worried. We've lots of sunsets ahead of us to make up for a disappointment or two along the way."

"All right, you have me where you want me. Now are you going to tell me what's going on?"

"First I have something I want to give you." She pulled a piece of paper out of her sweater. "It's not the real thing, that will come later, but I wanted something to mark the occasion." She handed the paper to Anna.

Anna looked at the writing and then at Karla. "I don't understand. This can't be what I think it is."

"It's exactly what you think it is. The house is yours again. Free and clear, under your name, to do with as you see fit."

"How!"

"I bought it back from the bank. You won't be getting a monthly check from the reverse mortgage anymore, but since I'll be staying here and paying rent, it won't matter." Karla had used the cash from the shop to buy Anna's house. For income she had the monthly payments Jim made to her for the house.

Anna brought the paper up to cover her face, using it as a shield, but not before Karla saw her eyes fill with tears. She'd never seen her grandmother cry and was unsettled. "I did this all wrong. I shouldn't have just dumped my surprise on you like this. I'm sorry."

Anna put the paper on her lap and wiped her eyes, but it did nothing to stop the tears. "I'm so confused. I don't know whether to be mad at you or just admit it's the nicest thing anyone has ever done for me." Finally she chanced a look at Karla. "How did you know how much this house meant to me?"

"You told me."

"I don't remember. I shouldn't have. I wouldn't have if I'd known you were going to do this."

"You didn't tell me so much in words, Anna, as you told me in memories."

"I'm sorry. I had no right to do that to you."

Karla took a tissue out of her pocket and gave it to Anna. "You healed my heart, Grandma. Without you I wouldn't have recognized what real love is. There was so much hurt and anger inside me before I came here that there wasn't room for you, let alone a man like Mark."

"You know he's the only man I ever thought was good enough for you."

She laughed. "That was pretty obvious when you started playing matchmaker."

The statement coaxed a smile out of Anna. "I just hate it when I'm being obvious. I'll have to work on that from now on."

Karla slipped her hand into Anna's checking to make sure she was staying warm. She could have let go once she found out what she wanted to know, but liked the way it felt and stayed. "There's something else I've been meaning to talk to you about."

"I'm afraid to ask."

"That money I found in your checkbook . . ."

"It's still yours, you know. I haven't spent a penny of it and don't intend to."

"Good, because I've decided what I want to do with it."

"All right, you have my attention."

"I'm going to rent a house on the coast—just you and me for an entire week."

Anna stared at the western sky and was quiet for a long time. Finally, still not looking at Karla, she said, "March is a good month. It's when Frank and I used to go to celebrate our anniversary."

"Then March it is."

"Look, the clouds are beginning to turn."

Wisps of salmon and pink marked the underbellies and fringes of the vanguard clouds from the storm sitting offshore. "It's going to be a good show tonight. Certainly worthy of another cup of tea."

"Don't go—you'll miss something for sure."

Karla sat back and propped her feet on the railing.

Anna noticed her shoes. "Penny loafers? I didn't think they made them anymore."

"I called around until I found a pair."

"Now why would you do that?"

"I had a penny I wanted to save and I couldn't think of a better place to keep it."

"I assume it has special meaning?"

"I found it on a day when I was feeling lost. Now I use it to make sure I never forget how lucky I am or how far I've come."

"Penny loafers were popular with the kids that lived in town when I was a girl. Only they wore dimes and used them for bus fare."

The sky had turned again, the salmon to rust, the pink

to orange, the muted colors giving way to depth and richness . . . precisely the way Karla's life had changed when she came home.

"Tell me what it was like back then," Karla said.

And Anna did.

A NOTE FROM THE AUTHOR

IN THESE DAYS OF MICROWAVES AND FIFTEEN—MINUTE meals, it still seems to be the kitchen—the conversations that take place there, the holiday dinners prepared there, even the time spent cleaning up afterward—that provides the spark of so many women's memories of home. The recipes passed from one generation to the next may be complex ethnic creations or ones taken from the label of a soup can; the origin doesn't matter. What really counts are the intensely personal and intimate feelings of home and family that can come with the whiff of something as simple as homemade soup.

My mother was an incredible, creative cook. She could take a bit of this and a dash of that and come up with something wonderful. I still use many of her recipes, and even though I'm always complimented on the results, it always seems that whatever I've made tasted better when she made it.

The applesauce cake I wrote about in *Things Remembered* was hers and is a particular favorite of mine. The persimmon cookie recipe came from my mother—in—law Marge Bockoven, and is a favorite of my son, Paul. The piecrust cookies, embarrassingly simple, are a holiday must for my other son, Shawn.

If any or all of the above sounds interesting to you, I'd be happy to share the recipes. And I'd love to have you share one or two of yours with me.

Georgia Bockoven
c/o HarperCollins Publishers

10 East 53rd Street
New York, NY 10022—5299

Oh, and about the peanut butter fudge . . I, like Anna, am just going to have to wait. My mother took the recipe with her when she died.

GEORGIA BOCKOVEN is an award—winning author who began writing fiction after a successful career as a freelance journalist and photographer. Her books have sold more than four million copies worldwide. Her first book for HarperCollins, *A Marriage of Convenience,* will soon be a CBS movie starring Jane Seymour and James Brolin. The mother of two, she resides in Northern California with her husband, John.

Dear Reader:

I hope you enjoyed reading this Large Print book. If you are interested in reading other Beeler Large Print titles, ask your librarian or write to me at

Thomas T. Beeler, *Publisher*
Post Office Box 659
Hampton Falls, New Hampshire 03844

You can also call me at 1-800-251-8726 and I will send you my latest catalogue.

Audrey Lesko and I choose the titles I publish in Large Print. Our aim is to provide good books by outstanding authors—books we both enjoyed reading and liked well enough to want to share. We warmly welcome any suggestions for new titles and authors.

Sincerely,